NEW ENGLAND AVIATORS

IN TWO VOLUMES

Volume I

NORMAN PRINCE

NEW ENGLAND AVIATORS

1914-1918

THEIR PORTRAITS AND THEIR RECORDS

WITH AN INTRODUCTION BY

A. LAWRENCE LOWELL

Volume I

Schiffer Military History
Atglen, PA

Cover artwork, *Red, White & Blue*, by James Dietz.
Image courtesy of the artist.

Library of Congress Catalog Number: 97-66730.

Printed in the United States of America.
ISBN: 0-7643-0345-7

We are interested in hearing from authors with book ideas on related topics.

Published by Schiffer Publishing Ltd.
4880 Lower Valley Road
Atglen, PA 19310
Phone: (610) 593-1777
FAX: (610) 593-2002
E-mail: Schifferbk@aol.com.
Please write for a free catalog.
This book may be purchased from the publisher.
Please include $3.95 postage.
Try your bookstore first.

TO

THE IMMORTAL MEMORY OF

THE AVIATORS OF NEW ENGLAND

WHO

WHETHER IN FRANCE OR IN AMERICA

FELL IN THE CAUSE OF

FREEDOM AND DEMOCRACY

NOTE

THE Committee takes this opportunity of expressing to Miss Caroline Ticknor its appreciation of her work in compiling and editing these records. She has been untiring in her devotion and has given her ability with great sympathy and interest. Without her assistance this memorial of faith and courage could not have been achieved.

MRS. CHARLES FROST ALDRICH
MRS. J. RANDOLPH COOLIDGE, JR.
MRS. J. BERTRAM WILLIAMS
Publishing Committee

PREFACE

In December, 1918, there was held in Boston a notable exhibition of portraits of New England Aviators; a collection so inspiring as to create a demand for its permanent preservation. And in response to this demand these volumes have been compiled. The Committee in charge of this project has striven to enlarge the original group, so as to include as many as possible of the New England Flyers, to be placed with their records in the accompanying volumes. It is too soon to attempt to offer any complete list of the New England Aviators; therefore, these volumes offer only a representative group of the flower of New England manhood whose courageous work in the air proved so vital a factor in the Great War.

Founded, as this work is, upon the original collection, which was thrown open to all New England Flyers, it necessarily includes many whose military service may seem of minor importance, yet all must realize, that, measured by true standards, no less fine service was rendered by the men who did their best in the American flying-fields, while longing to "get across," than by those who performed glorious service at the front. The heavy toll of life taken upon "inglorious" fields is voiced in the words of an aviator who wrote last January from Texas: "Since this field was opened about a year ago, there have been over forty men killed in crashes, and probably five times that number wounded. Of the sixteen men who came here to learn to fly with me, four are dead; six have crashed and been hurt more or less seriously. There are not many outfits which have contended for democracy on the shell-whipped fields of France which can show as high a percentage of killed and wounded."

In presenting the records included in this work, the Committee desires to state that it has had to contend with numerous obstacles. Questionnaires were sent out while the majority of the Flyers were still abroad, which made it difficult for their families to secure accurate data; some questionnaires brought back but scanty information; others failed to return at all. In calling for letters of especial interest, the Editor elicited, in many instances, a more ample response from those whose service seemed of lesser importance, while, on the other hand, but fragmentary items came in from many of those who had earned numerous citations. Moreover, in regard to the inclusion of the citations themselves the same problem arose; it was the desire of the compilers to tabulate them all, but only a portion could be obtained.

The aim of the Committee has been to make, out of dry military records, something like human documents, embodying the spirit of the men who served, as well as the outward facts concerning them. And if the *letter* of this work offers some unavoidable errors, the *spirit*, embodied in extracts from many sincere and beautiful documents, must atone for any faults in tabulation of data, and in the translation of certain questionnaires that needed a skilled interpreter.

There are a few men included in these volumes who technically belong outside of New England, but these either were in the original collection or were linked to New England by their traditions or associations. Portraits of some important Flyers could not be secured, and lack of space has made it necessary to omit others received after the assigned limit had been reached. The placing of some pictures two on a page is not significant of any distinction in value or importance, but merely the result of necessary economy of space, attained by putting in close proximity a number of the shorter records.

Had there been time and space, it would have added greatly to the value of this work to have included many more special articles dealing with various groups and branches of the Air Service. The compilers are very grateful for those which have been kindly contributed by interested Flyers.

Almost one hundred men included in these volumes gave their lives in the Service. One fifth of the contents of this work belongs to them, and to their families, to whose brave hearts these books, it is hoped, will bring comfort and satisfaction. To these heroic parents of brave sons, high tribute should be paid. They are worthy of every winner of a "gold star" and of that highest decoration, the "White Wooden Cross." They have been proud and patient, and, with a smile upon their lips, have given their best, believing that what they have given still remains theirs, bright and immortal; to them each "gold star" is a star of hope, and every "Croix de Guerre" a cross transfigured.

CONTENTS

Introduction. *By A. Lawrence Lowell* xv
The Faces of the Aviators. *By Joseph Edgar Chamberlin* . . . xvii
First Pursuit Group. *By Lieutenant James Knowles, Jr.* 47
First Day Bombardment Group 98
Twentieth Aero Squadron, First Day Bombardment Group. *By Lieutenant Karl C. Payne* 112
A Bit of Unintentional "Acrobatics." *By Lieutenant Samuel P. Mandell* 120
The Last Raid. *By Lieutenant Gardiner H. Fiske* 124
Ninety-Sixth Aero Squadron, First Day Bombardment Group. *By Lieutenant Arthur Hadden Alexander* 128
Eleventh Aero Squadron. *By Lieutenant Paul S. Greene* 100

Aviators

Abbott, George M., *Second Lieutenant* 428
*Adams, Briggs Kilburn, *Second Lieutenant* 254
Adams, Schuyler, *Ensign* 412
Alexander, Arthur Hadden, *First Lieutenant* 130
Amory, Roger, *Major* 414
*Angell, Cyril M., *Second Lieutenant* 172
Arnold, David B., *Lieutenant (j.g.)* 440
Ashley, John W., *Lieutenant (j.g.)* 442
Atwood, Edward Wilson, *Second Lieutenant* 106
Avery, Walter Roger, *First Lieutenant* 257
Babcock, Philip Rodney, *Captain* 188
Bacon, William Bartlett, *First Lieutenant* 326
Baldwin, Raymond Peacock, *First Lieutenant* 220
Barker, John de Forest, *Second Lieutenant* 470
*Barron, Robert James, *Cadet* 318
Batchelder, Sidney Spaulding, *First Lieutenant* 274
*Baylies, Frank Leaman, *Second Lieutenant* 6
Bazley, Halsey R., *Second Lieutenant* 458
Beaman, Bartlett, *First Lieutenant* 174
*Beauclerk, Sidney W., Jr., *First Lieutenant* 180
Berry, John E., *First Lieutenant* 145
Bigelow, Stephen Sohier, *Sergeant* 32
Blanchard, Carleton Woodman, *Second Lieutenant* 468
Blanchard, George Kinson, *Second Lieutenant* 468
*Blodgett, Richard Ashley, *First Lieutenant* 48
Bowditch, William Ingersoll, *Second Lieutenant* 460
*Bradley, John Watling, *Second Lieutenant* 334
Bradley, William George, *Second Lieutenant* 336
Briggs, Henry, *First Lieutenant* 164
Briggs, Russell, *Cadet* 166
*Bruce, Alexander Bern, *First Lieutenant* 94
Bryan, Mahlon Philip, *Second Lieutenant* 176

Buchanan, Douglas R., *First Lieutenant* 166
*Buck, Walter Francis, *Second Lieutenant* 292
Buckley, Harold R., *Captain* 67
*Bullard, Edward Lauriston, *Second Lieutenant* 204
Butler, Michael A., *Second Lieutenant* 466
Caldwell, Frederic Wyllis, *Second Lieutenant* 358
Cann, Frederick B., *Second Lieutenant* 458
Carlisle, Sumner, *Lieutenant* 211
Cassidy, John Alexander, *Second Lieutenant* 446
*Cate, Laurence Hill, *Ensign* 374
Chadwick, Noel, *Lieutenant (j.g.)* 402
*Chadwick, Oliver Moulton, *Corporal* 10
Chalmers, William Wallace, *First Lieutenant* 92
*Chapin, Elliot Adams, *First Lieutenant* 282
Chapin, Roger F., *First Lieutenant* 108
Chatfield, Sterling Russell, *First Lieutenant* 341
*Cheney, William Halsall, *First Lieutenant* 298
Chevalier, Godfrey de Courcelles, *Lieutenant Commander* . . . 418
Chevalier, John Bayard, *First Lieutenant* 416
*Clark, Robert FitzGerald, *Ensign* 376
*Clement, Frederic Percival, Jr., *First Lieutenant* 321
Cleveland, Robert L., *Second Lieutenant* 470
Clowes, Lloyd Roberts, *Second Lieutenant* 446
Codman, Charles R., *First Lieutenant* 136
Coggeshall, James, Jr., *Ensign* 444
Colton, Samuel H., *First Lieutenant* 74
Constan, Peter K., *Second Lieutenant* 301
*Coolidge, Hamilton, *Captain* 62
Cormack, William Sinclair, Jr., *Ensign* 444
Coward, Raymond S., *Second Lieutenant* 168
*Cowles, Donald B., *First Lieutenant* 160
Cowles, Francis W., *First Lieutenant* 158
*Craigie, Victor Raleigh, *Second Lieutenant* 268
Crocker, Charles T., III, *First Lieutenant* 84
Crompton, George, Jr., *Lieutenant* 408
Cunningham, Arthur Lawrence, *First Lieutenant* 80
Curtis, Frazier, *Private* 26
Cutler, Roger Wilson, *Lieutenant* 398
Davis, Roswell Emory, *Second Lieutenant* 462
*Davis, Philip Washburn, *Second Lieutenant* 78
Delano, Merrill Potter, *Lieutenant* 426
Dickinson, Melvin Story, *Second Lieutenant* 266
Dolan, Charles H., Jr., *First Lieutenant* 29
Duke, Leslie B., *Second Lieutenant* 450
Dunton, Gardner, *Second Lieutenant* 454
Dwight, Henry William, *Second Lieutenant* 178

CONTENTS

EATON, SHERBURNE, *Pilot* . . . 233
EDWARDS, JOHN WINTHROP, *First Lieutenant* . . . 338
ELLIOTT, JOHN MORSE, *Second Lieutenant* . . . 454
*ELY, DINSMORE, *Second Lieutenant* . . . 225
*EMERSON, WILLIAM KEY BOND, JR., *Second Lieutenant* . . . 170
ESTILL, JOE GARNER, JR., *First Lieutenant* . . . 340
FISKE, GARDINER HORSFORD, *First Lieutenant* . . . 122
FITCH, WILLIS STETSON, *First Lieutenant* . . . 216
FOSTER, WILLIAM WALLACE, *First Lieutenant* . . . 198
FREEMAN, TALBOT OTIS, *First Lieutenant* . . . 252
*FROST, HENRY BRADLEY, *First Lieutenant* . . . 270
*GILLETT, ROBERT SWIFT, *First Lieutenant* . . . 302
GOODSPEED, MORTON, *Lieutenant (j.g.)* . . . 406
GREENE, PAUL STEVENS, *First Lieutenant* . . . 104
GUILBERT, HORACE MOSS, *First Lieutenant* . . . 196
*HALL, JAMES GRANTLEY, *First Lieutenant* . . . 272
HALL, JAMES NORMAN, *Captain* . . . 22
HALL, ROY WALES, *First Lieutenant* . . . 144
HARTLEY, FRANCIS, JR., *Ensign* . . . 404
HARWOOD, ROBERT WALKER, *Second Lieutenant* . . . 348
HEADLE, MARSHALL, *First Lieutenant* . . . 346
*HILL, ARNOLD WHITTIER, *Lieutenant* . . . 262
HINCKLEY, NELSON C., *Second Lieutenant* . . . 448
HINDS, HORACE SARGENT, *Ensign* . . . 440
HITCHCOCK, HARRY C., *Second Lieutenant* . . . 448
HOCKERT, JENKIN R., *First Lieutenant* . . . 235
HODGES, CHARLES E., JR., *Ensign* . . . 410
*HOPE, MARTIN LUTHER, *Cadet* . . . 388
*HOPKINS, STEPHEN T., *Second Lieutenant* . . . 133
HORTON, CHARLES DABNEY, *Sergent-Pilote* . . . 250
HOYT, HOWARD C., *Second Lieutenant* . . . 364
HUBBARD, GARDINER GREENE, *Captain* . . . 264
*HUBBARD, JOHN LESTER, *First Lieutenant* . . . 290
HUGHES, GERARD HASTINGS, *First Lieutenant* . . . 206
HUGHES, GEORGE F., *Captain* . . . 208
*HULL, HOWARD B., *Second Lieutenant* . . . 320
*HUNT, JASON SOLON, *First Lieutenant* . . . 72
HURD, VOLNEY DALTON, *Second Lieutenant* . . . 356
HUTCHINS, HURD, *Lieutenant* . . . 434
*JEROME, GILBERT NELSON, *First Lieutenant* . . . 212
*JONES, CHARLES EDWARD, *Cadet* . . . 296
*JONES, FORREST DEAN, *Cadet* . . . 316
JUDD, EDWARD DAVID, *Lieutenant (j.g.)* . . . 248
*KEEP, FREDERICK ARTHUR, *Second Lieutenant* . . . 330
KELTON, ELIHU HOWARD, *First Lieutenant* . . . 82
KENNEY, GEORGE C., *Captain* . . . 202

KING, WILLIAM TROTT, JR., *Second Lieutenant* 450
KINSLEY, WILLBURT EDWARD, *Second Lieutenant* 185
KNIGHT, ARTHUR RAYMOND, *Second Lieutenant* 240
KNOWLES, JAMES, JR., *First Lieutenant* 59
LAMBERT, JOHN HOLME, *Captain* 194
LASELL, JOHN WHITIN, *Second Lieutenant* 328
LAVALLE, JOHN, JR., *First Lieutenant* 280
LITTLE, CHARLES GRAY, *Lieutenant* 426
*LOCHMAN, DEAN EDMUND, JR., *Lieutenant (j.g.)* 396
LOCKE, BRADFORD BROOKS, *First Lieutenant* 332
LOCKHART, W. LAWSON, *First Lieutenant* 200
LOOMIS, RALPH LANE, *Ensign* 230
LOOMIS, WILLIAM FITCH, *First Lieutenant* 228
LOVELL, WALTER, *Captain* 34
*LUFBERY, RAOUL, *Major* 2
*MANDELL, SAMUEL PIERCE, SECOND, *First Lieutenant* 149
McGRATH, MICHAEL FRANCIS, *Second Lieutenant* 452
McLENNAN, JOHN CHARLES EARLE, *Second Lieutenant* 142
MEANS, GARDINER COIT, *Second Lieutenant* 436
*MEEKER, WILLIAM HENRY, *Corporal* 236
MERRILL, GEORGE PARKER, JR., *Second Lieutenant* 456
*MESSER, RAYMOND B., *First Lieutenant* 308
*METCALF, HARRY HUBBARD, *Second Lieutenant* 312
MITCHELL, JOHN, *Captain* 56
MOORE, ROBERT LOWELL, *First Lieutenant* 232
MOORE, WALTER C., *Cadet* 472
*MORSE, EUGENE DORR, *Second Lieutenant* 310
MORSE, THOMAS ROBESON, *Lieutenant (j.g.)* 438
MUNN, ECTOR O., *First Lieutenant* 111
MURCHIE, HARRY FOSTER, *Second Lieutenant* 460
*NATHAN, THOMAS CUSHMAN, *First Lieutenant* 276
*NICHOLS, BRAYTON, *Second Lieutenant* 162
NOYES, STEPHEN HENLEY, *Major* 182
O'BRIEN, WILLIAM B., *First Lieutenant* 242
OSGOOD, FORREST C., *Ensign* 452
*PARSONS, ARTHUR MAXWELL, *Second Lieutenant* 306
PARSONS, EDWIN C., *Sous-Lieutenant* 14
PAYNE, KARL C., *First Lieutenant* 116
PEAK, LAWRENCE I., *First Lieutenant* 222
PERKINS, CHARLES KINGMAN, *First Lieutenant* 366
*PERKINS, ROGER CONANT, *Chief Quartermaster* 368
*PERO, DONALD CARY, *Ensign* 394
PERRIN, JOHN, *Lieutenant (j.g.)* 391
PHELPS, RALPH MAURICE, *First Lieutenant* 352
*PLUMMER, CHARLES W., *Second Lieutenant* 191
POLLARD, FRED DON, JR., *Second Lieutenant* 365

CONTENTS

POTTER, STANLEY B., *Cadet* 472
PRINCE, FREDERICK HENRY, JR., *Adjutant* 20
*PRINCE, NORMAN, *Sous-Lieutenant* 17
RAYMOND, ROBERT FULTON, JR., *Captain* 76
*RHENO, WALTER DAVIS, *First Lieutenant* 38
RICHMOND, ARTHUR L., *Captain* 370
*RILEY, FRANK W., *Ensign* 386
ROBINSON, CLARK, *Second Lieutenant* 219
ROLLINS, CARLE E., *Second Lieutenant* 184
*ROOSEVELT, QUENTIN, *First Lieutenant* 70
RYAN, HAROLD LYMAN, *Lieutenant (j.g.)* 424
SAFFORD, LOYAL R., *Second Lieutenant* 350
*SANGER, RALPH, *Captain* 304
SEARLE, RICHARD W., *Second Lieutenant* 372
SEWALL, SUMNER, *First Lieutenant* 52
SHEDD, PAUL W., *Second Lieutenant* 456
*SMITH, WINTHROP FLOYD, *Ensign* 378
SONNABEND, A. MORRIS, *Ensign* 442
SOULE, SEYMOUR, *Cadet* 362
SPEAR, GEORGE DANA, *First Lieutenant* 110
SPRAGUE, GEORGE E., *Chief Quartermaster* 278
STANLEY, CLARENCE, *Ensign* 464
STANLEY, GILBERT, *First Lieutenant* 154
STANLEY, LEONARD L., *First Lieutenant* 464
STARKWEATHER, RALPH, *Second Lieutenant* 462
*STARRETT, FRANK ELMER, JR., *Cadet* 42
STEARNS, RUSSELL FALCONER, *Corporal* 36
*STEARNS, WILLIAM ST. AGNAN, *First Lieutenant* 354
*STEWART, GORDON, *Cadet* 294
*SWAN, WILLARD FREDERICK, *Sergeant* 285
*TALBOT, RALPH, *Lieutenant (j.g.)* 383
TALBOT, ROBERT A., *Lieutenant (j.g.)* 422
TAYLOR, MOSELEY, *Lieutenant (j.g.)* 420
*TAYLOR, RAYMOND CLYDE, *First Lieutenant* 146
THAYER, SIGOURNEY, *First Lieutenant* 68
THOMAS, WALTER FREDERIC, *Second Lieutenant* 360
TORREY, WILLIAM WHEELWRIGHT, *Second Lieutenant* 432
TRAINER, H. POTTER, *First Lieutenant* 342
TRIDER, GEORGE H., JR., *Second Lieutenant* 324
TROWBRIDGE, CHARLES E., *First Lieutenant* 156
*TUTEIN, CHESTER ROBINSON, *Second Lieutenant* 87
VOGEL, HENRY W., *Second Lieutenant* 466
WARD, CHARLES LAKEMAN, *Second Lieutenant* 344
WARNER, DONALD D., *First Lieutenant* 152
*WEHNER, JOSEPH F., *First Lieutenant* 90
WELLMAN, ARTHUR OGDEN, *Second Lieutenant* 246

CONTENTS

WELLMAN, WILLIAM AUGUSTUS, *First Lieutenant* 243

WELLS, BENNETT, *First Lieutenant* 96

WENZ, EDWARD A., *Lieutenant (j.g.)* 430

WETHERALD, ROYAL WINTER, *Ensign* 260

*WILLIAMS, BERTRAM, *First Lieutenant* 138

WILLIS, HAROLD BUCKLEY, *Sous-Lieutenant* 44

WILSON, DONALD, *Ensign* 400

*WINTERTON, ROLAND JOHN, *Second Lieutenant* 314

*WOODWARD, LE ROY GATES, *First Lieutenant* 288

*WRIGHT, ARTHUR HOUSTOUN, *First Lieutenant* 380

INTRODUCTION

Modern warfare, with the vast number of men engaged, with its, organization and its efficiency, has tended to efface the individual as compared with the action of the mass; but in this war a new weapon developed which brought back the personal exploit of the individual warrior.

The range and precision of modern guns had, at the time this war broke out, rendered inadequate the former methods of observing operations on the field of battle. But just at that time aviation had been developed as a practical art to such a point that it could be used for observing the effects of artillery and the movements of the enemy. Airplanes became an essential means of information — the very eyes of the army. They could be used also to drop bombs upon the enemy's dépôts far to the rear.

All this involved on the part of the other army the need of interference with hostile observation and bombing planes; and as that could be done with very limited effect from the ground, armed planes were required that could attack and destroy the machines of the enemy. In accordance with the ordinary progress of warfare, the fighting planes of both sides became organized forces, trained to do battle with each other, manœuvring in squadrons with regular formations to give the greatest strength by mutual support. Although under the command of a leader of the squadron, the individual machines — like the separate ships in a fleet — were handled with a far greater independence than is possible with the small units of a land force; even more so, in fact, than is the case with warships; for in an encounter in the air the suddenness of the attack, the frequent surprises, the unexpected and rapid movements of the enemy, render necessary quick movements of attack and escape by single planes that leaves much to the personal skill, self-reliance, and decision of the aviator. He was the officer and crew of his own craft, for at most there were in ordinary fighting planes only two men, the pilot and the observer.

Conditions like this appealed strongly to young men of enterprise, initiative, and daring. The risk was, of course, exceedingly great; for to be beaten in an encounter meant almost certain death; and often that was true of a serious accident to the machine. Although death came quickly, it came in a form that to most people is peculiarly terrifying; but no such dangers deterred these young men. As Philip Washburn Davis, who was afterwards killed, wrote in a letter quoted in the following pages, "Once I had determined to get into the army, I wanted to get into something where individuality counts; and it does in aviation more than anywhere else. Even if the danger is greater, the value of the service is greater, too." Were it not that the large number of aviators distracts attention from the individual exploit, these men would appear as paladins of romance; and their spirit, their adventures, and their feats would abundantly justify their being so treated.

As compared with other arms, the proportion killed was large; the more so considering that a great part of the men were in active service only a few months, some only a few weeks. There are gold stars against 95 out of the 542 names.

Some facts about the history of these aviators are interesting. A very large proportion of them were college men, some having graduated and others having left before their academic course was completed. A number of them served with the British and French forces in the line or in the air before the United States entered the war; while others were members of one or other of the ambulance corps before that date. These were men who saw clearly from the early days of the war that it was a conflict for all that is most precious in civilization; and they felt keenly the longing to aid those who were fighting for moral standards in the world.

To gather and publish the records of the aviators from New England who took an active part in the war was an excellent project, which one may hope will be followed in the rest of the country; for whether they be dead or living, their deeds are worthy of any commemoration and honor that can be given.

A. Lawrence Lowell

Harvard University
November, 1919

THE FACES OF THE AVIATORS

By Joseph Edgar Chamberlin

[This article, reproduced by the kind permission of the author, was written on the occasion of the opening of the exhibition of the Aviation pictures.

Mr. Chamberlin's only son, Raymond Chamberlin, of the 102d Machine Gun Battalion, U.S.A., was killed in action in August, 1918.]

Wonderful faces of bravest boys! In the whole world there is nothing more significant than these photographs. We are told that God sifted three kingdoms to find the wheat for the planting of our American Nation. If that is so, here is another sifting of our whole Nation (in this collection mostly a sifting of our New England corner of it) to find this golden grain of buoyant adventure, of skill, of matchless courage, of willing sacrifice for the greatest end, that we see on these walls.

Faces and faces — faces of New England boys — faces all of boys, for the men of forty that we see among the French aviators are wanting here; faces, all of them, marked abundantly with that "sweet attractive kind of grace" that the old poet described as "continual comfort in a face"; not a hard face among them; faces of boys that look out on the world with that sort of expression that one would wear in opening a morning window on a sun-flooded world on a holiday; expectation of and confidence in a good world written in all these eager eyes, yet seriousness and devotion in every face.

In many of these young flyers' faces one sees, indeed, the smile. It is the native smile of that same "attractive grace." But always underneath it there lies the serious, achieving purpose, the consciousness of a great duty instantly assumed and cheerily borne. It is (so noted the observer of the aviators' faces who now writes these words) very like the expression that one sees on the graduates' faces on Commencement Day. There is the confident smile, but there is also the look of one fronting a big world in which there is but one thing to do, and that to acquit one's self a man; it is joy in the duty, but the duty unforgotten.

Certainly the Yankee race has never produced a handsomer type of young manhood than is shown by the photographs of these aviators. Old-time rolled velvet collars, purple broadcloth and brocaded waistcoats, with ambrosial locks to frame the faces, might have been more becoming than these stern khaki uniforms, reducing a man to his lowest terms, but the faces themselves were never, among our people, surpassed in beauty and expressiveness.

As far as the photographs of these aviators reveal the facial type of the young American of to-day of the best race, one would say that our evolution has produced in us a rounder, gentler face than that of the New Englander of old. The Puritan, on the whole, fades away; our picked men verge toward the Cavalier. For in spite of the return of the Puritan type here and there, few stern and no forbidding lineaments are to be seen. Nor is the Roman nose at all preponderant. The nose seems to be rather oftener a little *retroussé* than otherwise. Foreheads are not unduly high, nor the pale cast of thought very much in evidence.

No hollow cheeks, no sunken eyes; these are well-nourished sons of well-nourished parents, who for the most part have been sheltered from any other hardships or hard knocks than those which they have themselves sought in their sports. These are the faces that peace and plenty and comfort produce.

But what a vindication of our modern life, that it should produce no weakness as the result of all this kindly shelter, but should actually advance the race in strength! Nathan Hale could not have offered his life with a purer or less ostentatious spirit than you will find written in every one of these countenances.

Of those among the Missing who will never come back, and among those of the Golden Star, we should not, if they had absolutely known what was coming, have been fronted to-day with one smile the less, nor with a shadow on a single brow. Each one has the joyous look. He would have had it if he had known. He will wear it forever; it is always the same.

> Brave, good, and true,
> I see him stand before me now,
> And read again on that young brow,
> Where every hope was new,
> "How sweet were life!" Yet, by the mouth firm-set,
> And look made up for Duty's utmost debt.
> I could divine he knew
> That death within the sulphurous hostile lines,
> In the mere wreck of nobly-pitched designs,
> Plucks heart's-ease and not rue!

NEW ENGLAND AVIATORS

*RAOUL LUFBERY

LAFAYETTE ESCADRILLE; MAJOR, A.S., U.S.A.

Killed in action, May 19, 1918

SON of Mr. and Mrs. Edward Lufbery, of Wallingford, Conn.; was born in France in 1886; his father being an American and his mother a Frenchwoman. At the age of seventeen he ran away from his home, and began his career of travel and adventure. During the next four years he journeyed over France, Algiers, Tunis, Egypt, Turkey, and the Balkans, working at anything that came his way. In 1906 he returned to the U.S., and in 1907 entered the Regular Army; he spent the next two years in the Philippines, where he distinguished himself as a marksman (holding first place as rifleman in his regiment).

Leaving the army at the end of his two years' service, he continued his travels; he roamed over China and Japan, finally reaching India, where at Saignon, Cochin China, he saw his first aeroplane in 1910, and made the acquaintance of Marc Pourpe. This famous French trick-flyer, who was exhibiting in the Far East, engaged Lufbery as his mechanic, and soon found him an invaluable aid. For three years they travelled and worked together, and 1914 found them in France at the outbreak of the war. Pourpe at once enlisted in the Air Service, with N 23, and Lufbery wished to do the same, but being an American was forced to join the Foreign Legion; following which he was allowed to accompany Pourpe to the front as his mechanic.

On Dec. 2, 1914, Pourpe was killed, and Lufbery, longing to avenge his death, at once applied for permission to fly. After a few days he was given his brevet, and was enrolled in the celebrated Escadrille of Bombardment, the V 102. Six months later he was transferred to the newly organized Lafayette Escadrille, where he began those heroic exploits in the air that eventually won for him the title of "American Ace of Aces."

From this time on his success was rapid. On July 30, 1916, he brought down his first plane, over Étain, and a week later vanquished another; these successes won him his first citation from the French Government, which read:

Model of address, of coolness, and of courage. He has distinguished himself by numerous long-distance bombardments, and by daily combats

he has had with enemy aeroplanes. On July 30 he unhesitatingly attacked at close range a group of four enemy machines. He shot one of them down near our lines. Succeeded in bringing down a second on the 4th of Aug., 1916.

A third plane was brought down in flames a few days later, and shortly after, a fourth. Lufbery was promoted to Adjutant, and on Oct. 12, 1916, won his fifth victory over a huge three-seater Aviatik, shot down in flames during a bombing expedition against the munition factories at Karlsruhe. It was during this expedition that Norman Prince was mortally wounded.

Lufbery was now an "Ace," and according to the French custom was given a citation for each subsequent victory. He continued his successes, and on Dec. 27 shot down two planes in one day, only one of which, however, was officially credited to him; in one of these combats he narrowly escaped death. For these and other exploits he was awarded the Croix de Guerre with ten Palms, the Médaille Militaire, and named a Chevalier in the Legion of Honor. He was the first American to receive from England the British Military Cross, which was bestowed upon him on June 12, 1917; he also received three other English medals.

He was commissioned 1st Lieut. in June, 1917. During this month he brought down his tenth enemy plane; on this occasion, when flying alone at 18,000 feet altitude, he saw seven Boches at a distance, but observing that one of them was cut off from the others, he dived upon him, firing as he approached; after twenty-five or thirty shots, his gun jammed, but he had already accomplished his purpose, as his foe wavered and crashed into the German trenches.

When the U.S. entered the war, and began to prepare her own Air Service, the experienced fighting pilots, who had been doing their part for France, were given charge of the new American escadrilles. Both Lufbery and William Thaw, who had been original members of N 124, were commissioned Majors in the A.S., U.S.A. Lufbery's commission was received Nov. 7, 1917, and he was made Commanding Officer of the Lafayette Escadrille.

During the time of his service in France, Lufbery suffered much from severe attacks of rheumatism, which at times kept him in hospital, but although often enduring acute suffering, which was increased by the inclement weather, he continued to work with his Squadron, carrying on with unabated enthusiasm his active patrolling, and exposing himself to every risk.

On Sunday, May 19, 1918, Lufbery went aloft over Toul with his fighting Squadron. Enemy machines were at this time hovering over the American line. Seeing a German Fokker (a great armored plane, a single-seater triplane, the first of its kind that had been used) deep enough within the Allied territory to be cut off before it could escape, Lufbery darted swiftly to the attack. The exact details of the combat will probably never be known, but the American "Ace" was seen to fall in flames, and when 2000 feet from the ground, he was seen to jump from the blazing mass to instant death. When Lufbery's body was picked up, it was found to have been practically uninjured by enemy bullets, and it has been stated that had he been provided with a parachute attachment, his life might have been spared for further victories. Moreover, had his plane been equipped with a non-inflammable fuel tank, he would no doubt have scored his nineteenth victory. As it was, he stood officially credited with eighteen enemy planes, and was known to have brought down many more.

At Lufbery's death the title of "American Ace" passed to Lieut. Frank L. Baylies, upon whose death it was accorded to Lieut. David Putnam, of Brookline.

Lufbery's body was found where he fell, in a flower garden in the village of Maron. His machine crashed to earth in flames half a kilometre away and was burned to ashes. The American aviators who rushed to the spot where Lufbery lay, found him already covered with flowers by the peasants who had seen him fall. He was unwounded save by a bullet which had passed through the hand that held the control lever, and set his petrol tank on fire.

Lufbery's funeral was held on May 20, 1918, and he was buried with full military honors on the hillside back of the American lines. Six of his fellow flyers dropped roses on the bier and an eloquent tribute was paid by the French General, who said that Lufbery's work was typical of the union of America and France in the common cause. He closed his address with the simple words, "Au revoir."

*FRANK LEAMAN BAYLIES

LAFAYETTE FLYING CORPS, "STORK" ESCADRILLE
SECOND LIEUTENANT, A.S., U.S.A.

Killed in action, June 17, 1918

SON of Charles S. and Lydia Terry (Paige) Baylies; was born in New Bedford, Mass., Sept. 23, 1895. He was educated in the New Bedford Public Schools, and at the Moses Brown School, Providence, R.I. He was always interested in sports, and was an expert swimmer; he was also an expert automobile driver, one of his qualifications for the Ambulance Service.

He volunteered in the Automobile Sanitary Section, U.S.A., in May, 1916, and was on duty at the French front, on the Somme, at Verdun, and in the Argonne; then for three months in the Monastir sector, Serbia; where, in an order of March 25, 1917, he was cited for "perfect devotion and fearlessness" in evacuating wounded under bombardment, and was given the French Croix de Guerre, with palm. He served with the American Ambulance Corps from May, 1916, to May 11, 1917, when he enlisted in the French Aviation Corps, and was trained as a flyer at Avord, Pau, and Lake Cazaux. In Nov., 1917, he was sent to the front as a member of the "Stork" Pursuit Squadron, and he became one of the most famous aces of that famous Escadrille. He served first at Dunkirk, later at Verdun, then in the Champagne sector. After his sixth official victory he was cited by the French as a "chasing pilot of the highest class, who always seeks combat and leads marvellously the patrol of which he is chief. On April 12 he destroyed alone his fifth enemy aeroplane, and the following day he gained his sixth victory." He was then Sergeant of the Foreign Legion, pilot in Spad Squadron; and he refused a Captaincy in the American Aviation Service to keep the lower rank in his Escadrille.

Following Feb., 1918, eleven German planes were officially credited to Lieut. Baylies, and he was in reality a victor more than twenty times.

On May 13, 1918, he was transferred to the U.S. Aviation Signal Service Reserve Corps, and commissioned 2d Lieut. in an order dated May 20, 1918. On June 17, 1918, he fell in combat behind the German lines, near Montdidier, and was instantly killed. He was at first reported missing; a note, however, was thrown over

the lines by a German aviator stating that Frank L. Baylies, an American aviator, fell at Rellet and was buried in a private tomb.

Besides the Croix de Guerre with palms, the Military Medal, and the ribbons of the French Legion and of the Lafayette Flying Corps, Lieut. Baylies was given a medal by the Aero Club of America, and the French Legion of Honor.

On May 30, 1919, a handsome bronze tablet, given by the Daughters of the American Revolution, Fort Phenix Chapter, New Bedford, was placed in the Josiah Swift School which Lieut. Baylies had attended. The inscription is as follows:

> In Memory of Frank Leaman Baylies, American Ace, Member of the Lafayette Flying Corps, killed in action June 17, 1918. "Greater love hath no man than this, that a man lay down his life for his friends."

A letter to Lieut. Baylies's mother from Major Gros, commanding officer, A.S. Signal Reserve Corps, said in part:

> Your son met a glorious death. He was one of the shining lights of our Aviation. He was a soldier without fear and without reproach. You must apply to him the eloquent words spoken in the British Parliament with respect to aviators; you must not turn your mind on your sorrow, you must turn it towards all the glory which your son has won and the name which he will leave behind him when the story of this great war is written. He has taken his place by the side of all those heroes who gladly gave up that which is most precious of all, their lives, for the greatest ideal, the happiness of the human race.

In a dispatch to the *Chicago Daily News* dated July 8, 1918, Paul Ayres Rockwell paid tribute to the recently fallen Ace, as follows:

> One of the finest and highest-spirited figures that was ever revealed has disappeared from among us. To know Baylies was to like and admire him. His outstanding qualities were those which real heroes possess. Quiet, modest, and reticent on the ground, dashing, fearless, and indomitable in the air, Baylies goes down into history as one of the exceptional characters in war aviation.
>
> Baylies's record after reaching the front as a chasing pilot was unique. No other flyer in any army gained at the beginning of his career so many official successes over opposing pilots in so short a space of time. Baylies destroyed his first German airplane Feb. 19, 1918. On March 7 and 16 he gained his second and third victories; and on April 11 and 12 he had two more official triumphs. May was a wonderful month for the superb air fighter, confirmed victories being won May 2, 9, 10, 28, 29, and 31, making eleven enemy airplanes officially destroyed.
>
> Mention after mention was awarded to Baylies in the Army orders, and

many palms were added to his war-cross, ribbon, and military medal. Lately he was proposed for the Cross of the Legion of Honor, and also for the rank of Under-Lieutenant.

Citations

Order 57, March 27, 1917: "Frank Baylies, an American volunteer in the Automobile Sanitary Section No. 3, twice volunteered duty at the front and then for the Army of the Orient. He placed at the service of wounded men perfect devotion and fearlessness, being daily tested under bombardment. From Dec. 19, 1916, to March 27, 1917, during the evacuation of wounded from the Monastir sector, he exhibited contempt for the bombardment of cities, roads, and cantonments."

From an order dated March 9, 1918: "Frank Baylies, an American citizen, enlisted in the French Army before the United States declared war. He passed at his own request into chasing aviation, in which he displayed the very finest enthusiasm. On Feb. 18 he shot down single-handed an enemy aeroplane which crashed within our lines."

Order dated May 6, 1918: "An excellent chasing pilot; refused to enter American Aviation as an officer, not wishing to leave his French squadron; delivers daily combats; has destroyed alone his second enemy aeroplane."

Order dated May 29, 1918: "Frank Baylies is a brilliant, high-class chasing pilot. On May 9 and 10 he destroyed his seventh and eighth German aeroplanes."

Lieut. Baylies won four additional citations equally remarkable.

*OLIVER MOULTON CHADWICK

CORPORAL, ESCADRILLE 73, GROUPE DE COMBAT 12 (LAFAYETTE FLYING CORPS)

Killed in action, Aug. 14, 1917

SON of Austin Kilham and Julia M. (Moulton) Chadwick; was born at Lowell, Mass., Sept. 23, 1888. He prepared for college at Phillips Exeter Academy, 1907, where he was awarded the Yale cup for scholarship and athletics. He graduated from Harvard College in 1911, and from the Harvard Law School in 1914. He was one of the most popular men in his class, proving a leader in many undergraduate departments; he was coach of the Harvard freshman track team in 1915; assistant of the 'Varsity track team, of which he was asked to become coach; he attained a wide reputation for his skill as goal tend on the hockey team.

After graduation he entered the house of Stone & Webster as a member of the legal department, but at the outbreak of the war in Europe was filled with a desire to aid the Allied cause, and went to Canada to offer his services; finding that he could not enlist there as an American citizen, he decided to return and enter training. He attended the first and second Plattsburg camps, and in 1916 spent four months at the Mexican Border with Battery A, 1st Reg. Mass. F.A., N.G. On his return North he at once arranged for lessons in flying under Curtiss, at Newport News, and as soon as he had acquired proficiency in handling a plane he sailed for France, where he entered the French Foreign Legion, enlisting Jan. 22, 1917. He speedily obtained his license as pilot at the school of Pau, and having completed a course in aerial marksmanship at Cazaux, joined Squadron No. 12, under command of Major Brochard, July 29, 1917. After some practice flights on Spad aeroplanes, he took part in patrol flights and was particularly marked by his skill as a pilot.

On Aug. 3 Corporal Chadwick wrote:

I am now somewhere, and I can describe it no more definitely than by saying that I should rather be there than anywhere else. One of the first things I saw when arriving here was Capt. Guynemer. I saw him go up, and an hour later come back. In the meantime he got his 50th official, . . . and he must have dropped about as many more out of sight behind the German lines.

One of the other things of interest which I saw here was a machine which had been hit by several explosive bullets. They do a thorough job.

The men here are a splendid lot. It is the most famous group of escadrilles in the world and the finest commander. If I don't learn how to be a good Boche hunter, it will be my own fault. I am not at liberty to say where I am, or much about what is going on, but here is a generality drawn from the past, which will probably hold good for the future: Wherever the pot boils, there is to be found Groupe de Combat 12.

On Aug. 14 he was not scheduled to fly until afternoon, but anxious to get all the practice possible, he went to the field in the morning hoping that an extra man might be needed. A patrol was just going out, and being one man short, he was asked to fill the place. They set out at nine o'clock, and at 9.45, the patrol engaged in combat with an enemy squadron near the forest of Houthulst. An English patrol also took part in the fight, and seeing it attacked by an Albatross, Chadwick hastened to its assistance. At the same moment he was attacked from the rear by two enemy Albatross pilots and his machine was seen to fall towards the earth. It landed 1200 metres north of the village of Bischoff, exactly between the two lines. At the time of its fall, both French and Germans came out of the trenches and a skirmish took place about the machine without any definite result, the two parties shortly returning to their shelters. Two or three days later, a new French attack carried the lines forward to the exact place where the machine had fallen. The Spad was found with the body of a German beside it, but no trace of Pilot Chadwick. It was not until many weeks later that the certainty of his death was assured, and his burial place found marked with his name.

Baron d'Estournelles de Constant, Senator of France, wrote to Nicholas Murray Butler, of Columbia University, concerning the devotion and loyalty of Chadwick. He said:

He has literally flown to the defence of liberty, and might be likened to a young god. The letters which he wrote me filled me at the same time with admiration and anxiety, for he had but one thought. He was intensely eager to devote himself to the service at the earliest possible hour. I have often thought that he was one of those whom we describe as too good for this earth. When I consider such a loss, the only consolation which I find is that self-sacrifice such as that of Chadwick bears more beautiful fruit perhaps after death than during life. Such beautiful generosity awakens in souls still undeveloped unexpected inspirations and a desire to emulate. The heroic devotion of a single person is sufficient to animate suddenly the indifference of a crowd, of an army, of a nation, of a world. And then all humanity profits by the death of these magnificent young people, apparently wasted, but in reality most fruitful.

In July, 1919, the Croix de Guerre, awarded Chadwick by the French Minister of War, was personally presented to the aviator's father by Baron d'Estournelles de Constant.

Corporal Chadwick was awarded a blue ribbon decked with stars and the insignia of the Lafayette Escadrille, in recognition of service rendered, accompanied by the announcement:

The President of the Council, Minister of War, has decided to award a souvenir to the four directing officers and to the 214 pilots of the Lafayette Flying Corps, who in helping the cause of our people, fraternally joined the French ranks, sharing a great part of the perils and glories of war.

A war medal was awarded Chadwick by the Aero Club of America, "In recognition of Valor and Distinguished Service," in Jan., 1918, with an accompanying certificate on which was inscribed:

In recognition of the services rendered to France and her Allies for the cause of humanity this certificate has been issued to Serg't Oliver M. Chadwick who served during the European war in the capacity of pilot in the Lafayette Escadrille, killed on Aug. 14, 1917; thereby in a measure repaying the great debt which America owes France and contributing to the victory of Liberty and Civilization over military autocracy.

Croix de Guerre (with star) [1]

Le Colonel, Commandant la Division Aérienne
Cite à l'Ordre de la Division

CHADWICK, OLIVER MOULTON
Caporal, pilote, aviateur

Jeune pilote, venu au front après quelques mois d'École, a fait preuve d'une haute bravoure, d'un noble caractère et, malgré l'inexpérience des combats aériens, a afformé, des son arrivée dans une unité française (Spa 73), l'ardente volonté de prendre part à la lutte.

Au cours d'une mission à basse altitude, sur les lignes ennemis, a soutenu un dur combat au cours duquel il est mort en Héros.

Copie certifiée conforme au G.Q.G. le 7 juin.

Le Général Commandant l'aviation française
M. DUVAL

[1] The silver star is added to show that Corporal Chadwick was cited for bravery in the Army orders of his Squadron.

EDWIN C. PARSONS

SOUS-LIEUTENANT, ESCADRILLE LAFAYETTE, "STORK" ESCADRILLE

SON of Frederick D. and Grace M. (Steele) Parsons, of Springfield, Mass.; was born Sept. 24, 1892, at Holyoke, Mass. He was educated in the public schools of Springfield, and at Phillips Exeter Academy.

In Dec., 1915, he sailed overseas to enter the Ambulance Service. While at his first ambulance work at Neuilly-sur-Seine, Jan., 1916, was made Sergeant, and was later given charge of a section of the Ambulance at Mrs. Whitney Warren's Hospital at Juilly, near the Soissons front.

While there he made his application to enter the Aviation Service, and in April, 1916, his papers arrived. He served three days in the Foreign Legion (during which time he took the oath of allegiance to France for the duration of the war). His first training was at Buc where he was made Corporal after three months' work. From there he was transferred to the school at Avord for training in "pursuit flying"; then to Cazaux for machine-gun work; and to Pau for "group flying." About Dec. 8, 1916, he went to Plessis-Belleville for final training, and was there when "demanded" by the Escadrille Lafayette which he joined Jan. 24, 1917.

He was made Sergeant in Feb. and won his first honors — being cited with two others in the order of the day for having had three aerial combats the day previous.

He brought down his first Hun in Sept., 1917, and was awarded the Croix de Guerre.

From Nov., till Jan., 1918, he was at home on leave, and upon his return, the Lafayette (N 124) being taken over by America, he joined the French 124, but in April was assigned to the Cigognes or "Stork" Escadrille (Spad 3). He was commissioned Sous-Lieutenant in the fall of 1918.

He got most of his enemy machines while with this organization, receiving the silver stork after his third. He has eight officially confirmed enemy planes to his credit.

He has the right to wear the Croix de Guerre with eight palms, the Médaille Militaire, and *fourragère*, the latter awarded the Escadrille as a group, after winning its 150th plane, and the silver stork.

He also received the Cross of Leopold, the Belgium War Cross,

and Medal of the Aero Club of America. He was awarded the William Pynchon Medal by the Publicity Club of Springfield in 1918.

Citations

Sept. 4, 1917 N 124

Bon pilote de chasse qui exécute avec entrain les missions qui lui sont confiées. Le 4 septembre a attaqué et abattu un avion ennemi en pièces sur Neuilly (1er avion).

Citoyen américain fait preuve depuis deux ans, déjà comme pilote de chasse d'un dévouement absolu, d'une joyeuse bravoure. Le 6 mai 1918 a abattu seul son 2e avion ennemi.

Excellent pilote de chasse a abattu seul le 17 mai 1918 son 3e avion ennemi.

Excellent pilote de chasse, exécute avec intelligence toute mission; a abattu le 19 mai 1918 son 4e avion ennemi.

Pilote très énergique, plein de courage et d'entrain, le 20 mai 1918 a abattu son 5e avion ennemi.

Citoyen américain, pilote d'élite, exécutant avec gaieté les missions les plus ingrates, vient encore le 29 août d'abattre seul son sixième avion ennemi dans des conditions difficiles (dated 5 septembre 1918).

Excellent pilote de chasse remarquable pour son audace bravoure et dévouement, a abattu le 26 septembre 1918 son septième ennemi.

Pilote de chasse exceptionale pour son courage, un vrai modèle pour ses camarades, le 1er octobre 1918 a descendu très bas dans les lignes ennemis et abattu son huitième avion ennemi dans les très durs conditions.

On June 17, 1918, Lieut. Parsons accompanied Lieut. Baylies on his last flight. The latter's swift machine carried him far ahead of his companion, who saw him in combat with four enemy planes before his machine went down over the enemy's lines. It was days before his comrades received the news of Baylies's fate.

Lieut. Parsons avenged his late companion's death by bringing down a Hun machine which approached him camouflaged as a French plane. After a hot fight, Parsons gained a position above his adversary and after firing a burst of not over ten shots, the enemy dropped like a stone from a high altitude.

During the month of Oct., 1918, being ill, he was given a *permission* and was at Biarritz when the Armistice was signed. He has since returned to America.

*NORMAN PRINCE

Sous-Lieutenant, Lafayette Escadrille

Killed in action, Oct. 15, 1916

Norman Prince was the younger of the two sons of Frederick Henry and Abigail (Norman) Prince and the grandson of Frederick Q. Prince, a former Mayor of Boston, and of George H. Norman, of Newport, R.I. Born Aug. 31, 1887, at Prides Crossing, Mass., he received his early education under private tutors in this country and in Europe and completed his preparation for college at Groton. He was graduated at Harvard College in the class of 1908, receiving a *cum laude* with his degree of Bachelor of Arts. He received a degree of Bachelor of Laws from the Harvard Law School three years later and was admitted to the bar, beginning the practice of his profession in Chicago. He devoted much of his time to the study and practice of aviation at a time when flying was popularly regarded as a mere sport rather than a practical utility in this country.

At the outbreak of the World War, in 1914, he offered his services to France as a volunteer aviator, taking passage abroad in Dec. of that year, and receiving his preliminary training at the Military Aviation School at Pau. Having won a certificate of proficiency in four months, he distinguished himself by his skill and bravery in many air raids against the enemy, winning at once the confidence and admiration of his commander and comrades.

At the beginning of his active service he conceived the idea of bringing the American aviators, together with some of those of the Foreign Legion, into a single squadron, not only that the Americans might be associated in closer comradeship, but also that their achievements might become more distinctive and thus redound to the glory of their own country as well as to that of the Allies. With this end in view he was primarily and chiefly instrumental in organizing the Lafayette Escadrille. Originally carrying the Tricolor, this famous squadron subsequently had the distinction of carrying the first American flag that appeared on any of the battle-fields of the World War, after the United States became a co-belligerent.

The Lafayette Escadrille became famous for skill and daring in the battle-fronts and Prince soon achieved the ranks of Sergent, Adjudant, and Lieutenant successively, and was actively engaged in 122 aerial engagements in northern France. He was credited officially with five Boches brought down in battle, not to mention four others not officially recorded.

On Oct. 12, 1916, while descending from an aerial raid on Oberndorff, his plane struck an aerial cable near Luxeuil, Alsace. In the collision his machine was overturned and wrecked, Prince receiving injuries from which he died at the neighboring Gérardmer Hospital three days subsequently.

He was given all the honors of military funeral, which was held on the Luxeuil aviation field and was attended by a large representation of the Allied military divisions. The body was borne to a neighboring chapel, there to rest until the end of the war in accordance with the military regulations regarding the temporary disposition of those dying at the battle-fronts.

Citations

Croix de Guerre, with two stars, and four palms

First Star, won for being cited in L'Ordre du Jour of his Division for having been the only one of twenty-five aviators to reach Douai in 1915.

First Palm, won for being cited in L'Ordre du Jour of the French Army for having brought down an enemy avion.

Second Palm, for having brought down two enemy avions on the same day — at the same time receiving the

Third Palm, cited in L'Ordre du Jour for having brought down a fourth enemy avion, and for meritorious service in a raid on the Mauser Ammunition Works at Oberndorff — at the same time receiving the Médaille Militaire.

He was also awarded the Croix de la Légion d'Honneur.

In writing of the founding of the Lafayette Escadrille, Elliot C. Cowdin, one of its original members, has said:

Norman Prince had spent many years and made many friends in France, and felt it his privilege and duty to serve her in the hour of need. He conceived the idea of forming an aero squadron composed exclusively of Americans, to join the French Army. Prince arrived in Paris early in January, 1915. He consulted with his French friends, of whom Lieut. Jacques de Lesseps was the most enthusiastic, and was instrumental in getting the French War Department to listen to Prince's ideas and plans. He solicited the aid of several prominent Americans then residing in Paris, but they all declined to be identified in any way with the scheme, so that Prince had to fight his own battle single-handed. The French Government told him they could not use his services, as Aviation was so popular among the soldiers that they had more aviators than they could use.

Prince was not to be denied, and kept plodding along on his own account, calling on such of his French friends as might be influential, trying to convince them that it was essential and would be most beneficial to France if she would accept an American squadron.

The only men upon whom he depended for pilots were Frazier Curtis, then flying in England, and Norman Read, then in Paris, and doing what he could to help Prince. The situation looked hopeless, but Prince was ever determined. . . . He finally obtained permission to form a squadron of six pilots, all to be Americans, with previous flying experience.

Cowdin has described the various discouragements through which the founders of the Squadron passed before perfecting their organization. Accidents reduced their number after the quota was complete. Curtis had two bad smash-ups and was forced to withdraw; Andrew Ruel (another of the group) was injured; and after some months Prince and Cowdin found themselves alone, with their hopes sadly dimmed. At last, however, assisted by Dr. Gros, at Paris, with M. de Sillac and Mr. Frederick Allen coöperating, the project was carried through. Cowdin writes:

Early in May (1916), we were all mobilized at the Alsatian front as the Lafayette Squadron, with French officers, Capt. Thénault and Lieut. de Laage, in command. The original members, besides those officers, were Norman Prince, William Thaw, Victor Chapman, and Kiffin Rockwell, of the Foreign Legion; James McConnell, who had already done good work in the American Ambulance before joining the French Aviation; Bert Hall, and myself. We remained but a short time in Alsace and were then transferred to the Verdun sector, where we were joined by such men as Lufbery, Masson, Clyde Balsley (who was severely wounded the first week), Dudley Hill, Lawrence Rumsey, and Chouteau Johnson.

The Squadron increased steadily, so that at the end of the following year a total of 325 men had joined it, counting those training in various schools. Of this number more than twenty-five gave their lives, and there were a number wounded and taken prisoner.

Norman Prince fortunately lived long enough to see his long-cherished ideas successfully carried out, and the Lafayette Squadron at the height of its success.

FREDERICK HENRY PRINCE, Jr.

Lafayette Escadrille

Son of Frederick Henry and Abigail (Norman) Prince; was born in Boston, on April 10, 1885. He was educated at Groton School and at Harvard College.

With his younger brother Norman, he volunteered for service before the U.S. entered the war, and on the latter's return from his Christmas furlough at home in 1915, sailed with him for France early in 1916. He enlisted in the French Army, Jan. 29, 1916; brevetted a pilot, May 21, 1916, at Buc; returned to Pau for training on Morane and Nieuport, was made a Brigadier; continued training at the Aerial Gunnery School at Cazaux, returning to Pau for the D.A.C. (Division d'Application de Combat); then to the G.D.E., where he waited for a place in Escadrille N 124 (Lafayette), joining on his brother's death Oct. 15, 1916. At the end of Feb. he was ordered to Pau as monitor, where he was made Maréchal des Logis; after six weeks he was returned to the Escadrille, then at Ham, where after a few days he was ordered back to Washington, D.C. In Sept., 1917, he was sent back to France to G.D.E. and from there ordered to report to the Chief of Liaison attached to the 26th Division, at Neuchâteau. There he remained until the middle of Jan., 1918, having been promoted to Adjudant. He was then sent to Le Bourget as convoyer, remaining until honorably discharged in April, 1918, to enter the U.S. Army.

During his service he took part in 22 aerial engagements.

Married, July 14, 1917, to Mary Elizabeth Harding, daughter of Hon. William P. G. Harding, of the Federal Reserve Board, Washington.

Brother in Service —

Norman Prince, Sous-Lieutenant, Lafayette Escadrille; killed in action, Oct. 15, 1916.

JAMES NORMAN HALL

Captain, A.S.A., U.S.A.; Escadrille Lafayette (Spad 124); French Squadron, Spad 112; One Hundred Third Pursuit Squadron, U.S.A., Flight Commander, Ninety-Fourth Pursuit Squadron

Son of Arthur Wright and Ella (Young) Hall, of Colfax, Ia.; was born in Colfax, April 22, 1887. He attended the Colfax High School; Grinnell College, from which he graduated in 1908; and the University of Chicago. For five years he made his home in Boston.

In the spring of 1914 he went to England, intending to spend a year in traveling and cycling, but on the outbreak of the war he enlisted with the 9th Battalion, Royal Fusiliers (British), London, on Aug. 18, 1914.

He spent the following winter in Aldershot and Folkestone drilling, and went on active duty in France with the 9th Royal Fusiliers on May 30, 1915. Throughout the summer he was in the trenches of Flanders, at Messines, Ploegsteert Wood, Loos, and Armentières. In Sept., 1915, he narrowly escaped death by stepping into a dugout just a moment previous to the explosion of a large German shell which killed seven men in his squad. He was shortly promoted to be Lance Corporal in charge of a machine-gun section, and was starting for an officers' training camp on Dec. 1, 1915, when he was presented with his discharge from the British Army, which, unknown to him, his friends in Boston had been active in securing for him because of the illness of his father in Colfax, Ia. He returned to the United States immediately, visited Iowa, found his father much improved, and settled in Boston where he spent the winter lecturing and working on his book "Kitchener's Mob." In June, 1916, he attended the Officers' Training Camp at Plattsburg, N.Y.

He returned to England in July, intending to continue literary work, but instead enlisted in the French Aviation Service on Oct. 13, 1916. He trained in the French aviation schools at Buc (Seine-et-Oise), Avord (Cher), and Le Plessis-Belleville (Oise), and was assigned to the Lafayette Escadrille. On June 26, 1917, he had an encounter with seven German airplanes, was shot through the shoulder and lungs, and fell 12,000 feet to what seemed certain death. But fortunately he was picked up alive and taken to a hospital near Paris, where he soon recovered. Reports of his death reached

America, but he wrote from the hospital at Neuilly to a friend that he was alive.

When he left the hospital on Sept. 22, 1917, he returned to the front as a pilot in the French Squadron, Spad 112. A fortnight later he was transferred to his old unit, the Lafayette Escadrille, with which he served, with the rank of Sergeant, until his transfer to the United States Air Service. He was commissioned Captain, A.S.A., U.S.A., on Jan. 26, 1918, and was kept on active duty with the Escadrille Lafayette which had just become the 103d Pursuit Squadron, U.S.A.S. On March 29, 1918, he was assigned to the 94th Pursuit Squadron as Flight Commander. He was shot down in combat on May 7, 1918, near Pagny-sur-Moselle, back of the German lines. He tells the story of this encounter in his book, "High Adventure."

Again it was reported that he was dead. But on May 8, a German airman flew over the Allied lines, and dropped a note saying that Hall was safe.

Capt. Hall returned to America shortly after, and on March 10, 1919, was discharged from the service at Garden City, N.Y.

Citations

Médaille Militaire

HALL, JAMES NORMAN (active de l'Escadrille N 124)

Réformé, après avoir été mitrailleur dans une armée Alliée, s'est engagé comme pilote à l'Escadrille La Fayette. Dès son arrivée a montré un courage splendide et le plus pur esprit de sacrifice. Le 26 juin 1917 a foncé seul sus sept avions ennemis, faisant l'admiration des témoins du combat, blessé grièvement dans la lutte a réussit à ramener son appareil dans nos lignes.

(Pour prendre rang du 29 juin 1917)

La présente nomination comporte l'attribution de la

Croix de Guerre avec palme

Signé: MAISTRE

Médaille Militaire

Monsieur HALL, JAMES, Caporal pilote (active) à l'Escadrille N 124, est informé que par arrêté ministériel du 13 septembre, à 1917, rendu en application du décret du 13 août 1914, la MÉDAILLE MILITAIRE lui a été concédée.

Il aura droit au port l'insigné de la décoration et aux arrérages attachés à celle-ci à compter du vingt-neuf juin 1917.

La présente concession sera régularisée ultérieurement par une loi spéciale.

Paris, le 29 octobre 1917

Pour le Président du Conseil
Ministre de la Guerre, et par son Ordre
Le Lieut. Colonel, S/Chef du Cabinet
Signé: F. JODINOT

Au G.Q. le 21 janvier 1918

Le Général Commandant la IVe Armée cite à l'Ordre de l'Armée:

Excellent Pilote de chasse, déjà blessé en combat aérien, revenu au front, y fait preuve des plus belles qualités de hardiesse et d'allant. Le 1 janvier 1918, a descendu un monoplace ennemi dont une aile s'est détachée et est tombée dans nos lignes.

Le Général Commandant le IVe Armée
Signé: GOURAUD

le 4 avril 1918

Le Général Commandant la IVe Armée cite à l'Ordre de l'Armée,

Capitaine HALL, JAMES NORMAN, de l'Escadrille Lafayette

Pilote d'une grande bravoure, qui livre journellement de nombreux combats. A abbatu deux avions ennemis.

Le Général Commandant le IVe Armée
Signé: GOURAUD

D.S.C.

G.H.Q. American Expeditionary Forces *April 10, 1918*

The Commander-in-Chief has awarded the Distinguished Service Cross to James Norman Hall, Captain, Air Service, Flight Commander 103d Aero Squadron. On March 26, 1918, while leading a patrol of three, he attacked a group of five enemy fighters and three enemy two-seaters, himself destroying one and forcing down two others which were very probably destroyed, the fight lasting more than twenty minutes.

By Command of General Pershing:
Signed: FRANK C. BURNETT
Adjutant General

Capt. Hall has also been awarded the Croix de la Légion d'Honneur.

le 9 mai 1918

Le Général Commandant la VIIIe Armée, cite à l'Ordre de l'Armée

Capitaine HALL, JAMES NORMAN, à pilote à l'escadrille américaine, 94.

Brilliant pilote de chasse, modèle de courage et d'entrain qui a abattu recemment un avion ennemi, a trouvé une mort glorieuse dans un combat contre quatre monoplaces dont un a été descendu en flammes.

Le Général Commandant la VIIIe Armée

FRAZIER CURTIS

ESCADRILLE AMÉRICAINE (LAFAYETTE), SECOND GROUPE D'AVIATION

SON of Greely Stevenson and Harriet (Appleton) Curtis; was born in Boston, July 18, 1876. He attended Mrs. Shaw's, and J. P. Hopkinson's private schools, and graduated (*cum laude*) from Harvard College in the class of 1898 (A.M. '99). He played on his class football team and on the Harvard second eleven. He was married June 16, 1909, to Gladys Margaret Roper.

In Sept., 1914, Curtis sailed for England, where he tried to enlist in the Air Service. Being rejected on account of his age and nationality, he returned to the U.S. hoping to take back to Europe a Burgess-Dunne seaplane, which might be of assistance in his next application. At Marblehead he met Norman Prince and discussed with him the idea of creating an American Escadrille in the French Army. Returning to England he tried again unsuccessfully to enter the British service. In Feb. he went to Paris, and with Prince organized the American Escadrille, later called the Lafayette.

Curtis trained with the Escadrille at Pau, and later at the Camp d'Avord, until disabled by two accidents; his machine catching fire at about 2000 feet, followed five days later by an axle breaking in two places on landing. After a week in the hospital he was given 45 days' sick-leave. At the end of his furlough he applied to be transferred from a bombing-machine, on which he had been hurt, to a fighting-machine. In answer to this request the French War Office gave him an honorable discharge as unfit for further flying, on Aug. 8, 1915.

After four months' rest in England, he returned to the U.S. and in March, 1916, organized the Harvard Flying Corps, but his health again broke down and he had to give up his work and go to California to recuperate.

It is believed that Curtis was the first American pilot to go over to Europe to offer his services to the Allied Air Force, having sailed from Boston on the Arabic, Sept. 2, 1914.

Frazier Curtis's father, Greely S. Curtis, organized and commanded the 1st Mass. Cavalry in the Civil War. His grandfather served aboard the U.S.S. *Chesapeake* and U.S.S. *Constitution* in the War of 1812, and his great-grandfather was one of the "Boston Tea Party."

The following letter of appreciation was sent to Curtis by his French Commander:

MON CHER CURTIS:

Vos deux lettres, ainsi que votre résiliation d'engagement me sont arrivées, et j'ai fait part de cette dernière au ministère. Nous avons bien regrettés que votre état de santé ne vous permette pas de continuer votre entraînement et vous empêche ainsi de devenir le hardi pilote que vous promettiez d'être, d'après vos excellents et rapides progrès à l'école d'aviation d'Avord.

Sans ce malencontreux accident, au cours de vos épreuves du Brevet Militaire, vous auriez en 48 heures, terminé ce B.M. Vous auriez ainsi complété une brilliante escadrille avec vos camarades venus en même que vous et qui se sont également fait remarquer pour leurs qualités de sang-froid et d'énergie.

Soyez certain, mon cher Curtis, que nous garderons le meilleur souvenir de vous et de vos charmants camarades, et croyez bien, je vous prie, à l'assurance de mes meilleurs sentiments.

Signé: HUSSIGNY

CHARLES H. DOLAN, Jr.

Lafayette Escadrille, First Lieutenant, A.S., U.S.A., One Hundred Third Aero Squadron, Third Pursuit Group

Son of Charles H. and Anne (Mainwaring) Dolan; was born at Boston, Mass., Jan. 29, 1895. He graduated from Mechanic Arts High School, where he was secretary and treasurer of his class; studied electrical engineering for one and a half years at Mass. Institute of Technology. Chief inspector of a munition works in England for one year. Installing engineer in France for Sperry Gyroscope Company, 1915–16. Joined French Air Service, Aug., 1916, and assigned to Lafayette Escadrille.

Lieut. Dolan has given the following summary of service, which contains an admirable outline of the activities of the Escadrille:

I joined the French Foreign Legion as a 2d-class soldier in Aug., 1916. I immediately transferred to the Air Service, was sent to the old Blériot School at Buc on the hills surrounding Versailles. I took preliminary instruction, and on the moving of the school went with it to Avord. I got my license and went through the School of Perfection work on Nieuports there. From Avord I went to Pau, Basses Pyrénées, to the School of Acrobatics and Combat, where I took my final training before going into reserve at the front. I was in reserve about ten days at G.D.E. at Plessis-Belleville, near Paris, when I was ordered to join the Lafayette Escadrille N 124 at Ham. On the Somme, James MacConnell, Roland Hoskier, and Genêt were killed. Our sector on this front was from Moy to Anizy-le-Château, during the great German retreat in 1916.

From there we went to the Aisne, and from the Aisne to Dunkirk (St.-Pol). But because of very bad weather, we did very little flying in this sector which ran from the sea to Armentières. We were then ordered to Verdun, where we lost Willis as a prisoner, and MacMonagle killed. The Squadron was here cited for the first time. After this attack the group of which the Squadron was a part was ordered to Chaudun to patrol the Chemin des Dames from Coranne to La Fère. The battle of Chemin des Dames was fought in a drizzle and fog and none of us flew over 200 feet. Campbell was killed in this battle.

From here we were ordered, in the middle of winter on six hours' notice, to go to Champagne, and in anticipation of a German winter attack, which never occurred. We spent the winter practically on the same spot that Attila, "King of the Huns," occupied in the year 451 when he overran the Franks, between the towns of Le Cheppe and La Noblette. Our sector which we patrolled here was from Reims to the Forest of Argonne.

While here Edward Laughlin and Stuart Walcott, American boys in a French Squadron in our group, were killed. It was here in Champagne that we transferred to the American Expeditionary Forces and were taken over as an American unit known as the 103d Aero Pursuit Squadron, under command of Major William Thaw, Nov., 1918, and I was made Engineer Officer in addition to my flying duties. As such, we continued with American personnel to operate under the direction of the French, and moved shortly after to Fismes, where we were signally honored by the French by being given the sector from Reims to Noyon — the longest sector given to a pursuit squadron — to patrol, being the only pursuit squadron on a front of 65 miles; and at that we carried the fight into the enemy's country, because of the German concentration on the Somme where all the Allied Aviation was also concentrated.

In the early part of June we were ordered north to Dunkirk, and had our aerodrome on the border of Belgium at Leffrinckoucke. While here we acted in unison with a French photo squadron, which did some of the most wonderful aerial photography of the war. We also acted with the French Army of the North and the Northeast, at the battle of Mont Kemmel.

We were again cited in the Order of the Army and were granted the privilege of wearing the *fourragère* and the colors of the Croix de Guerre.

Because of extensive bombing we had to move our field to another site southwest of Dunkirk near the town of Steene. The sector we patrolled was from the sea to the Forest of Nieppe, including the Ypres salient, and as far south, sometimes, as Béthune.

The first of July we were ordered to join the American Army, 2d Pursuit Group, at Toul, in the St.-Mihiel sector, which we patrolled from St.-Mihiel to Bey.

Just before the battle of St.-Mihiel, while in this sector, Major Thaw was given command of the 3d Pursuit Group, Capt. Robert Rockwell took command of the old Lafayette Squadron — now the 103d — and as the 3d Pursuit Group we participated in the battle of the First American Army. We were felicitated for our work and lost very few men.

We moved with the First Army when they moved up in the Argonne, and between the Argonne and the Meuse patrolled the Verdun salient from St.-Mihiel to Argonne.

Our aerodrome at this time was at Lisle-en-Barrois. It was on Oct. 16, 1918, that I was ordered home to report to the Office of the Director of Military Aeronautics, Washington, D.C., to be used in an advisory capacity on pursuit work; and with my chum, Major David McK. Peterson, went to Carlstrom and Dorr Fields, Arcadia, Fla., where the most advanced pursuit and aerial gunnery schools in the country were. There I was put on the Control Board and also made Engineer Officer at Carlstrom Field. After Major Peterson's death, I was transferred to the O.D.A.S. Information Group, Washington, D.C., where I now am.

STEPHEN SOHIER BIGELOW

Sergeant, Foreign Legion, and Escadrille Lafayette, N 124, Group 13

Son of Joseph S. and Mary C. Bigelow; was born at Boston, March 18, 1894. He graduated from Groton in 1911, and from Harvard College in 1915. He attended the Plattsburg Training Camp in 1915, and April 13, 1916, enlisted in the Foreign Legion at Paris, France. In June he entered the Air Service and was trained at Dijon, Buc, Avord, Pau, Cazaux, and Plessis-Belleville; he received his Brevet as Military Aviator on Sept. 7, 1916, and on Oct. 18, he was brevetted as *Pilote Aviateur* No. 4651. He was attached to the Escadrille Lafayette N 102, and later to N 124. On April 28, 1917, he was detailed with four others to act as *garde d'honneur* chosen to represent the Escadrille Lafayette, at the ceremonies performed at the monument of Lafayette. On June 21 he had a miraculous escape from five enemy planes which attacked while he was protecting French machines engaged in photographing the enemy's position. He landed safely, as did the photographers, a large hole in the wing of his machine being the only casualty. On June 24 and June 30 he had two successful engagements with enemy planes; on June 25 he was mentioned in the official report on American flyers. On Aug. 22 he was attacked by several German planes, but escaped unhurt, and on Aug. 23, being attacked by eight German flyers, his machine was crippled and he was wounded about the head and face. On Sept. 14, 1917, he was officially cited in Army orders and shortly afterwards decorated with the Croix de Guerre.

Citation

Sergeant Bigelow, an American volunteer pilot, engaged six Germans on Aug. 22, while protecting a bombing squadron. He was slightly wounded, but repelled the enemy.

In Jan., 1918, he was honorably discharged from Hospital No. 6, being pronounced physically unfit for further active service.

Brothers in Service—

Joseph S. Bigelow, Jr., American Ambulance Field Service; 1st Lieut., U.S.A., Aviation Signal Corps, A.E.F.

Arthur G. Bigelow, American Ambulance Field Service; Private, U.S.A., A.E.F.

WALTER LOVELL

Captain, Lafayette Escadrille

Son of Wallace D. and Josephine (Hastings) Lovell; was born at Newton, Mass., Sept. 9, 1884. He was educated at Milton Academy, Newton High School, the Stone School, Boston, and Harvard College, A.B. 1907. He was a member of the 1st Corps Cadets, M.V.M.

In Feb., 1915, he enlisted with the American Ambulance Field Service in France, and was made second in command of Sec. 3, which did remarkable service in Alsace. He received the Croix de Guerre for his work there. In 1916 he transferred to Aviation, and joined the Lafayette Escadrille, with which he did such notable service as to win the Croix de Guerre of Aviation, and the Médaille d'Argent of the Aero Club of France. He was credited with two German planes officially and with four unofficially. While in the American Service he was in charge of assigning personnel for the Air Service Squadrons at Colombey-les-Belles. In Aug., 1918, he came to the United States for purposes of instruction. In Jan., 1919, he resigned at Washington, D.C.

Capt. Lovell was married to Hélène du Bouchet on April 15, 1918, and has taken up his residence in Paris.

From Lieut. Lovell's Ambulance Service citation one reads:

> Has always given proof of a noteworthy spirit and constantly set the example of courage to the other drivers.

Brothers in Service —

- Endicott Remington Lovell, Capt., U.S.A., 301st Reg't, F.A., 76th Division.
- Philip Gray Lovell, 1st Lieut., U.S.A., 101st Reg't, F.A., 26th Division.

RUSSELL FALCONER STEARNS

CORPORAL, LAFAYETTE FLYING CORPS, ESCADRILLE S 150,
GROUPE DE COMBAT 16
SECOND LIEUTENANT, U.S. MARINE FLYING CORPS

SON of Walter Henry and Abbie Harris (Razee) Stearns; was born at Pawtucket, R.I., Jan. 4, 1896. He was educated at Lake Placid School and at the University of Virginia, class of 1918.

On Jan. 8, 1917, he enlisted in the American Ambulance Corps for two months. He then transferred through the Foreign Legion to the Aviation Service of the French Army. He was sent to Camp Avord, and presently became a member of the Lafayette Flying Corps. He was brevetted at Jévisy and had intensive flying at Pau, and Plessis-Belleville.

During his training at Jévisy, Lieut. Stearns wrote to his family on June 23, 1917, as follows:

> We are a few miles out of Belfort which I like immensely and which gets bombed often. The German machines fly over our airdrome quite frequently, and then the anti-aircraft guns get busy and we have quite a time. My work consists of escorting bombing-planes, patrolling, and hunting. I am given my regular machine to-morrow, which I regret to say is a type out of vogue and which enables the crafty Hun to make circles around me. However, our entire escadrille changes to Spads in ten days, and there is no better machine out than that. . . . Aviation is a great game which requires perfection in all a man's faculties, and I am trying to keep myself in the best physical shape possible, one false step might mean the end. . . . I have become a fatalist as every aviator does, and am prepared to accept whatever awaits me.

For two months and a half, late in 1917, he flew at the front, his first flight over the German lines being as a member of Escadrille 150, Groupe de Combat 16. On one occasion while travelling over the lines alone, three German planes attacked him, but he eluded them and returned in safety. He was located in the Alsace-Lorraine section. In May, 1918, he received furlough from France, and then entered the U.S. Service, of the Marine Flying Corps. He was sent to Florida as 2d Lieut. He was honorably discharged on account of nervous breakdown.

*WALTER DAVIS RHENO

FIRST LIEUTENANT, A.S.A., U.S.A., ESCADRILLE 80, LAFAYETTE SQUADRON

Died of pneumonia, Oct. 10, 1918

SON of Simeon L. and Clara (Pratt) Rheno; was born in Vineyard Haven, Mass., on Feb. 26, 1895. He was educated in the public schools of Vineyard Haven. In the latter part of 1916, he abandoned the automobile business in which he was engaged in New York City, sailed for France, and enlisted in the Foreign Legion, in Paris, on Dec. 19, 1916. In Jan., 1917, he applied for transfer to the Aviation Service, and in Feb. started his training at the École d'Aviation Militaire at Buc, near Versailles, continuing at Pau and at Avord. On May 10, 1917, he received the French Military License. After perfection air work in the one-man combat machine known as the Fighting Chasse, the fastest of fighting machines in use at the front, he was ordered to the war zone on July 1, 1917. He was sent to Verdun on July 16 to join fighting Squadron N 80 of the Groupe de Combat. On his arrival at Verdun, he found awaiting him notice of 21 days' leave of absence in the United States, but did not accept it, because he did not wish to return home without having seen active service. It was at this time that he made the wager that he would down a German machine within a month. This he accomplished on Aug. 18, when in a fighting chasse with one gun, he downed a two-man German Albatross carrying four guns, after an 11-minute combat. For this engagement he was cited and decorated. On this occasion Rheno received the following letter from Dr. Edmond Gros, dated Aug. 23, 1917:

> Bravo! I think you hold the record for shortness of time you were at the front before bringing down your Boche. When you get your citation send me a certified copy and I'll see if we can give you a money prize.
>
> The Associated Press has heard of your exploit and I have no doubt that you will be a hero in every aviation camp of America very shortly — all prospective aviators in the United States will envy you.
>
> Very truly yours
>
> (*Signed*) EDMOND GROS

On Sept. 6, he won his second combat, defeating a one-man German Albatross scout machine in a one-minute fight. For this exploit, when still a pilot, without higher title, he won the Croix de

Guerre as a member of the Lafayette Squadron, French Aviation Corps. On Sept. 12, 1917, he defeated his third machine, a one-man German Albatross, for which he received official confirmation. He also brought down seven other machines which fell too far within German territory for confirmation by the French observation posts, but which were confirmed by comrades flying with him, a confirmation not considered official.

On Sept. 18, 1917, he left for Paris to secure his passport for the leave granted him in America in the first days of his stay at the front. He received his passport Sept. 19, 1917, and revisited the United States the following Nov. wearing the second palm on his Croix de Guerre with a third on its way. On his return to the front, he was transferred to the American Forces with the commission of a 1st Lieut.

He died at the American Hospital at Neuilly-sur-Seine, on Oct. 10, 1918, of pneumonia, and was buried in the New Cemetery in Neuilly, France.

Confirmations (Official)

14th Fighting Group
Escadrille N 80 — *Postal District, no.* 8, *August* 31, 1917

No. 4141.

Captain GLAIZE, Commander of Escadrille N 80, certifies that Corporal WALTER DAVIS RHENO, a Pilot in the Escadrille, brought down a German biplane "Albatross" after twice attacking it, on the 18th of August, 1917, at 7.40 P.M. Corporal RHENO was piloting the "Spad" No. 1298, Type S VII, 140 H.P. Motor.

The Captain Commanding the Escadrille

14th Fighting Group
Escadrille N 80 — *Postal District, no.* 8, *Sept.* 16, 1917

No. 487.

Captain GLAIZE, Commander of Escadrille N 80, certifies that Corporal WALTER DAVIS RHENO, a Pilot in the Escadrille, brought down a German monoplane "Albatross" after once attacking it, on the 6th day of September at 10.10 A.M. Corporal RHENO was piloting the "Spad" No. 1776, Type S VII.

The Captain Commanding the Escadrille

WALTER DAVIS RHENO

Citation

Croix de Guerre

14 *Groupe d'Escadrille*
de Combat *S.P.* 8 *septembre* 1917

Extrait de l'Ordre Général No. 889

Le Général Commandant la IIe Armée à l'ordre de l'Armée:

. . . .

Le Caporal Rheno, Walter Davis, pilote à l'Escadrille N 80

Très bon pilote américain montre de grandes qualités d'audace et d'entrain; le 18 août a abattu un biplane ennemi qui s'est écrasé dans ses lignes.

Signée: Le Commandant de G.C. 14

Brother in Service —

Winthrop C. Rheno, honorably discharged from the Army at Camp Devens, Oct. 28, 1918.

*FRANK ELMER STARRETT, Jr.

Cadet, Lafayette Escadrille

Killed in airplane accident, Dec.. 1917

Son of Frank Elmer and Lena Dora (Hoehm) Starrett; was born in Athol, Mass., on July 16, 1893. He graduated from the Athol High School, from Worcester Academy, Worcester, Mass., and from Brown University. He played football and baseball at Worcester Academy; at Brown, he was manager of the track team, member of the Beta Theta Pi Fraternity, the Camarian and Sphinx Clubs.

He entered the American Ambulance Field Service, Nov. 1, 1916, and served six months in France, in Red Cross Section 5–646, which won the Croix de Guerre, and green and yellow *fourragères*. He afterward enlisted in the French Aviation Service, and was assigned to the Lafayette Escadrille. He was among the first 200 men to train at Tours, France, in Aug., 1917, a group called the "Stranger Legion," made up of American boys who had volunteered with the French before the United States entered the war. He was detained in the hospital for some time by illness so that he fell behind his class, but on his return from the hospital, he continued his training (on the Caudron G–3 type). In Dec., 1917, as Starrett was making the first lap of the triangle from Tours to Pontleroy, which was part of the trial test, he was first seen by the mechanics at the field, about 500 metres from the ground, heading for the airdrome. Suddenly the plane peeked over and dived for the earth about two kilometres from the hangars, never redressing. Starrett died instantly. He was buried at Tours with full military honors by the French and American officials. Just at the time of his accident he had been planning to return home on a furlough. In a memorial discourse delivered before the students of Brown University some time after his death, the Dean said that Frank Starrett was a man whom all Brown men might well emulate, and whose memory should be ever cherished by the university.

Brother in Service —

Arthur H. Starrett, Cadet, A.S.A., U.S.A.; Sergeant, 1st class, in 139th and 32d Aero Squadrons. In service in France for 14 months.

HAROLD BUCKLEY WILLIS

Sous-Lieutenant, Lafayette Escadrille

Son of John B. and Myrta (Gale) Willis; was born at Boston, Mass., Feb. 9, 1890. He attended the Newton High School, and graduated from Harvard College, class of 1912. He served in Battery A, M.V.M., 1913–14.

He enlisted in the American Ambulance Field Service in Feb., 1915, and arrived at the western front, with Section 2, at Pont-à-Mousson, in April, 1915. From Feb. to May he served with the Ambulance at Verdun. He was cited, July 4, 1915, "for rescue of wounded under fire," offensive Bois-le-Prêtre, "Croix de Guerre with Star."

In June, 1915, he enlisted in the Foreign Legion of the French Army, and transferred to 2d Groupe d'Aviation. He was brevetted pilot on Blériot, at Buc. He trained successively at Nieuport Perfectionnement School, at Avord; Machine-Gun School, Cazaux; Combat and Acrobatics, at Pau; Spad, at Plessis-Belleville.

He arrived on the Somme front with the Lafayette Escadrille (N 124), in March, 1917, under Capt. Théraul and Lieut. Thaw. Served during the Somme retreat to the Hindenburg line, March to April, 1917; the offensive of Aisne, April and May, 1917; the Ypres offensive, July and Aug., 1917; Verdun, 1917.

He was awarded the silver medal of Ligue Aéronautique de France, in May, 1917, and recommended for Order of Leopold, by C.O. 13th Groupe de Combat, July, 1917. Proposed for Sous-Lieut. in French Army, July, 1917, and cited for Croix de Guerre with palm, Aug., 1917; he was also recommended for Majority to U.S. Aviation, by Com. Féquant, C.O. 13th Groupe de Combat, Aug., 1917.

On Aug. 18, 1917, Lieut. Willis was shot down behind the enemy lines at Verdun, and was interned in the prison camps of Montmédy, Carlsruhe, Landshut, Gütersloh, reprisal camp Eutin, Bad Stuer, Mecklenburg-Schwerin, Magdenburg, Wurzburg, and Villingen, during 14 months of captivity.

After several attempts, Lieut. Willis, disguised as a German guard, made his escape from the American camp at Villingen on Oct. 4, 1918, in company with Lieut. Isaacs, U.S.N., and Lieut. Puryear, U.S.A. This plan was accomplished by means of an intricate and

coördinated plot of many American and Polish officers, electric lights being short-circuited, barbed-wire palisades and cordons of guards being pierced at several points simultaneously. Isaacs and Willis crossed the Black Forest mountains together, travelling at night by means of luminous compasses, and aided by the stars, hiding by day. After a week they arrived at the Rhine frontier of Switzerland, which was crossed by swimming.

On arriving at Paris, Lieut. Willis was awarded the Médaille Militaire, and permitted to return to the Argonne front. Returning to the U.S. in 1919, he was honorably discharged.

Citations

Croix de Guerre

Citation à l'Ordre du Service de Santé de la 73me Division, N° 19.

Par application du décret du 23 avril 1915, sur la Croix de Guerre, le Médecin Divisionnaire cite à l'ordre du jour du service de santé de la 73me Division —

Monsieur WILLIS, HAROLD, conducteur à la S.S.A.A.

A toujours fait preuve d'un courage et d'une hardiesse dignes des plus grands éloges, notamment pendant l'attaque du 4 juillet; s'offrit pour aller chercher des blessés dans un endroit très périlleux et eut sa voiture criblée d'éclats d'obus.

En campagne le 5 octobre 1915

Signé : D. W. VIELE
Le Médecin Chef

A l'Ordre de l'Armée

Ordre du Général Commandant la 2me Armée, N° 889 du 10 sept. 1917.

Le Général Commandant la 2me Armée cite à l'Ordre de l'Armée:

WILLIS, HAROLD BUCKLEY, sergent pilote à l'escadrille N 124 (G.C. 13) (mort en combat):

Citoyen américain engagé au service de la France. Véritable modèle pour ses camarades d'escadrille par son courage et sa haute conception du devoir. A fourni par des reconnaissances de nombreux et utiles renseignements. Est tombé 18 août au cours d'un combat contre deux avions ennemis qui venaient attaquer des avions de bombardement qu'il escortait.

FIRST PURSUIT GROUP

By Lieutenant James Knowles, American Ace, Ninety-Fifth Aero Squadron

After the arrival of the 95th Squadron at the Gengoult airdrome, the 1st Pursuit Group was officially formed on May 5, 1918. The Group was composed of the 94th and 95th Squadrons. Although these Squadrons had been on the front since the middle of Feb. they had not operated over the front to any extent because the pilots of the 94th, although they had planes, had no machine guns, and the 95th with machine guns had no planes.

On May 31, 1918, the 27th and 147th Squadrons joined the Group, thus bringing it up to full strength. At that time the Group was operating with the 8th French Army at Toul, and up to June 25 had shot down 58 Boche planes, 27 of which were confirmed. Toward the end of June, the Group moved to Touquin, in the Château-Thierry sector, and started operations there. The preponderance of German aviation on that sector necessarily caused very heavy losses, the Group losing 36 pilots in a period of about six weeks, although credited with 38 Hun machines destroyed.

During all this time the Group was attached to the 6th French Army and did not operate with the American Army until the St.-Mihiel offensive in Sept.

On Sept. 1, 1918, the Group moved to Enze-la-Pétire, where it stayed until the Armistice. At Dumey, the St.-Mihiel attack, "low flying on the offensive" was the order. This was also done through the Argonne-Meuse attack, and at no time did any pilot in the Group fly at more than 600 metres, except as a voluntary patrol. Ground and balloon "strafing," and attacks on enemy réglages and observation machines constituted the day's work.

On Oct. 7, 1918, the 185th, a night-flying Chasse Squadron, joined the Group. From Sept. 12 to Oct. 12 the Group shot down 104 planes and balloons officially; an average of almost one victory for each Squadron.

At the Armistice the Group was credited with 285 victories, 201 of which were official, and had suffered 72 casualties. To show the calibre of the 1st Pursuit Group, one needs only mention Capt. Edward Rickenbacker, Maj. Raoul Lufbery, Capt. James Norman Hall, and Capt. David Peterson.

*RICHARD ASHLEY BLODGETT

FIRST LIEUTENANT, A.S., U.S.A., NINETY-FIFTH AERO SQUADRON

Killed in action, May 17, 1918

SON of Edward E. and Mabel (Fuller) Blodgett; was born in Brookline, Mass., June 27, 1897. He attended the Newton High School, and Lawrenceville, N.J., where he was prominent in athletics. He entered Williams College in the class of 1919, and during his freshman year played on his class football team and was captain of the hockey team; the following year was on the 'Varsity football squad. He was an admirable musician and played on several instruments; he was a member of the Sigma Phi Fraternity.

In 1916 he attended the Officers' Training Camp at Plattsburg, and when war was declared he volunteered for six months' ambulance service abroad, leaving college in his sophomore year. He sailed for France May 5, 1917, and when on arrival he found the ambulance service overcrowded, he signed for six months' duty as a munitions truck-driver, during which time he won a commendation from the French Commander, for "courage and coolness displayed under violent bombardment July 28, 1917."

Before the time of his camion service had expired, he was transferred to Aviation, training at Tours, Issoudun, and graduating from the School of Acrobatics. He was an able and enthusiastic flyer, and it was believed he would surely become an ace. When the 95th Pursuit Squadron was formed, he was assigned to it and accompanied it to the Toul sector; and about March 1 he was one of a famous trio that went over the lines patrolling without guns between Épernay and Reims at 5500 metres.

As soon as the guns arrived he was eager to try them, and on May 9 he wrote:

> At last we've got guns on our planes. You know we were at the front for six weeks without them; my first trip over the lines with a gun, I got in a fight with two German biplanes. There were four of us (all in monoplane fighters) and we split up and two attacked each plane.
>
> There was a Major with me and first thing his gun jammed. That put it up to me; so I went in hell bent for election. I manœuvred as much as possible so his machine-gunner could n't shoot at me, and let him have it. I shot two hundred and sixty rounds into him. I followed him all the way to his airdrome, killing his observer, and I think starting a fire, as he let out clouds of smoke. My comrades were all split up and the last time they saw me I was following the German right home. They thought surely the

anti-aircraft would get me, as I was very low, but they did n't even shoot at me. I ran out of gas just after re-crossing the lines into France and they thought surely I had been brought down, until I telephoned in. It was a pretty exciting game.

Most of our work is far back of the German lines, as they won't come to meet us usually. In the last two days, however, there have been two new German pursuit squadrons in our sector, supported by another squadron of Von Richthofen's circus, or all aces. They have brought down two of our men, one of them James Norman Hall, author of "Kitchener's Mob," and whom I saw shot down last summer while he was with the French on his second trip over the lines. This time in German territory; so we don't know whether he survived or not. The other fell in flames.

We have caused so much damage here that they are out for revenge, and there's going to be hell breaking loose. It's a great game and you have to keep on the watch every second. Even when shooting one man, you have to watch another does n't drop on you. But, Dad, we're giving them hell. We're winning. We're showing fight and ability and we're fighting cleanly and cleverly. The cost is awful, but it's far worse for them. This sector is going to see some terrible casualties, but we've got to do it.

If I go out, you can know that I went game; that before I went I brought one down; that we're beginning to get up against the best, but that we make him pay heavily for his victory.

On May 17 Blodgett and Lieut. Sewall went out in the morning to protect an observation plane; during an attack by hostile pursuit planes, Blodgett engaged one German and drove him down behind the enemy lines. When the two pursuit planes started back with the observation plane, Blodgett was flying very high. When on the return of the other planes he failed to appear, it was supposed that he had gone off by himself to look for another German; when he finally appeared, his flying in coming down attracted some attention, as he seemed to be trying to land some distance from the airdrome. Suddenly his machine crashed to the ground, and though help arrived promptly the fall had proved fatal. There were two bullet holes through the bottom of the machine, and the conclusion was that Blodgett had been in a fight, was wounded in the head, but had been able to get almost back when he lost control of his machine.

He was buried with full military honors, at Sebastopol, France, and lies next to Major Lufbery, who was killed the following day. He was known as a daring and efficient flyer and acted as instructor while still a cadet. He received his commission as 1st Lieut. Dec.,

1917, and was leader of the first American patrol to patrol the front in aviation; he was, in the absence of his ranking officer, Flight Commander, and he drove a fast fighting monoplace, capable of making 140 miles an hour.

Major Davenport Johnson, of the 95th Aero Squadron wrote of Blodgett:

> We had become very fond of Dick and deeply feel his loss, and the one idea is to avenge him, which we have done to date, by bringing down four enemy planes (official), and six others which were too far in the German lines for the infantry to see from the ground. His memory is always fresh in our minds, as he was the first of our number to give all for his country.

Lieut. Alden Bradford Sherry, who had been with Blodgett both in training and in the Ambulance Service, wrote:

> His kindness and cheerfulness towards others, his sunny nature and his simplicity of character, all endeared him to us. Out here on the front it was his ability as a flyer, his quick perception of his duty, and his great zeal in carrying out his work, without any thought of the risk involved, which made our admiration for him almost as great as our affection. He was flying all the time and was almost unhappy when he was not in the air. His impetuosity and his enthusiasm had a most marked influence on his entire squadron, which was most apparent to my squadron which was working with his. . . . The first day he flew over the lines he attacked a two-man German plane and brought it down single handed. The combat took place so far behind the lines that none of the French and American observers saw the German fall, or he would have received official recognition of his victory.

Citation

American Field Service in France
Lettre de Félicitations

Le Chef d'Escadron, Directeur des Services Automobiles aux Armées, adresse ses félicitations au Personnel du 3e Peloton de la Section-Groupe Américaine Génin, placé sous les orders du Chef de Peloton H. E. Cox, pour le sang-froid et le courage dont il a fait preuve dans la nuit du 28 juillet 1917, au cours d'un déchargement dans un dépôt soumis à un violent bombardement.

Signé: Doumenc

SUMNER SEWALL

First Lieutenant, A.S.A., U.S.A., Ninety-Fifth Aero Squadron, First Pursuit Group

Son of William D. and Mary L. (Sumner) Sewall of Bath, Me.; was born in Bath, June 17, 1897. He fitted for college at the Westminster School, Simsbury, Conn., and entered Harvard College with the class of 1920. He attended the Officers' Training Camp at Plattsburg, N.Y., in July, 1916. In the second half of his freshman year he left college to sail with the American Ambulance Field Service, with which he served in France from Feb. 17 to Aug. 20, 1917.

He enlisted in the American Air Service in Paris on Aug. 23, 1917, and was assigned to Tours for preliminary training with the 3d Platoon on Sept. 2. He was transferred to the 3d Aviation Instruction Centre at Issoudun. He subsequently took a course in aerial gunnery at Cazaux, and was commissioned 1st Lieut. on Dec. 8, 1917. In Feb., 1918, the 95th Pursuit Squadron was formed at Issoudun, and Lieut. Sewall was assigned to it. On March 1, with Lieuts. Blodgett and Wooley, he went over the line on the first patrol without machine guns at 5500 metres, in a type 28-metre Nieuport between Épernay and Reims. Later, the Squadron was sent to Château-Thierry, where Lieut. Sewall succeeded in bringing down several Boches. In Sept. the 95th Squadron moved to Rembercourt, took part in the St.-Mihiel drive, and continued on through the Argonne offensive until the Armistice was signed. During these two drives, Lieut. Sewall was officially credited with 7 Boches, and became an Ace in Oct., 1918. He was recommended for promotion at the close of the war. The French Government awarded to him the Legion of Honor, and the Croix de Guerre with a palm. From his own Government he received the Distinguished Service Cross with one oak leaf. He was made a member of the Order of Leopold, by King Albert I of Belgium. In Jan., 1919, the Aero Club of America awarded him its medal. He was honorably discharged at Garden City, N.Y., on Feb. 20, 1919.

Recommendation for Promotion

On Nov. 27, 1918, Lieut. Sewall received this letter from the Chief of the Air Service, A.E.F.:

The exceptionally meritorious service which you have rendered with

the American Expeditionary Forces resulted in a recommendation for promotion in grade submitted by your superior officers. The Chief of Air Service approved the recommendation, but unfortunately instructions from the War Department discontinued all promotions of officers on the 11th inst. making it impossible to confer the reward which you have so well earned.

While communicating the above information, the undersigned takes this opportunity of thanking you personally for the assistance contributed toward the American air successes in the great war now drawing to a close.

(Signed) MASON M. PATRICK
Major General, N.A.
Chief of Air Service

Order of the Crown

On Feb. 12, 1919, Lieut. Sewall received from the Chief of the Belgian Mission in France, the letter which follows:

My dear Lieutenant:

The KING, Albert I of Belgium, has given me instructions to inform you that He has bestowed upon you the

Ordre de la Couronne

with the rank of "Chevalier."

His Majesty desires that this honorary distinction be conveyed to you as a token of His esteem and in recognition of the valuable services you have rendered the common cause.

The medal will be handed over to you by the Adjutant General.

Please accept my most cordial greetings.

I am, my dear Lieutenant,

Very truly yours
(Signed) J. M. CINAUT
Chief of the Belgian Mission

Citations

D.S.C.

First Lieutenant SUMNER SEWALL, Air Service, 95th Aero Squadron

For repeated acts of extraordinary heroism in action near Menil-la-Tour, France, June 3, 1918, and near Landres St.-Georges, France, Oct. 13, 1918. On June 3 Lieut. Sewall with two other pilots attacked a formation of six hostile planes. Though his comrades were forced to withdraw because of jammed guns, he continued to fight for fifteen minutes and succeeded in sending one of his adversaries down in flames. On Oct. 18, while on voluntary patrol this officer saw an American observation plane being attacked by a German machine (Fokker type), accompanied by eight other hostile planes. He immediately attacked and destroyed the Fokker and was in turn attacked by the other eight planes. By skilful manœuvring he evaded them and escorted the observation plane back to our lines.

(Signed) PERSHING

An oak leaf to be worn with the D.S.C. was awarded to Lieut. Sewall on Dec. 28, 1918.

First Lieutenant SUMNER SEWALL, Air Service, 95th Aero Squadron

For the following act of extraordinary heroism in action near Rocourt, France, July 7, 1918, Lieutenant Sumner Sewall is awarded an oak leaf to be worn with the Distinguished Service Cross awarded him 10 Dec. 1918. Lieutenant Sewall fearlessly attacked a formation of five enemy planes (Type K Fokker) and separating one from the group, pursued it far behind the enemy's lines and sent it down in crash, following it within 30 metres of the ground in spite of severe fire from a machine gun, rifles, and anti-aircraft guns, bullets from which passed through his clothing.

(Signed) PERSHING

Legion of Honor and Croix de Guerre (awarded Nov. 30, 1918)

Ier Lieutenant SUMNER SEWALL, à l'Escadrille américaine 95:

Pilote ardent en combat, ayant une haute conception de son devoir, le 3 juin, a attaqué, avec sa patrouille, une formation ennemie de 6 avions, a poursuivi l'un d'entre eux jusqu'à 200 métres du sol et l'a abattu. Au cours des opérations Marne-Aisne, s'est dépensé sans compter, descendant un avion ennemi en flammes et forçant un deuxième adversaire à attérir.

Au Grand Quartier Général, le 30 novembre 1918.

LE MARÉCHAL DE FRANCE
Commandant en Chef les Armées Françaises de l'Est

JOHN MITCHELL

CAPTAIN, A.S.A., U.S.A., NINETY-FIFTH AERO SQUADRON FIRST PURSUIT GROUP

SON of Walter J. and Eva B. (Sherlock) Mitchell; was born at Cincinnati, Ohio, Oct. 15, 1895. He attended the Fay School, Southboro, Mass., and St. Mark's School, Concord, N.H., and graduated from Harvard College.

He enlisted (from Manchester, Mass.) at Key West, Fla., on March 1, 1917; was trained at Miami, Fla., Essington, Pa., and at M.I.T. He was commissioned 1st Lieut. June 27, 1917, and went overseas Sept. 1, 1917, continuing his training at Issoudun and Cazaux, France, and joined the 95th Squadron.

At Toul he was credited with helping members of his squadron to bring down two Boches, and at Château-Thierry he did excellent work in patrolling and strafing infantry formations. During a "dog fight" with Richthofen's circus, he divided the honors with Lieut. Heinrichs in bringing down one of the circus.

The following are official confirmations of several combats in which he was engaged:

I, Captain David McK. Peterson, A.S., Sig. R.C., certify that First Lieutenant John Mitchell, of the 95th Squadron, has been engaged in the following mentioned combats with the enemy, the results of which have been officially confirmed by the French and American military authorities:

(*a*) On May 27, 1918, Lieutenant Mitchell encountered three enemy airplanes over Apremont. He dove on the last airplane in the formation, and after firing a burst of forty shots, it crashed to the ground. (Confirmed in Operations Report No. 18, Hdqrs. 1st Pursuit Group, June 16, 1918.)

(*b*) On May 30, 1918, Lieutenant Mitchell at 8.15 A.M. encountered two enemy airplanes in the vicinity of Apremont, who turned and headed toward the lines. He caught up with the rear German airplane, and fired 185 rounds from above. The German dove into a nose-dive and crashed to the ground in flames. (Confirmed in Operations Report No. 18, Hdqrs. 1st Pursuit Group, June 16, 1918.)

(*c*) On July 5, 1918, Lieutenant Mitchell, near Priez, encountered six enemy Albatross monoplanes. He attacked the highest one and engaged in a running fight, lasting twenty minutes, which terminated by the German bursting into flames. (Confirmed in Operations Report, Hdqrs. 1st Pursuit Group, Order No. 59.) Attest: DAVID MCK. PETERSON

On Aug. 1, 1918, Lieut. Mitchell was commissioned Captain, and on Oct. 13, 1918, he was placed in command of the 95th Squadron.

JOHN MITCHELL

Citations

D.S.C. (awarded Dec. 31, 1919)

JOHN MITCHELL, Captain, Air Service, 95th Aero Squadron. For extraordinary heroism in action near Beaumont, France, May 27, 1918. Seeing three enemy planes flying east over Apremont, at 2500 metres, Captain Mitchell unhesitatingly attacked the three machines, which were in close formation, despite the fact that a fourth, hovering above, threatened to close in and join the enemy formation. He succeeded in shooting down the enemy machine, which proved to be a biplane returning from an important mission.

(Signed) PERSHING

Croix de Guerre, with Palm (awarded Nov. 29, 1918)

Lieutenant-Pilote JOHN MITCHELL, à l'Escadrille américaine, 95:

Excellent pilote de chasse, possédant les plus belles qualités militaires. Le 27 mai 1918 a attaqué et descendu un biplane ennemi dans ses lignes. A attaqué, le même jour, une formation ennemie et a forcé un appareil à attérir. Le 5 juillet a attaqué six monoplanes et en a abattu un en flammes.

Signé: PÉTAIN

JAMES KNOWLES, Jr.

First Lieutenant, A.S., U.S.A. Ninety-Fifth Aero Squadron
First Pursuit Group

Son of James and Laura (King) Knowles, of Cambridge, Mass.; was born at Cincinnati, Ohio, Dec. 27, 1896. He was educated at the Peabody School, Cambridge, and at Phillips Andover Academy. He entered Harvard College in the class of 1918. He was a member of the 'Varsity baseball team for two years and won several prizes on both school and college track teams.

He was examined and accepted for aviation at Washington on April 7, 1917, and trained at the Ground School, Ohio State University, Columbus, Ohio, till July, 1917. He was then ordered overseas, sailing July 23. He had his preliminary flying training at Tours, France, being among the first American Army Aviators to be trained in France. He was sent to the 3d Aviation Instruction Centre, Issoudun, France, received his advanced training there, and was commissioned 1st Lieut. Nov. 20. After three months' work he was ordered to Cazaux, where he rapidly completed the course in aerial gunnery. Later he was sent to the front and attached to the 95th Aero Squadron, 1st Pursuit Group, with which he remained until the Armistice, seeing active service in the Toul, Verdun, Château-Thierry, St.-Mihiel, and Argonne offensives. He was awarded the Croix de Guerre with one palm, the Distinguished Service Cross with one oak leaf, the Aero Club of America Medal, and was officially credited with five Boches destroyed in combat.

Following Jan., 1919, Lieut. Knowles was stationed at Tours, France, in the office of the Assistant Chief of Staff of the Air Service, working on Historical Records Data and the Official Government Records of the Air Service. He returned to the United States, March 13, 1919.

D.S.C.

For extraordinary heroism in action near Montfaucon, France, 9 October, 1918. While on a voluntary patrol over the enemy's lines, Lieutenant Knowles observed three enemy Fokkers attacking one of our balloons. He unhesitatingly attacked, and in a bitter combat that lasted for five minutes, he succeeded in bringing one of the enemy planes down in flames and driving off the others.

(Signed) T. D. Milling,
Colonel, A.S., U.S.A.

JAMES KNOWLES, Jr.

Croix de Guerre

[Translation] Lieut. Pilot James Knowles, Jr., of the American 95th Squadron. Excellent chasse pilot, very aggressive, who never loses opportunity to engage in combat. On July 25, 1918, he brought down an enemy biplane protected by six monoplanes.

(Signed) PÉTAIN, *Marshal of France*
Commander-in-Chief of the French Army of the East

Military Record of Lieut. Knowles's Family

Lieut. James Knowles, Jr., is a direct descendant of Richard Knowles, Plymouth (1630), William Munroe (1640), of Lexington, and Captain Jonathan Parker, the minute man of Lexington.

Capt. Richard Knowles the first was a sea-captain, owner of the ship in which he came to America in 1630; and his descendants took part in all the Colonial wars, the Revolution, and the War of 1812. Capt. John Knowles, his son, of the Militia, was killed by the Indians near Taunton in 1675. His son, Colonel Samuel Knowles, was of the Militia. His son, Samuel Knowles, Colonel in the French Wars, commanded a company at the storming of Crown Point. Col. Willard Knowles, of the Revolutionary War, died in 1786. Next, Capt. Winslow Knowles, captured in Cape Cod Bay by the British, was taken to Provincetown to the frigate Spencer, Capt. Raggett, and released to obtain ransom. Instead, he fitted out a privateer manned by his fellow townsmen, and met with considerable success.

*HAMILTON COOLIDGE

CAPTAIN, A.S., U.S.A., NINETY-FOURTH AERO SQUADRON
FIRST PURSUIT GROUP

Killed in action, Oct. 27, 1918

SON of J. Randolph, Jr., and Mary (Hill) Coolidge; was born at Brookline, Mass., Sept. 1, 1895. He prepared for college at Groton School, where he was senior prefect, captain of the school eleven, and pitcher of the nine. He entered Harvard College in the class of 1919; was vice-president of his freshman class and played on the freshman baseball team, and was in the 'Varsity football squad in 1916.

He attended the Plattsburg Training Camp in the summer of 1915, and the Curtiss Flying School at Buffalo in the summer of 1916. In March, 1917, he entered the U.S. Service at Key West, Fla., enlisting in the Aviation Section, Signal Corps, training at Miami, Fla.; graduating from there June 5, 1917, he was sent to the 1st Ground School at M.I.T. In July, 1917, he sailed for France and was stationed at Headquarters Office in Paris, where he was engaged in organization work.

He was commissioned 1st Lieut. on Sept. 29, 1917, and on Oct. 12 was assigned to the 3d Aviation Instruction Centre at Issoudun, where he helped to organize and develop the great flying school. Graduating from there second in his class he was for a time Commander of a Squadron of 150 men, later becoming tester of planes, from Dec., 1917, to June, 1918, averaging from 15 to 20 flights a day. On June 16, with his friend, Quentin Roosevelt, he joined the 94th Squadron, 1st Pursuit Group, at the front at Toul.

On July 7 he wrote:

> I got a Boche to-day, or rather Jim Meissner and I together got one. . . . Four of us attacked a single biplace Rumpler and we all peppered away without result for several minutes. He was fighting for his life and gave us all a good fight! Suddenly it occurred to me that it would be much more to the point to get under his tail where I should be out of range from his rear gun and at the same time have a chance to soak some of the shots into him at close range; as I did so, Jim Meissner appeared. The other two of our group had jammed and left the scrap. We both shot at the Boche, and a scond later, great hot, red flames burst out from beneath his fuselage. I shall never forget the sensation of seeing a stream of flaming tracer bullets from my guns sink into its body and almost instantly flames bursting out as we dove at great speed through the air.

On Sept. 27 he shot up a German supply train, himself flying alone four times up and down the hapless column. Then came four victories together. He wrote:

On Oct. 2 I picked up a Halberstadt biplace fighter over the lines. My guns jammed after about 50 rounds, but I kept manœuvring with him to keep him occupied till help arrived. Help did arrive in the form of seven more of my companions! We cut the old boy off from their lines and started driving him home. But one of the boys growing impatient, put a few incendiaries into him and brought him down in flames. . . . The next day, Oct. 3, two of us attacked enemy balloons ten kilometres behind their lines at 4.35 P.M. I hardly had time to think of Archie-fire and streams of machine-gun bullets that flew by, as I dove on my balloon. I could see my incendiaries pour into the old gas-bag and the observer jump out in his parachute. A few seconds later the flames burst out and down it went. . . . My companion, a boy from another squadron, was ahead of me and about to attack another balloon, when I suddenly saw a formation of seven Fokkers above. He never saw them. My shriek of "Look out, Walter!" never got beyond my mouth because of the roaring exhaust; it was hideous; in a second they were upon him. Just a glimpse of the poor boy in the midst of these devils was all I could catch before the whole mess went circling to the ground. When I reached the spot they were careering around like a flock of buzzards over a freshly killed prey. I was so mad I saw red and dove upon the nearest of them. He did n't see me, so I waited till I was close upon him, then I riddled him with bullets. Then I was completely surrounded, but my situation was so futile that I was strangely calm. I tried to keep head on to the attackers. In a few more seconds they would have had me in such an unequal combat, when a Spad flashed down from the sky, and then another and another! The protection, five Spads, had arrived. For fifteen minutes, we milled together, rolling and tumbling, Spad, Fokker, Fokker, Spad. Gradually we edged towards the lines, and finally crossed them with the Fokkers in hot pursuit. The day was not over yet, however. After the main bunch had gone home a few of us were still out on the lines. The Boches evidently thought we had all gone, for they sent an observation plane sneaking over to do some quick reconnaissance work. Three of us spotted him almost simultaneously a few kilometres in our lines. We raced at him together and ten seconds later he was in flames. He sailed on a little, about 200 feet above the ground, then tottered and crashed in a final burst of flames. If all my victories are officially confirmed I shall be an "ace," five victories.

Two planes and a balloon were added to his record in the ensuing fortnight, and on Oct. 3, 1918, he was promoted to a Captaincy, and offered the command of another squadron. He wrote:

By some queer arrangement I have become a Captain. Here's the way it strikes me. I don't want any position higher than the one I hold now, that of Flight Commander, where I lead in person my little band of 6 or 8 on their stunts. I am afraid they are going to make me a Squadron Commander, when I shall have to tell my men to do things, instead of being able to lead them personally. I *don't want* a position of authority or responsibility where one sits in a chair. If they will leave me alone, a simple pilot and flight leader, I won't mind being a Captain—voilà!

On Oct. 27, while leading a protective patrol over Grand Pré, Capt. Coolidge was struck by anti-aircraft fire and instantly killed. He lies buried where he fell at Chevières. He was an ace, having brought down 12 planes or balloons. He was officially credited with 8.

He has been awarded the Croix de Guerre with palm, a citation by General Pershing, and the Distinguished Service Cross.

Arthur Woods, Colonel in the Air Service, who saw Capt. Coolidge at the front three weeks before his death, wrote to his parents:

Ham was his own splendid self, genuine and modest and confident. He had a score then of 4 Hun balloons and 2 planes. He was proud of the work of his Group, which since the 1st of Sept., with only 8 casualties, had officially been credited with 92 balloons and planes. Like American boys they had devised new ways of doing things, and some of their balloon tactics had come from Hamilton and had results that as far as I could find had not been equalled at all by other American or British Groups.

Hamilton gave far more to his country than simply the results of his own work as pilot in patrolling his sector and fighting the German. He was a sunny and steadying power among boys who were living in cold and wet and cheerlessness, who were high-strung by nature, and were growing more taut every day, for they were flying those little Spads in all weathers, were hunting out the enemy and engaging him even if he were vastly superior in number, and the battle was so continuous they could get no proper leave for rest.

Citations

Croix de Guerre, with palm

Après approbation du Général Commandant en Chef les forces expéditionnaires américaines en France, le Maréchal de France, Commandant en Chef les Armées Françaises de l'Est, cite à l'Ordre de l'Armée:

. . . .

Lieutenant-pilote Hamilton Coolidge, à l'Escadrille 94:

Pilote de grand courage. A abattu en flammes, le 7 juillet 1918 un biplace ennemi dans la Région de Grisolles.

Le Maréchal de France
Commandant en Chef les Armées Française
Pétain

HAMILTON COOLIDGE

D.S.C.

For extraordinary heroism in action near Grand Pré, France, Oct. 27, 1918. Leading a protection patrol, Capt. Coolidge went to the assistance of two observation planes which were being attacked by 6 German machines. Observing this manœuvre, the enemy sent up a terrific barrage from anti-aircraft guns on the ground. Disregarding the extreme danger Capt. Coolidge dived straight into the barrage and his plane was struck and sent down in flames.

First Lieutenant HAMILTON COOLIDGE, A.S., 94th Aero Squadron, for distinguished and exceptional gallantry at Bonnes, France, on 7 July, 1918, in the operation of the American Expeditionary Forces.

In testimony thereof, and as an expression of appreciation of his valor, I award him this citation.

JOHN J. PERSHING
Commander-in-Chief

Awarded on 27 March, 1919

HAROLD R. BUCKLEY

CAPT., A.S., U.S.A., 95TH AERO SQUADRON, 1ST PURSUIT GROUP

SON of Daniel H. and Mary A. Buckley of Springfield, Mass.; was born at Westfield, Mass., on April 4, 1896. He was educated at Phillips Andover Academy, where he was a member of the track team, the football squad, and captain of the swimming team.

In March, 1917, he entered the American Ambulance Service and served for 4 months in France; enlisting in the U.S. Air Service, in Paris, Aug., 1917. He trained at Tours, during Sept. and Oct.; at Issoudun, Nov., 1917, to Feb., 1918; and at Cazaux in March, 1918. He joined the 95th Aero Squadron, 1st Pursuit Group, and served at the front from March, 1918, until the signing of the Armistice. During this period he was in the Champagne sector in March; Toul sector, May and June; Château-Thierry drive, July and Aug.; St.-Mihiel drive, first part of Sept.; Argonne drive, Sept., Oct., and Nov., 1918. He was commissioned 1st Lieut. on Dec. 12, 1917; and on Nov. 1, 1918, he was commissioned Captain. He was awarded the Croix de Guerre; D.S.C. with oak leaf; medal of Aero Club of America; and officially credited with five Boches.

Croix de Guerre

Citation à l'ordre du Corps d'Armée.

Le Lieutenant-Pilote HAROLD R. BUCKLEY, 95th Escadrille américaine, chef de patrouille, calme et déterminé. A attaqué les avions et les saucisses, et mitraillé les troupes sur la terre d'un hauteur faible. Le 30 mai 1918, avec sa patrouille, est livré combat à deux avions ennemis, dont l'un a été descendu, l'autre a été forcé de descendre désemparé. PÉTAIN

D.S.C.

Awarded for extraordinary heroism in action at Perles, France, Aug. 10, to Lieut. Harold R. Buckley, 95th Aero Squadron.

Lieut. Buckley was on a patrol protecting a French photographing machine when they were suddenly set upon by six enemy planes. Lieut. Buckley attacked and destroyed the nearest and the remainder fled into their own territory. He then carried on with his mission until he had safely escorted the photographing machine back to its own aerodrome.

A bronze oak leaf for extraordinary heroism in action near Remonville, France, Sept. 25–26, 1918.

Lieut. Buckley dove through a violent and heavy machine-gun and anti-aircraft barrage and set on fire an enemy balloon, as it was being lowered into its nest. The next day, while leading a patrol he sent down in flames an enemy réglage machine, which was engaged in work over our lines.

SIGOURNEY THAYER

First Lieutenant, A.S., U.S.A., Ninety-Fifth Aero Squadron
First Pursuit Group

Son of Rev. William G. Thayer, D.D., and Violet (Otis) Thayer; was born at Southboro, Mass., March 24, 1896. He was educated at St. Mark's School, 1908–14, and at Amherst College, 1914–17, A.B. *causa honoris*, 1918. At St. Mark's he was on the school football and track teams; at Amherst he was captain of the track team, and won his "A" in track.

He enlisted in June, 1916, in Battery A, 1st Mass. Regt., F.A., N.G., and went to the Mexican Border. Returning from Mexico, he was transferred to Aviation, and trained at M.I.T. Ground School from April to Aug., 1917. From Aug. to Oct. he trained at Mt. Clemens, Mich., Aviation Camp. From Oct. to Dec. he was stationed at Mineola, N.Y., and was commissioned 1st Lieut. on Dec. 10, 1917. From Dec., 1917, to March, 1918, he was at Lake Charles, La.; and at Mineola, N.Y., in March, 1918. Receiving overseas orders, Lieut. Thayer sailed for England on March 4, and went from England to Issoudun, France, and from there to Haussiment-sur-Marne. He was first attached to the 99th Aero Squadron, then to the 12th Squadron, with which he went through the St.-Mihiel and Argonne–Meuse offensives, acting as Flight Commander from the end of Aug. until early in Oct., 1918. He was then transferred to the 95th Pursuit Squadron, as chasse pilot, and served until the Armistice, when he was attached to Aviation Headquarters, at Paris, going as courier to England. He returned to the U.S. in April, 1919.

Lieut. Thayer was cited in General Orders Sept. 13, 1918: "For gallantry in action near St.-Mihiel, France."

Brothers in Service —

William G. Thayer, Jr., 2d Lieut. U.S. Infantry.
James Appleton Thayer, 2d Lieut. U.S. Infantry.

*QUENTIN ROOSEVELT

First Lieutenant, A.S., U.S.A., Ninety-Fifth Aero Squadron
First Pursuit Group

Killed in action, July 14, 1918

Son of Theodore and Edith Kermit (Carow) Roosevelt; was born at Washington, D.C., Nov. 19, 1898. He was educated at Groton School, Groton, Mass., the Episcopal High School, Alexandria, Va., and at Harvard College, class of 1919. Prior to enlistment he attended the Officers' Training Camp at Plattsburg.

He enlisted about April 30, 1917, at Oyster Bay, N.Y., and trained for the Air Service at Mineola, N.Y. He was commissioned 1st Lieut. in April, 1917, and sailed overseas on July 23, 1917, on the S.S. *Orduna*, landing at Liverpool. From there he was sent to Paris, where he remained at Aviation Headquarters until Oct., when he was sent to Issoudun in command of the flying cadets and served as Instructor. On finishing there he went to Cazaux, Aerial Gunnery School, Feb. 28, 1918, and remained there for three weeks, returning to Issoudun to stay until the first of June in charge of one of the fields. About the first week in June he was sent to the American Acceptance Park at Orly, near Paris, and from there was assigned as tester of planes at Villacoublay, a French field near Orly.

He received orders to go to the front and joined the 95th Aero Squadron, 1st Pursuit Group, on June 15, 1918. On July 14, 1918, he was killed in action, falling near Chamèry, about 3 or 4 kilometres southeast of Fère-en-Tardenois.

Brothers in Service —

Theodore Roosevelt, Lieut.-Col. 26th Infantry, 1st Division, U.S.A. (20 months with A.E.F.; gassed and wounded).

Kermit Roosevelt, Capt. B.E.F., Light Armored Motor Battery, Mesopotamia; Capt. U.S.A., Field Artillery (20 months with A.E.F.).

Archibald Roosevelt, Capt. U.S.A., 26th Infantry (14 months with A.E.F.; invalided home).

*JASON SOLON HUNT

First Lieutenant, A.S., U.S.A., Twenty-Seventh Aero Squadron, First Pursuit Group

Killed in action, Aug. 1, 1918

Son of Bertron A. and Nettie B. Hunt; was born at Johnson, Vt., Jan. 24, 1894. He prepared for college at the High School in Johnson, Vt., and graduated from the University of Vermont in 1915. He entered the Harvard Law School in the fall of 1915, leaving there at the end of the second year to attend the 1st Officers' Training Camp at Plattsburg in May, 1917. At the time of his graduation from the University of Vermont, he was captain of the University Battalion and the following Nov. he was commissioned 1st Lieut. in the State Guard.

In July, 1917, he was one of 25 men sent from Plattsburg to Toronto to take up Aviation. From Canada he was sent to Texas to continue his training, where he was commissioned 1st Lieut. in Feb., 1918, and sent overseas attached to the 27th Squadron, 1st Pursuit Group.

With this Squadron he did excellent work, and on Aug. 1, while in the Château-Thierry sector, he was sent out on a mission with five other planes to protect an observation machine. When the formation was well within the enemy territory they were attacked by some 20 German planes; the protection planes did their best to shield the observation machine, which started for home with the photographs that had been taken. In the fight that followed, all but one of the American machines were shot down. Two of the aviators, although wounded, afterwards recovered in German hospitals, but Lieut. Hunt was probably instantly killed, although his family have been unable to obtain the exact details regarding his death, or to ascertain the place of his burial.

The observation machine which Lieut. Hunt was helping to protect was able to reach its own side of the line, carrying the photographs, which proved to be of great value although the pilot, who was fatally wounded, lost control of his plane before he could make a landing and it fell killing him and his observer.

Brother in Service —

Bertron A. Hunt, Jr.; served in Co. E, 101st Ammunition Train, in the 26th Division, A.E.F.

SAMUEL H. COLTON

First Lieutenant, A.S., U.S.A., Twenty-Seventh Aero Squadron, First Pursuit Group

Son of Samuel H. and Elizabeth (Slater) Colton; was born at Worcester, Mass., Feb. 2, 1895. He attended Worcester Academy and graduated from Bowdoin College in 1917. During the summer of 1915 he served for six months with the American Ambulance Field Service in Belgium.

He enlisted at Boston on July 16, 1917, and trained at the Princeton Ground School, Princeton, N.J. He completed his course there on Sept. 14, 1917, and sailed within the week for England. His first six months abroad were spent in training at Foggia, Italy. He trained for two months at Tours; three months at Issoudun, and one at Orly. He was commissioned 1st Lieut. May 13, 1918.

On Sept. 1, 1918, he was transferred from Orly to Rembercourt and attached to the 27th Squadron, 1st Pursuit Group. From this time until the signing of the Armistice he flew over the front with this Squadron, participating in the splendid work done by the 1st Pursuit Group, especially during the St.-Mihiel and Argonne-Meuse attacks.

Lieut. Colton was officially credited with bringing down two enemy planes. Among the many exciting encounters in which he took part was one north of Grand Pré, where he was attacked during the early morning patrol by a number of Fokkers. Other Americans came to his assistance and during the fighting Colton managed to separate one of the enemy planes from its group and downed it after five minutes of combat.

Lieut. Colton was honorably discharged at Camp Mills, Mineola, N.Y., Feb. 10, 1919.

Brothers in Service —

James H. Colton, Temporary Ensign, U.S. Navy.
John B. Colton, U.S. Naval Reserve.
Sydney Colton, U.S. Medical Corps.

ROBERT FULTON RAYMOND, Jr.

CAPTAIN, A.S., U.S.A., TWENTY-SEVENTH AERO SQUADRON
FIRST PURSUIT GROUP

SON of Judge Robert Fulton and Mary E. (Walker) Raymond, of Newton Centre, Mass.; was born in New Bedford, Mass., on March 15, 1895. He was educated in the public schools of New Bedford and Newton, and at Tilton Academy, Tilton, N.H. He graduated from Wesleyan University, Middletown, Conn., in 1917, receiving the degree A.B. *in absentia*, because of attendance at Plattsburg.

In 1915, and again in 1917, he attended the Plattsburg Camp, enlisting there in the Air Service in May, 1917; he trained with the Royal Flying Corps at Toronto, and at Camps Mohawk and Borden, in Canada, in the autumn of 1917. He was then assigned to Hicks Field, Fort Worth, Tex., where he remained throughout Dec., 1917, and Jan., 1918. He was commissioned 1st Lieut. in Jan., 1918, and sailed from New York in Feb. with the 27th Aero Squadron. He saw service with this Squadron, 1st Pursuit Group, in the Toul, St.-Mihiel, and Château-Thierry sectors. On June 24, 1918, he brought down his first plane, a German two-seater, and was awarded the D.S.C. by General Pershing. He was commissioned Capt. June 24, 1918. On July 16, 1918, he was shot down over the enemy lines at Château-Thierry, but was uninjured. For the next five months he was a prisoner in German prison camps, at Rastadt, Landshut, and Fürstenfeldsbruk. He was released on Dec. 5, sailed for America, and was honorably discharged in Feb., 1919, at New York.

D.S.C.

For extraordinary heroism in action near Château-Thierry, France, June 24, 1918. Lieut. Raymond piloted one machine in a formation of three which were escorting three reconnaissance planes over enemy territory. On account of motor trouble, he was unable to keep up with his companions, and while thus detached, was attacked by an enemy machine. In spite of the condition of his engine and his presence far within the German lines, Lieut. Raymond vigorously attacked the German plane and destroyed it, after which he succeeded in rejoining his patrol.

Capt. Raymond was also awarded the Croix de Guerre with the palm, by the French Government.

Brother in Service: Allen S. Raymond, Corporal, U.S.A., 306th Brigade, Heavy Tank Corps, A.E.F.

*PHILIP WASHBURN DAVIS

BREVET, LAFAYETTE CORPS, SECOND LIEUTENANT, NINETY-FOURTH AERO SQUADRON, FIRST PURSUIT GROUP

Killed in action, June 2, 1918

SON of S. Warren and Maria E. (Washburn) Davis; was born at West Newton, Mass., March 10, 1888. He was educated at the Newton High School, class of 1904, and at Harvard College, A.B. 1908. He made records in hurdling and tennis at college, and later in tennis clubs. After leaving college he entered the office of Lee, Higginson & Co., where he remained for two years. Subsequently he went into business for himself, as partner in the firm of Chamberlain & Davis, investment securities.

Previous to the war he was a member of the 1st Corps of Cadets, M.V.M. In May, 1917, he sailed overseas determined to do his part in the Ambulance Service; he reached Paris, June 2, 1917, and three days later wrote:

> I have enlisted in the Aviation Squadron, the Lafayette Escadrille. I decided that it was the only right thing to do. You cannot imagine at home — of course, I could n't — what this war really is. How everybody has got to do his share to save the world from the Boches . . . they need aviators badly and they are very important in the conduct of the war. . . . Now that the U.S. is in the war I think our men should be at the front. . . . Once I had determined to get into the Army, I wanted to get into something where individuality counts and it does in Aviation more than anywhere else. Even if the danger is greater the value of the service is greater too.

He trained at Avord, Pau, and Cazaux, receiving his Brevet Oct. 26, 1917. He was transferred to the U.S. Service, was commissioned 2d Lieut. on Jan. 6, 1918, and was assigned to the 94th Squadron (Major Lufbery's). With this Squadron he took part in several actions. On June 2, 1918, Lieut. Davis made his last flight. Capt. Douglas Campbell was leading the patrol when four of the American planes were attacked by five or six Germans. After a hot fight the Germans were driven off, but Lieut. Davis was seen to fall in flames.

He was buried near Burly Wood (Richecourt), north of Seicheprey. (See record of Lieut. Arthur Lawrence Cunningham.)

Sister in Service —

Amelia W. Davis, in Y.M.C.A. canteen and library work abroad, from Oct., 1917, until the Armistice.

ARTHUR LAWRENCE CUNNINGHAM

First Lieutenant, A.S., U.S.A., Ninety-Fourth Aero Squadron, First Pursuit Group

Son of John F. and Mary Elizabeth (Ryan) Cunningham; was born at Everett, Mass., Dec. 15, 1895. He prepared for college at the Medford High School, where he was valedictorian, and Major of High School Battalion; he entered Harvard College in the class of 1918, and was winner of Price-Greenleaf, and three other scholarships.

On May 26, 1917, he went overseas with the Harvard Ambulance Unit, and after a month in Paris with that organization, enlisted July, 1917, in the Foreign Legion, Lafayette Escadrille. He trained for some months at Avord, Pau, and Cazaux, and in Jan., 1918, was commissioned 2d Lieut. and assigned in Feb. to the 94th Squadron, 1st Pursuit Group, and participated in all the great drives.

On May 7, 1918, he took the air in answer to a challenge from a German aviator and found five others in hiding behind clouds. Attacked by six Germans, he fought until his machine gun jammed, then succeeded in reaching the American lines with his plane riddled with bullets.

On June 2, 1918, while returning from escorting a British Bombing Squadron along the Rhine Valley, Lieut. Cunningham and Lieut. Philip Davis, of Newton, were cut off from their seven other companion flyers, and attacked by a squadron of German planes. Lieut. Davis's machine burst into flames and he fell five miles back of the enemy lines. Lieut. Cunningham circled around, but could do nothing, as his machine was riddled with bullets, but he succeeded in reaching the American lines unharmed. He was convinced that they had brought down two enemy planes, but he was too far over the German lines for official verification. On Aug. 1, 1918, he was commissioned 1st Lieut. and in Sept. made Assistant Operations Officer, and later Operations Officer, on Major Hartney's staff, for the 1st Pursuit Group.

After the signing of the Armistice, he rejoined the 94th Squadron and was transferred to Coblenz, Germany, with the Army of Occupation.

Brother in Service —

John P. Cunningham, Ensign U.S. Navy.

ELIHU HOWARD KELTON

First Lieutenant, A.S.A., U.S.A., One Hundred Eighty-Fifth Aero Squadron, First Pursuit Group

Son of George Howard and Ruth (Coolidge) Kelton, of Hubbardston, Mass.; was born in Waltham, Mass., on Jan. 4, 1897. He was educated at the Boston Latin School, at the Gardner High School, and at Harvard College.

He enlisted in Cambridge, Mass., on Aug. 20, 1917, and was immediately assigned to the Ground School, M.I.T., where he remained until Oct. 13. He sailed for France on Nov. 1, 1917. He was trained at Issoudun, France, from Nov. 16, 1917, to Feb. 10, 1918, and was subsequently student and instructor at the School of Aerial Gunnery at Cazaux, from Feb. 10 to May 1, 1918. He was then given preliminary work in flying at Tours from May 1 to June 20, and advanced work in flying at Issoudun from June 20 to Aug. 18, 1918. He later took a Pilot's Gunnery Course at Cazaux from Aug. 18 to Sept. 1, and acted as Ferry Pilot at Orly from Sept. 1 to Sept. 8. He was assigned to the 185th Squadron on Sept. 9, transferred to the 27th Squadron on Oct. 1, and transferred back to the 185th Squadron for night pursuit work on Oct. 18, 1918. He was shot down and taken prisoner on Oct. 30. He was confined in the Karlsruhe Prison Camp, from which he escaped on Nov. 20, 1918, and reached Strasbourg by walking all night. He was attached to the 41st Aero Squadron, 5th Pursuit Group, on duty with the Army of Occupation in Coblenz, Germany. He was commissioned 1st Lieut. on June 9, 1918.

Citation

For distinguished and exceptional gallantry, Oct. 24–30, 1918.

CHARLES T. CROCKER, III

First Lieutenant, A.S.A., U.S.A., Ninety-Fourth Aero Squadron, First Pursuit Group

Son of Charles T. and Fay (Bigelow) Crocker; was born in Fitchburg, Mass., in 1896. He was educated at Fay School, Southboro, Mass., and at St. George's School, Newport, R.I. At the latter school he was on the football and hockey teams.

In 1913 he enlisted in Battery A, M.V.M., at Boston, Mass. In 1915 he joined the American Ambulance Service in France, sailing on the U.S.S. *Sussex* which was torpedoed in the English Channel. The Ambulance Unit with which Lieut. Crocker served received the Croix de Guerre for its excellent work. In 1915 he was recalled from France, to go to the Mexican Border with Battery A, then 1st Mass. Reg't, F.A., N.G.

He was transferred to the Aviation Service in 1918, and after 10 weeks' technical training at the M.I.T. Ground School, was sent abroad, and stationed at Issoudun, France, for practical flying. In July, 1918, he was sent to the front, attached to the 94th Aero Squadron, 1st Pursuit Group. Just previous to the Argonne drive, Lieut. Crocker was one of two pilots to volunteer for a low flight far beyond the German lines over Stenay, to ascertain the movements of the German troops. He performed the mission successfully, and was recommended for the D.S.C.

At last accounts Lieut. Crocker was with the Army of Occupation at Coblenz, Germany.

Citations

Recommendation for D.S.C. October 29, 1918

On Sept. 27, 1918, a call for volunteers to fly at a very low altitude to Stenay-sur-Meuse was made. Lieut. Crocker was one of the first to volunteer. To successfully fulfil this mission, it was necessary for Lieut. Crocker to pass twice through a very intense barrage and on account of atmospheric conditions at such a low altitude that his plane was in easy range of machine guns on the ground. In fact, the visibility was so poor that it was impossible for other planes to work. During the entire trip, he was under continual and intense shell and machine-gun fire, but in spite of this, and the fact that he was well within the lines of hostile country, he, by skill, courage, and determination, brought to a successful conclusion a mission, the hazardous nature of which made his safe return almost impossible. The information he was able to furnish our forces was of a

most valuable nature, especially at that particular time, and aided materially in the success of our operations.

Lieut. Crocker has been on active service at the front with this Squadron since Sept. 5, 1918, during which time he has displayed a marked desire for work of the more arduous and dangerous nature. On numerous occasions, he has voluntarily performed missions which called for the highest courage and devotion to duty. He has made many valuable reports on the condition of enemy bridges, roads, and movement of troops. This information has been obtained by him under the most perilous conditions and which often necessitated penetrating the German lines from thirty to fifty kilometres while flying at an extremely low altitude.

E. V. Rickenbacker
Captain, Air Service, U.S.A.

Belgian Legion of Honor Cross

France, 12th February, 1919.

My dear Lieutenant, —

The King, Albert I, of Belgium, has given me instructions to inform you that He has bestowed upon you the

Ordre de la Couronne

with rank of "Chevalier."

His Majesty desires that this honorary distinction be conveyed to you as a token of His esteem and in recognition of the valuable services you have rendered the common cause.

The medal will be handed over to you by the Adjutant General.

Please accept my most cordial greetings.

I am, my dear Lieutenant,

Very truly yours

J. M. Cinaut
Chief of the Belgian Mission

*CHESTER ROBINSON TUTEIN

Second Lieutenant, A.S., U.S.A., One Hundred Eighty-Fifth Aero Squadron, First Pursuit Group

Killed in accident, Nov. 17, 1918

Son of E. Arthur and Edith (Robinson) Tutein; was born at Revere, Mass., May 17, 1895. He attended the Revere and Winchester public schools and graduated from the Winchester High School. He was finishing the third year at M.I.T. at the time of his enlistment with the American Ambulance Field Service in May, 1917. He was prominent in athletics, being on the High School football team and captain of the boat crew. At Tech he continued his interest in athletics; he was a member of the Athletic Committee, entered the school meets and was prominent on the hockey team, of which he was elected captain just before enlistment.

He left New York on June 20, 1917, with the American Ambulance Field Service, staying in that service until Nov. 19, 1917. On arriving in France he was assigned to the Section Groupe Américaine, Convois Automobiles, T.M. 526, Peloton C, serving as conductor of camions in the region of the Aisne and the Chemin des Dames.

On Dec. 4, 1917, he enlisted in the Air Service, in Paris, but was not called until early in the new year; in the meantime he found employment in the A.E.F. Post-Office in Paris.

About Jan. 1, 1918, he left Paris for the Cadet Flying Camp at St.-Maixent. He received his commission as 2d Lieut. on May 17, 1918.

About May 29 he was transferred to the 2d Aviation Instruction Centre at Tours. He left Tours for the 3d Aviation Instruction Centre at Issoudun, where he finished Sept. 30, and awaited orders to go to the Gunnery School at St.-Jean-des-Monts, where he arrived Oct. 21. He left there Nov. 10, arriving at the front near Bar-le-Duc on the morning of Nov. 11, just after the Armistice was signed. "Well," he wrote, "Roy Youmans and I are assigned to the First Pursuit Group (the best) and we go out this afternoon. We may fly to-morrow, but we are all pretty low. The Armistice is signed and we will not be able to get any Boches."

On Nov. 20, the Commanding Officer of the 185th Squadron wrote to the parents of Lieut. Tutein of his death on Nov. 17:

> Chester had been flying over the field for some time. I had been watching him and admiring his flying which was of the best. Suddenly he seemed to lose control of his plane on a turn and spun straight to the ground. Death was of course instantaneous, so that there was absolutely no pain or suffering. I had not known your son very long, as he came to my squadron Nov. 12. I really knew him much better than some of the pilots who have been with me much longer. He was always willing and cheerful about his work. . . .
>
> Chester was buried at 3 P.M. Nov. 18, at Base Hospital No. 6, at Suilly (France). We held a military service. I obtained as many flowers as was possible and left a permanent wreath on the grave.

The 185th Squadron, of which Lieut. Tutein was a member, was trained in Texas under English tables of organization, and subsequently was sent to England, where it saw duty before going to France. On Oct. 7, 1918, it was assigned to the First Pursuit Group, being equipped with Sopwith Camel machines with Monosoupape motors. Its duties were to establish a barrage over the American line of searchlights against enemy night-bombing machines. This was the first attempt at night-flying chasse made in the American Air Service. A schedule of night patrols was maintained over the searchlight positions and all along the lines where it was known that enemy bombers were apt to cross. Extremely bad weather during Oct. and the early part of Nov. prevented the Squadron from doing much work. The Squadron engaged in five combats, but because of lack of searchlights did not bring down any enemy planes.

Brother in Service —

Dexter A. Tutein, Ensign, U.S. Navy.

*JOSEPH F. WEHNER

First Lieutenant, A.S.A., U.S.A., Twenty-Seventh Aero Squadron, First Pursuit Group

Killed in action, Sept. 20, 1918

Son of Frank W. and Johanna (Nelson) Wehner; was born in Boston, Sept. 20, 1895. He attended the Everett High School and Exeter Academy. At both institutions was captain of the football team; at Exeter, he was stroke on the crew.

Prior to the entrance of the U.S. into the war, he did Y.M.C.A. work in prison camps in Germany, leaving when diplomatic relations were severed. In June, 1917, he enlisted in the Air Service in New York City. He trained at Austin, Texas, and after graduating at the head of his class was sent to Scott Field, Belleville, Ill. Here he also did exceptionally fine work. He was commissioned 1st Lieut. Jan. 9, 1918, and about Feb. 1 sailed for England, where he was two weeks in training. He was then assigned to the 3d Aviation Instruction Centre at Issoudun, France. In June, 1918, he was at the front, taking part in the big drive. On Sept. 15 he found an enemy patrol of eight machines attacking a single American observation plane; he attacked promptly, and succeeded in destroying one of the enemy machines, and forcing another down. He convoyed the American plane to safety. For this exploit he received the D.S.C. On Sept. 16, 1918, he destroyed two enemy balloons, and was awarded a bronze oak leaf. He was reported missing in action on Sept. 18, and on Sept. 20 his death in action inside the German lines near Serronville, was officially given out. He was buried at Serronville France.

D.S.C.

For extraordinary heroism in action near Rouvres, France, Sept. 15, 1918. While on a mission Lieut. Wehner found an enemy patrol of eight machines attacking a single American observation machine. He immediately attacked, destroying one and forcing another down out of control, his own plane being badly damaged by enemy machine-gun fire. He managed to convoy the American plane to safety. A bronze Oak Leaf is awarded to Lieutenant Wehner for the following act of heroism in action near Mangiennes and Réville, France, Sept. 16, 1918. Amid terrific antiaircraft and machine-gun fire, Lieut. Wehner descended, attacked, and destroyed two enemy balloons. One of these balloons was destroyed in flames after it had been hauled to the ground and was resting in its bed.

WILLIAM WALLACE CHALMERS

First Lieutenant, A.S., U S.A., Ninety-Fourth Aero Squadron, First Pursuit Group

Son of Dr. and Mrs. James Chalmers, of Framingham, Mass.; was born in Columbus, O., May 23, 1891, and is now living in Hartford, Conn. He graduated from the Fitchburg High School in 1909, and from Middlebury College, B.S. 1913. He played on the 'Varsity football team four years.

He enlisted in S.E.R.C., on May 21, 1917, at Columbus, O., and trained at the Ohio State University Ground School from May 21 to July 14, 1917. On July 23 he sailed overseas, and was trained at Tours, Issoudun, and Cazaux. He was commissioned 1st Lieut. on Nov. 20, 1917.

From March to May, 1918, Lieut. Chalmers acted as ferry pilot at Paris, and saw active service with the 94th Aero Squadron at Toul and Château-Thierry. At Château-Thierry he was captured by the enemy, being shot down 15 kilometres behind the German lines. He was held prisoner for the remainder of the war, but was released after the Armistice, on Nov. 29, 1918.

Lieut. Chalmers sailed from Brest for America on Jan. 29, 1919, and was discharged at Garden City on Feb. 18, 1919.

Married, May 14, 1919, Katherine Williamson.

Brother in Service —

Robert Burns Chalmers, Ambulance Section 511, now with the French Army of Occupation.

*ALEXANDER BERN BRUCE

First Lieutenant, Ninety-Fourth Aero Squadron, First Pursuit Group

Killed in action, Aug. 17, 1918

Son of David and Carrie E. (Wainwright) Bruce, of Lawrence, Mass.; was born at Seattle, Wash., May 3, 1894. He graduated from Phillips Andover Academy in the class of 1911; a member of the Cum Laude Society, and was on the honor-roll for four successive years. He graduated from Harvard College in 1915; a member of the Phi Beta Kappa, with highest honors in scholarship. He was a member of the Harvard Gymnasium athletic team, and of the Harvard chess team.

On graduation from college he taught mathematics and chemistry at Phillips Andover Academy, until his entry into the Service. He attended the Officers' Training Camp at Plattsburg in 1916. In March, 1917, he helped to organize the Andover Ambulance Unit, and sailed with its 23 members to France, April 28, 1917. Soon after arriving in Paris, he and his Unit volunteered for camion service with the French Army, where he remained until allowed to enter the U.S. Air Service, in Sept., 1917. He was trained at Issoudun, Cazaux, and elsewhere; and was commissioned 1st Lieut. on Jan. 22, 1918. After the big German drive was turned, he was assigned to the 94th Aero Squadron, 1st Pursuit Group.

Lieut. Bruce met his death in combat at Les Cruaux, on Aug. 17, 1918. In an engagement with the enemy, his patrol was attacked from above, and when their gas was almost exhausted the Americans retreated; but Lieut. Bruce and another pilot of his patrol brushed wings. Lieut. Bruce, losing control of his machine, started to fall. But after falling 1000 metres, he regained partial control, and made a tight spiral during the remaining 2500 metres. The pilots above noticed that he was trying to spiral into an open field, but he missed that and landed in a forest. His machine struck some tall trees, nose first, at an angle of about 30 degrees, and Bruce's neck was broken by the fall of nearly two miles.

Lieut. Bruce was buried where he fell, in the Commune of Chéry-Chartreuve, Aisne, France.

BENNETT WELLS

First Lieutenant, A.S.A., U.S.A., One Hundred Forty-Seventh Aero Squadron, First Pursuit Group

Son of Herbert Clifford and Amy C. (Bullard) Wells, of Wayland, Mass.; was born in Cambridge, Mass., Nov. 16, 1894. He was educated at Cambridge Latin School and at Harvard College, class of 1918; leaving college during his sophomore year to go to France. He sailed on May 5, 1917, to join the American Field Service in France, driving an ammunition truck to and from the front for six months. He then transferred to Aviation, in Sept., 1917, enlisting in U.S.A.S. He was trained in the American Aviation School in France, and was then sent as chasseur to the front. He was commissioned 1st Lieut. about Feb. 1, 1918, and was assigned to the 147th Aero Squadron, 1st Pursuit Group, Zone of Advance.

While in active service Lieut. Wells took part in the great battle of Château-Thierry.

FIRST DAY BOMBARDMENT GROUP

As its name implied, the 1st Day Bombardment Group was America's first attempt at such work and mistakes were naturally to be expected. Unfortunately no adequate use was made of the experience of the Allies, and both in tactics and equipment much was learned only by a needless sacrifice of many lives. Two of the Squadrons, the 20th and the 12th, were the first to be equipped wholly with American machines — De Haviland 4's, with Liberty motors. These machines quickly earned the soubriquet of "flaming coffins," from the vulnerability of the gasoline tank. In the De H. 4's these tanks were directly between the two men. They thus not only made a third distinct vital spot as target for the enemy — the engine, the pilot, and the gas tank — but separated the pilot from his observer, so that all communication had to be indirect, a tremendous handicap not only against coöperative work, but to that moral support which direct contact of one person with another can give.

These tanks were not protected with the usual cork or rubber lining which, in case they were punctured by a bullet, closed up after it and prevented the fatal leakage which means "flames." The gas, too, was fed to the engine by pressure, which was thus simultaneously stopped by the unchecked puncture and could only thereafter be supplied by hand pumping. Already the type of machine had been discarded by the Allies as superannuated. Some idea of how far it fell short of expectations can be formed when it is known that the bomb racks were constructed to hold 10 bombs, and though at first it was attempted to fly with 4, it was subsequently necessary to cut the number to 2. The machines were also without the armored seats then in fairly frequent use, and because of the relative position of the gasoline tank and the wings, the pilot's view was much more circumscribed than in the machines whose tanks were forward. In such antiquated machines these boys were asked daily to face death. They knew the weaknesses, for they had been trained in Allied "ships" of the best type.

In tactics there was a similar lack of understanding. Before the formation of the American Bombing Group late in Aug., but little attention had been paid by the Germans to the flyers in the American sector. It was thus taken for granted that even a single bomber might be sent out alone. But immediately upon the advent of the 1st Day Bombing Group the Germans moved several of their crack circuses down to oppose them. Thus in pitiable small groups these American boys were called upon to meet tremendously predominating forces. The Allies had long abandoned small formations and sent their bombers only in large numbers.

The first flight over the enemy lines which the 20th Squadron was called upon to make was an example of the fearful odds they had to meet. That they met this crisis successfully is recorded in the following citations accorded their Group.

Citations

Commendation of work of First Day Bombardment Group

September 19, 1918

1. The work of the 1st Day Bombardment Group during the battle of St.-Mihiel, and in the operations after it, has been such as to bring out the praise and appreciation of all the troops of the Allied Service participating in the operations.

This Group, under most difficult conditions, with new equipment, and Pilots and Observers, who had recently come up on the front, has shown a devotion to duty and initiative which has not been exceeded by any troops on the front.

2. The work of the 1st Bombardment Group has materially aided in hindering hostile concentration troops, troop movement along the roads, and in sweeping the enemy back, thereby making lighter the work of our own pursuit aviation along the immediate front.

3. I desire that all members of the Group be informed of the high regard in which their work is held throughout the Army.

(Signed) W. S. Mitchell
Colonel, A.S., First Army

Telegram

Headquarters A.E.F.
Chief of Air Service

First Day Bombardment Group —

Excellent work done by the officers and men of your Group during the recent offensive deserves and has received hearty commendation; congratulations to you and your command on the record you have made for yourselves and for the Air Service. It is good to know that we can rely upon you to keep up this fine work which counts for so much in bringing about the results desired.

(Signed) *General* Patrick

ELEVENTH AERO SQUADRON

By First Lieutenant Paul S. Greene

Some light may be shed on the fortunes of the 11th Squadron by the fact that most of its members started operations on Friday the 13th of September, 1918. On account of the tremendous speed — on paper — of the American de Haviland, the Squadron, together with the 20th, was detailed to protect the Spad patrols of the 1st Pursuit Group operating from Toul in the St.-Mihiel drive.

When it was demonstrated that the D.H. 4's could not keep up to pursuit planes, let alone protect them, the Squadron was sent back to its proper work of day bombing, making its maiden raid the 14th. On that day two teams were lost, 1st Lieut. Edward T. Comegys and his observer being killed, and 1st Lieut. Fred T. Shoemaker, and his observer, 2d Lieut. Robert R. Groner, wounded and taken prisoner.

Hard luck only waited until the very next day before following up his first blow with one plainly labelled knockout. Out of a formation of six planes which crossed the lines, only one succeeded in staggering back in a riddled condition. The extent of this calamity was very much intensified when taking into account who the missing men were.

We started out with four pilots and one observer who had seen service over the lines. These officers were 1st Lieut. Thornton D. Hooper, our Commanding Officer; 1st Lieuts. John C. Tyler, Roger F. Chapin, and Cyrus G. Gatton, flight-leading pilots; and 1st Lieut. Harry H. Strauch, flight-leading observer. Of these, all, except Gatton, whose motor fortunately refused to carry him over the lines, were lost.

This catastrophe left the Squadron with only one man capable of leading a flight, and not enough machines to make one in any case, so, as the St.-Mihiel drive was already quieting down, the Squadron was given a few days in which to get new planes and reorganize.

In that time a new Commanding Officer, Capt. Charles L. Heater, D.F.C., arrived with experience gained on the British front, and 1st Lieut. Vincent P. Oatis was trained as flight leader, so that when the group left Amanty for Maulan to commence the Argonne battle, the 11th was again in condition to do its share in the operations.

With the ranks again filled up to normal, the 11th was able to lend half a dozen teams to the 96th in order to fill up their depleted roster and these flew the French Bréguets with some success after their own so-called "flaming coffins" or D.H. 4's.

During the month of Oct. the 11th was quite fortunate. We succeeded in dropping more bombs than any Squadron except the 96th, whose machines carried twice as many as ours, and most of the casualties of the group were borne by the 20th and 96th. Also the dog belonging to Adj. Joe Molten died.

At this time there was a shortage of observers and a call made for volunteers among the enlisted men of the Squadron. They responded almost to a man and three were picked for training. Among them one was wounded, and another made half a dozen successful raids. Neither was given any reward, not even an observer's wing. Nothing could speak higher for the spirit of the men than going with eyes open into such a forlorn adventure, more especially as at the time they were sleeping in the hangars under the planes and standing in a foot of mud in the rain to eat their meals.

In the last raid that weather permitted, on Nov. 6, we lost two of our best teams, including the ever-faithful Gatton, than whom no man ever more deserved decoration by his Government. The other men lost were 1st Lieuts. Dana E. Coates and George Bures, and 2d Lieut. Loren S. Thrall.

On the day following the signing of the Armistice, 2d Lieut. Lawrence J. Bauer was fatally injured in obeying an order to make a practice flight in weather in which it was almost impossible to get off the ground. This was the last casualty in the Squadron and one of the most unnecessary.

From that time practically no flights were made, and the pilots began to be sent in small groups in the general direction of home, to separate and probably never again have the chance to meet and discuss the grievances and misadventures which made the "Bewilderment Group" famous throughout the Allied Flying Corps.

Copy of Roll of Officers of the Eleventh Aero Squadron

(Taken from the Thanksgiving 1918 Dinner Programme)

STAFF

Captain Charles L. Heater, A.S.	Commanding
1st Lieut. Jos. G. B. Molten, A.S.	Adjutant
1st Lieut. Charles F. Netzel, M.C.	Surgeon
2d Lieut. Sigbert A. G. Norris, A.S.	Operations Officer
2d Lieut. George T. King, A.S.	Engineering Officer
2d Lieut. Warren N. Cromley, O.C.	Armament Officer
2d Lieut. Frank Katlinsky, A.S.	Asst. Arm. Officer
2d Lieut. Henry W. Ulmo, A.S.	Supply Officer

PILOTS	OBSERVERS
1st Lieut. Thomas M. Ring	1st Lieut. Paul S. Greene
1st Lieut. Walter A. Stahl	2d Lieut. Hasell D. Archer
1st Lieut. Clifford Allsopp	2d Lieut. George W. Perry
1st Lieut. Charles G. Slauson	2d Lieut. James S. Yates
1st Lieut. W. F. Halley	1st Lieut. C. J. Griffen
1st Lieut. P. W. Louden	2d Lieut. Sheldon C. Crane
1st Lieut. Vincent P. Oatis	2d Lieut. Ramon H. Guthrie
1st Lieut. Paul D. Nelson	1st Lieut. Ernest G. Noring
1st Lieut. Robert B. Porter	2d Lieut. James L. Patton
1st Lieut. Alfred C. Cooper	2d Lieut. John A. Richards
1st Lieut. Ralf A. Crookston	2d Lieut. Henry D. Lawrence
1st Lieut. Sydney E. Brewster	1st Lieut. Horace N. Jones, Jr.
1st Lieut. Uel T. McCurry	2d Lieut. William T. Parrish
1st Lieut. Guy H. Gale	2d Lieut. Morton F. Bird
1st Lieut. Donald T. Malcolm	2d Lieut. James G. Curtin
2d Lieut. John L. Garlough	2d Lieut. William J. Kelly
2d Lieut. John E. Osmun	2d Lieut. Robert C. Payton
2d Lieut. Harlan L. Shrader	2d Lieut. Philip J. Edwards
1st Lieut. F. L. Koons	2d Lieut. R. S. Williams
1st Lieut. George Spear	2d Lieut. E. W. Atwood

EXTRA OBSERVERS

2d Lieut. W. C. Craig
2d Lieut. R. H. Williams
2d Lieut. C. W. Reading
2d Lieut. E. N. Kinsley
Corporal Jacobs

ELEVENTH AERO SQUADRON

FRITZ'S GUESTS

1st Lieut. Thornton D. Hooper
1st Lieut. Fred T. Shoemaker
1st Lieut. Roger F. Chapin
1st Lieut. Ralph R. Root
2d Lieut. Clair B. Laird
2d Lieut. Robert R. Groner
2d Lieut. Horace Shidler

MISSING

1st Lieut. Dana E. Coates
1st Lieut. Cyrus G. Gatton
1st Lieut. George Bures
2d Lieut. Lorin R. Thrall

IN MEMORIAM

1st Lieut. Harry H. Strauch
1st Lieut. Lester S. Harter
1st Lieut. Edward T. Comegys
1st Lieut. McCrea Stephenson
2d Lieut. Arthur S. Carter
2d Lieut. Lawrence J. Bauer
2d Lieut. Harold Sayre
1st Lieut. John C. Tyler

PAUL STEVENS GREENE

FIRST LIEUTENANT, A.S. U.S.A., ELEVENTH AERO SQUADRON
FIRST BOMBARDMENT GROUP

SON of Henry Brooks and Amy B. (Stevens) Greene, of Reed's Ferry, N.H.; was born in Boston, Mass. on Oct. 28, 1892. He was educated at the Methuen High School, and at Amherst College, class of 1916. In Feb., 1916, he left college to join the Norton-Harjes Ambulance Unit, Section 5, with which he served at Verdun, Vosges, Oise, Aisne, and Chemin des Dames; the Unit being cited for bravery in the month of March. He returned to the U.S. in Sept. to finish his senior year at Amherst, but when war was declared, was released from college, and on April 28, 1917, sailed again overseas, and rejoined the Harjes Unit.

On Sept. 5, 1917, he enlisted in the Air Service, U.S.A., at Paris, and trained at Tours, Issoudun, Clermont-Ferrand, Gondrecourt, Chartres, Châteaudun, and Orly. He was commissioned 2d Lieut. on Dec. 27, 1917. On March 20, 1918, he was commissioned 1st Lieut. and in Aug. was assigned to the 11th Aero Squadron, serving as bomber, at St.-Mihiel and in the Argonne, and remaining with the Squadron at the front until the Armistice was signed. On Oct. 4, 1918, he brought down a Hun plane; when flying at a low altitude, he and his pilot, Lieut. Theo. M. Ring, were attacked by a large number of enemy machines. He wrote the following day:

> I had the narrowest escape anybody could have. We were attacked by Boches variously estimated from 15 to 40, and my pilot did n't know it! We sailed along way behind, and they all hopped on. I did n't know which one to shoot at.
>
> One devil got right behind my rudder and I had to shoot part of our tail to get him out of it. Then one got real nasty and loomed up nice and close and I knocked him off. He emitted a lot of smoke and went into a vrille, or spinning nose-dive, and fell to earth. Two other men saw this, and I expect it to be confirmed. My first Boche! May there be many happy returns. I went on fighting a lot more, when both my guns jammed. I thought then we were done, but at the critical moment our chasse planes came along in a multitude and Mr. Boche beat it.

Lieut. Greene was honorably discharged at Garden City, N.Y., on Feb. 7, 1919. He has written a short account of the 11th Squadron which is included in this volume. (See pages 99 to 102).

EDWARD WILSON ATWOOD

Second Lieutenant, A.S., U.S.A., Eleventh Aero Squadron, First Day Bombardment Group

Son of Thomas West Wilson and Grace Eveleth (Tobie) Atwood; was born at Portland, Me., June 27, 1897. He fitted for college at the Portland High School, and entered Bowdoin College in the class of 1920; he was a member of the Psi Upsilon Fraternity.

He joined the R.O.T.C. at Bowdoin in the spring of 1917, and was among those chosen to attend the Officers' Training Camp at Plattsburg, but being under age was not admitted.

He enlisted at Portland, Me., Aug. 23, 1917, and was assigned to the School of Military Aeronautics, M.I.T. from which he graduated with the 18th Army Aviation Squadron, Nov. 10, 1917. He sailed for France Nov. 23, 1917, and continued his training at the 1st Corps School at Gondrecourt, March 9–25, 1918, and at the École de Bombardement Aérien, Le Crotoy, Somme, March 29 to May 29, 1918. He attended the 7th Aviation Instruction Centre, Clermont-Ferrand, as student for two months. He joined the 11th Aero Squadron, 1st Day Bombardment Group, Nov. 2, 1918, and was with them until Dec. 4, 1918.

He was commissioned 2d Lieut. May 18, 1918, and was honorably discharged at Garden City, N.Y., Feb. 19, 1919.

ROGER F. CHAPIN

First Lieutenant A.S.A., U.S.A., Eleventh Aero Squadron First Day Bombardment Group

Son of Charles Taft and Annie W. Chapin of Ashmont, Mass.; was born in Boston, Mass., on Aug. 23, 1892. He graduated from the Dorchester High School, where he played on the football team for two years. For three years he belonged to the 1st Squadron, Mass. Cavalry. He enlisted at the Officers' Training Camp at Plattsburg, on May 14, 1917, was transferred to the Air Service in June and assigned to M.I.T. for ground work. On completing the course there, July 30, 1917, he was sent to Mineola, N.Y., for preliminary flying. He completed the R.M.A. flying tests on Sept. 17, and was commissioned 1st Lieut. on Nov. 14, the date on which he sailed overseas. He completed his advanced training at the 3d Aviation Instruction Centre at Issoudun, France, in March, 1918, and proceeded to Clermont-Ferrand for a two months' course in Day Bombardment. He was ordered out with a French Day Bombing Squadron, Escadrille Bréguet No. 127 (Groupe de Bombardement 5), about the middle of June. While attached to this Escadrille, Lieut. Chapin took part in the Château-Thierry offensive on July 15, and during Aug. was at the Fismes-Soissons-Mondidier front. At the end of Aug., he was recalled to go out with the new American Day Bombing Squadron, No. 11, and took part in a number of raids through the St.-Mihiel offensive. On Sept. 18, Lieut. Chapin and his observer, Clair B. Laird, of Algona, Iowa, were brought down back of the enemy lines north of the Chambley-Toul sector by enemy machines. The observer had been wounded by the fire of machine guns. Both men were captured, and kept as prisoners of war until Nov. 28, 1918, when they were exchanged through Switzerland. Lieut. Chapin received the Croix de Guerre for his services with the French. He was honorably discharged at Mineola, N.Y., in April, 1919.

Croix de Guerre

Le Chef d'Escadron, Vuillemin, Commandant l'Escadre, cite à l'ordre de l'Escadre 12:

Chapin, Roger, 1° Lieutenant Pilote, américain, de l'escadrille Br. 127: Excellent pilote, toujours volontaire pour les missions périlleuses. A pris part aux bombardements des 15 et 28 juillet et des 10 et 11 août, 1918, qui not causés à l'ennemi des pertes considérables.

Signé: Vuillemin

GEORGE DANA SPEAR

First Lieutenant, A.S.A., U.S.A., Eleventh Aero Squadron
First Day Bombardment Group

Son of Frank N. and Julia (Smith) Spear, of Walpole, Mass.; was born in Walpole, on Nov. 18, 1895. He was educated in the public schools of Walpole and graduated from M.I.T. in 1917. He enlisted in the Aviation Service in Boston, on July 2, 1917. After a ground course at M.I.T. he sailed overseas in August to finish his training in England.

He attended the School of Military Aeronautics in Oxford, Eng., and was soon after sent to Grantham, Eng., for an instructor's course in machine guns. He was then ordered to Scampton, in Lincolnshire, to learn the working and managing of a squadron. On Feb. 1, 1918, he was sent to Waddington, Lincolnshire, for actual flying training, and thence to Bircham-Newton, Norfolk, for work in fighting. He was then ordered to London, and there assigned to the Central Despatch Pool in London for ferry duty. On Sept. 10 he proceeded to France with the A.E.F. After three days at Tours, he was sent to the First Air Dépôt at Colombey-les-Belles. He was there fortunately able to join the 11th Aero Squadron which was made up of a number of men with whom he had trained. He reached Amanty, the Squadron Headquarters, in time for the last of the St.-Mihiel drive, and was with the Squadron throughout the entire Argonne offensive, and until the middle of Dec., 1918. Passing through the casual camps at Colombey-les-Belles, Tours, and Angers, he arrived at Brest on Jan. 30, 1919, and sailed for the United States on Feb. 2. On his arrival, Feb. 9, he was ordered to Garden City, N.Y.

ECTOR O. MUNN

First Lieutenant, A.S., U.S.A., Eleventh Aero Squadron
First Day Bombardment Group

Son of Mr. and Mrs. Charles A. Munn, of Manchester, Mass.; was born at Washington, D.C., April 11, 1891. He attended the Westminster School, Simsbury, Conn., and graduated from Harvard College, class of 1914.

He served for three years in the Mass. National Guard, and on June 11, 1917, enlisted in the Aviation Service, at Manchester, Mass. He attended the Ground School at M.I.T. and was sent from there to Mineola, N.Y., for further training.

He sailed overseas for France, attached to the 98th Squadron, and trained at Tours, and later at Clermont-Ferrand for day bombing.

He was commissioned 1st Lieut. Oct. 4, 1917.

Lieut. Munn joined the 11th Aero Squadron, 1st Day Bombardment Group, at the front, and with them saw active service until the signing of the Armistice. He returned to the U.S. and on July 16, 1919, resigned from the Service at Washington, D.C.

He had two brothers in the Service; one acted as Assistant Military Attaché at the Army Embassy at Paris, and the other as Assistant Naval Attaché at the American Embassy, Paris.

TWENTIETH AERO SQUADRON, FIRST DAY BOMBARDMENT GROUP

By Lieutenant Karl C. Payne

On Sept. 7, 1918, the 20th Aero Squadron was ordered to Amanty, Meuse, to join the 1st Day Bombardment Group which at that time consisted of one Squadron, the 96th.

Operations began Sept. 12, 1918, the opening day of the St.-Mihiel push. Three of the Squadron were sent to do Army reconnaissance. 1st Lieut. G. M. Crawford, our first casualty, was taken prisoner Sept. 12, while attempting a reconnaissance mission in the rain. The other officers were sent to Toul to operate with the 2d Pursuit Group. At this time it was believed that our planes, the Liberty D.H. 4's, could be used as biplace fighters. However, this proved impractical and the Squadron was assigned to daylight bombing.

The morning of Sept. 13 we made our first bombing raid, and since the 20th was the first off the ground, it achieved the distinction of being the first Squadron of American-built machines to drop bombs on the enemy. In spite of adverse conditions due to lack of familiarity with planes and work, the Squadron made eight raids in three days.

Capt. Cecil G. Sellers and Lieut. K. C. Payne were fortunate in being the first to receive Distinguished Service Crosses, the official citation being as follows:

> For extraordinary heroism in action near Longuyon, France, Sept. 16, 1918. Starting on a very important daylight bombing mission with five other planes, Capt. Cecil G. Sellers, Pilot, and Lieut. Karl C. Payne, Observer, went on along when the other five planes were forced to turn back. On crossing the German lines they were attacked by three enemy planes. Keeping the enemy at bay they went on, reached the objective, and dropped their bombs on the railroad junction, cutting the line. On the way back four more planes joined the attack, but they kept them off and reached the Allied lines.

Other decorations were soon to follow, however. Lieut. J. Y. Stokes, Observer, and Lieut. A. F. Seaver, Pilot, started on an early morning raid which had Étain as its objective. All the planes in the formation with them dropped out before the lines were crossed. They sighted another American formation headed for the same objective and followed. Before the objective was reached, their plane was struck by anti-aircraft fire and thrown into a vrille. They straightened out and followed the formation, which was, by this time, far ahead of them. After dropping their bombs on the objective, their motor stopped entirely and they were attacked by an enemy plane. Lieut. Stokes held him off while his pilot managed to glide to our lines. The action brought both the D.S.C.

During the time the Squadron operated from Amanty, it lost but one man over the lines while one man was killed and one injured, in a crash in the field. Among the objectives were Dommery-Baroncourt, Gorze, Bayonville, Longuyon, and Mars-le-Tour. Nine successful raids were made. The Squadron — with the Group — was cited for devotion to duty during the St.-Mihiel offensive, and four Distinguished Service Crosses were won.

On Sept. 23, 1918, we moved from Amanty to Maulon, near Ligny-en-Barrois. It was from the latter field that we did the major part of our work and suffered virtually all of our casualties.

Our most disastrous raid was the operation of Sept. 26, 1918. Out of a formation of seven planes, five were lost over the lines and one returned with a dead observer. A portion of a letter written by 1st Lieut. E. C. Leonard, one of the observers who was wounded and taken prisoner, gives an idea of the fight:

> The flight leader made a very sharp turn to the right after we dropped our bombs on Dun-sur-Meuse. Phil [1st Lieut. P. H. Rhinelander] and Harry [1st Lieut. H. C. Preston] slipped below the formation to avoid a collision. We were attacked by five Fokkers. "Coop" [1st Lieut. M. C. Cooper] and I dropped below the others to help Phil and Harry, when twelve Fokkers came at us from above, diving through the formation. I could n't swing my guns fast enough, for they were on all sides at once — about a million lines of tracer smoke coming the wrong way.

It was always the aim of the German flyers to break up a formation, for they could then attack each plane separately. The plane thus attacked would be without the efficient protection of the other members of the formation.

In this raid, 1st Lieut. W. Clarkson Potter stuck to the leader, 1st Lieut. Sidney Howard, after the leading observer, 1st Lieut. E. A. Parrott, had been killed, and thus protected the rear of the leading plane. Lieut. Potter was awarded the D.S.C. for this act, but was himself shot down and killed a few days later.

The officers lost on this raid were: Lieut. P. H. Rhinelander and

Lieut. H. C. Preston (killed); Lieut. Harris and Lieut. E. Forbes (killed); Lieut. H. P. Matthews and Lieut. E. A. Taylor (killed); Lieut. G. B. Wiser and Lieut. Glen Richardson (prisoners); Lieut. M. C. Cooper and Lieut. E. C. Leonard (prisoners); Lieut. E. A. Parrott was brought back dead.

Probably the Squadron's most successful raid was over Montmédy on Nov. 4, 1918. Montmédy at that time was the headquarters of the German army. It was also a most important railroad centre and directly in the main line of communications. We were over the town at 2.20 P.M. Sixteen 155 mm. penetration bombs were dropped, all of which found their mark. We left the town in flames. On the return to our lines we were attacked by seven Fokkers, two of which were shot down. All our planes returned safely. (The "Montmédy cocktail" is very well known to the New England members of the 20th.)

On Nov. 5 was the last and one of the most disastrous operations in our history. We were, after we had dropped our bombs, attacked by three patrols of Fokkers. The first patrol was driven off. During the fight with the second, 1st Lieut. K. G. West, Pilot, and 1st Lieut. Wm. Frank, Observer, were shot down in flames. Both flyers were of the original quota. Lieut. Frank had been wounded and recommended for the D.S.C. Lieut. West was one of the best pilots in the Squadron and a veteran of many raids. A lull in the fight made it possible for all to observe the red ball of flame as it tumbled to the earth, 13,000 feet below.

The third German patrol shot down two planes. Lieut. Brooke Edwards and Lieut. Karl C. Payne, with the motor riddled, the gas tank punctured, the controls shot away on one side, and out of ammunition, were fortunate enough to make a landing even behind the German lines. The third American plane to fall was driven by 1st Lieut. Samuel Mandell. Lieut. R. W. Fulton was the observer. The plane went down partially out of control. A few hundred feet off the ground "Sam" straightened it out, and then sideslipped and smashed. Mandell was killed; Fulton came through without a scratch. (See Lieut. Mandell's record, pp. 149-51.—*Ed.*)

On the day that the Armistice was signed, there was a picture taken on the field at Maulon. The survivors of the original flyers in the 20th stood together. There were six: Capt. C. G. Sellers,

Lieut. Gardiner Fiske, Lieut. A. F. Seaver, Lieut. Sidney Howard, Lieut. J. Y. Stokes, and Lieut. W. S. Holt. These officers, either due to skill or good fortune, but probably a share of both, managed to get back from every raid. They were all flight leaders and three were winners of the D.S.C.

At one time during the operations north of the Argonne Forest, it was necessary to call for volunteers among the enlisted men to fly over as machine-gunners. Sgt. 1st class Fred C. Graveline, Corp. Raymond C. Alexander, and Pvt. 1st class Hoyt M. Fleming came forward and carried on with the work.

The 20th lost 20 officers over the lines, had 2 men killed on the field, and 1 observer brought back dead, during the time we operated from Maulon. Some of the objectives were Montmédy, Grand Pré, Tailly, and Buzancy. The original members of the Squadron were given personal citations for devotion to duty.

KARL C. PAYNE

First Lieutenant, A.S.S.C., Chief Observer, Twentieth Aero Squadron, First Day Bombardment Group

Son of Edward F. and Mae (Chatwin) Payne, of Belmont, Mass.; was born in Cambridge, Mass., on June 18, 1896. He was educated at the Belmont High School, the Browne and Nichols School in Cambridge, and M.I.T. At the Browne and Nichols School he was prominent in athletics, and was captain of the football and hockey teams. He attended military classes at Norwich University, Northfield, Vt., in the spring of 1917, and in the summer trained with the Harvard R.O.T.C.

He enlisted in Cambridge, Mass., on July 20, 1917, and was assigned to the Ground School at M.I.T. in the fall of 1917. He was sent overseas in Nov. and was trained at French flying schools at Issoudun, Clermont-Ferrand, Châteaudun, and Chartres. He was commissioned 1st Lieut. about June 18, 1918, and spent the following summer at the front in the St.-Mihiel and Argonne sectors. He was made Chief Observer of the 20th Aero Squadron, and made over 16 successful bombing raids during the great offensives. He was awarded the D.S.C. on Sept. 16. On Nov. 5 he went over the lines on a bombing expedition, and when the formation returned, his plane was missing. This is the account of the experience which Lieut. Payne sent to his family in a letter dated Nov. 24:

The next day I went over with Brooke Edwards. We were flying protection in the rear. We bombed Mouzon, north of Stenay, and turned right going east. The leader made a great turn and took us away over Montmédy. The Boches were waiting for us there and about forty of them jumped us. We were only eight. It was a real fight. We got the first one to come up, but there were a lot behind him. I was running short of ammunition and the bullets were snapping close to my ears. Then the gas tank was hit low and the gas ran out. At the same time I was shooting at a devil that had come up rather too close. My left arm was across my chest, the wrist being about over my heart, when I felt a bump and saw my glove torn just above the wrist. I lost the use of that arm, but I could n't help but smile to have my arm over my chest just at that moment. I turned to tell Brooke that I was hit and out of ammunition and the gas tank was punctured. As I turned I saw him put his hand up to his head. Naturally I thought he had got a load of lead. I sat down and took control of the plane from the rear seat. I put the plane into a steep nose-dive. We outdared the Huns by going down nearly vertically. Finally, having dropped

from about 14,000 to 2000 feet, we could see the infantry below us — and it was German infantry. Brooke took control of the plane and levelled out, trying to glide without motor to our own lines. However, as soon as we levelled out, the Huns — three of them — caught up with us and the bullets snapped close again. They shot the fur off my collar and I saw it flying up as the bullet passed through. Then they shot through my sleeve up near my shoulder. I had about ten bullets left and feel pretty sure that I got one of the Huns with these. But the game was up, they drove us to the ground in the German infantry.

They were round us the minute we landed. And I really believe that, but for a German non-com who ran up, I would not be writing this now. But the non-com came and they dressed my arm. Then they marched us back, to the artillery and the artillery took us back to Loupy.

Lieut. Payne was later taken to Virton and finally to Karlsruhe Prison. He escaped from Karlsruhe on Nov. 20 with several other officers, and reached Strasbourg, Lorraine, on Nov. 22.

Citation

For extraordinary heroism in action, near Longuyon, France, Sept. 16, 1918. Starting on a very important daylight bombing mission with five other planes, Lieut. Payne, observer, went on alone when the other five planes were forced to turn back. On crossing the German lines, he was attacked by three enemy planes. Using his guns to keep the enemy at bay, he went on, reached his objective, and dropped his bombs on the railroad junction, cutting the line. On the way back four more planes joined in the attack, but keeping them at bay with his guns, he reached the Allied lines.

(Signed) PERSHING

Offizielle Zahlen.

Die zwischen dem 1. und 30. September eingebrachte Kriegsbeute der Armeen der Entente auf der Westfront beträgt:

2.844 Offiziere
120.292 Mann
1.500 Geschütze
über **10.000** Maschinengewehre.

Die **Gesamtbeute**, die von den verbündeten Armeen auf **allen** Kriegsschauplätzen zwischen dem 15. Juli und 30. September eingebracht wurde, betragt:

5.518 Offiziere
248.494 Mann
3.669 Geschütze
über **23.000** Mäschinengewehre.

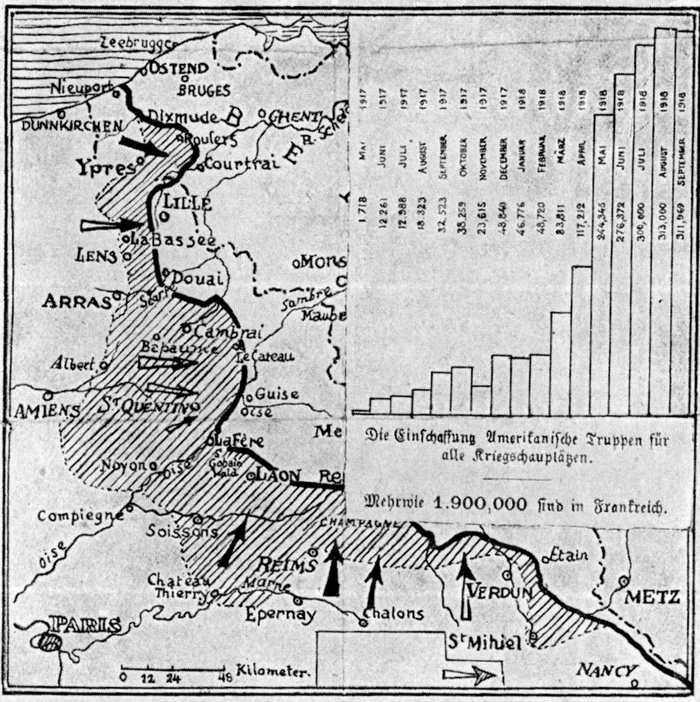

Der Deutsche Rückzug von 15 Juli an 10 Oktober 1918.

Einige Fragen an die Deutschen Soldaten.

1. Werdet Ihr jemals wieder so stark sein als im Juli 1918?
2. Werden Enre Gegner täglich stärker oder schwächer?
3. Haben Euch die grausamen Verluste die Ihr 1918 erlitten habt, den Siegfrieden gebracht, den Euch Eure Führer verprochen haben?
4. Habt Ihr noch leiseste Hoffnung auf einen Sieg?
5. Wollt Ihr Euer Leben lassen in einem hoffnungslosen Kampf?

A SAMPLE OF THE STUFF WE DROPPED OVER THE LINES

A BIT OF UNINTENTIONAL "ACROBATICS"

By Lieut. Samuel P. Mandell

(Account of how his observer, Lieut. Fiske, was thrown from his plane when two thousand feet in the air.)

I HAD the thrill of my life yesterday. We were flying formation in these great big busses and the machine I had had, two camera guns on it, one for the pilot and one for the observer. Old F—— was standing up on the seat in back shooting away with his camera gun at a scout machine that was flying around us. At the same time I dove to get a shot at him with my gun. I heard sort of a crash behind, and after I had straightened out looked around to see what it was. Lo and behold, a man in a leather coat holding onto the tail of my machine. I could hardly believe my eyes, but F—— had fallen out of his cockpit when his gun broke loose from its fastenings and I had nosed over. The first thought that came to me was: Will he have strength enough to hold on till I get down to the ground? I put the machine in the gentlest glide I could and started for home, as I could not land where I was up on the mountain-tops. All this happened at about 700 metres. God help him if he had fallen. F—— all this time was lying with his body across the fuselage right next to the vertical stabilizer on the tail. As I watched him over my shoulder, he gradually wound his way up the fuselage. He got a-straddle of it and gradually slid up, caught hold of the tourelle, and dove head first into his seat. About ten years' weight came off my shoulders by this time. It was the funniest sight in the world to see the expression on that face as he scrambled up the fuselage and fell face first into the cockpit with only his heels sticking out. All that saved him was the little wooden spars that hold the covering of the fuselage breaking and making a sort of a hole in which his body stuck as it struck. As we were in formation, some of the other men saw it. They said that F—— left the fuselage bodily and flew through the air for a space of five feet till he struck the vertical stabilizer that knocked him back on to the fuselage. Of course, it is hard to believe, but it is Gospel truth. All the time it was happening we were going at the rate of 100 miles per hour at least.

F—— to-day is reposing in bed, having been excused from all formations. He will never come any nearer death at the front, and nothing can ever scare me any more than this did.

A Bit of Unintentional "Acrobatics"

How an Observer Was Thrown from His
Plane 2000 Feet in the Air
and Came Back

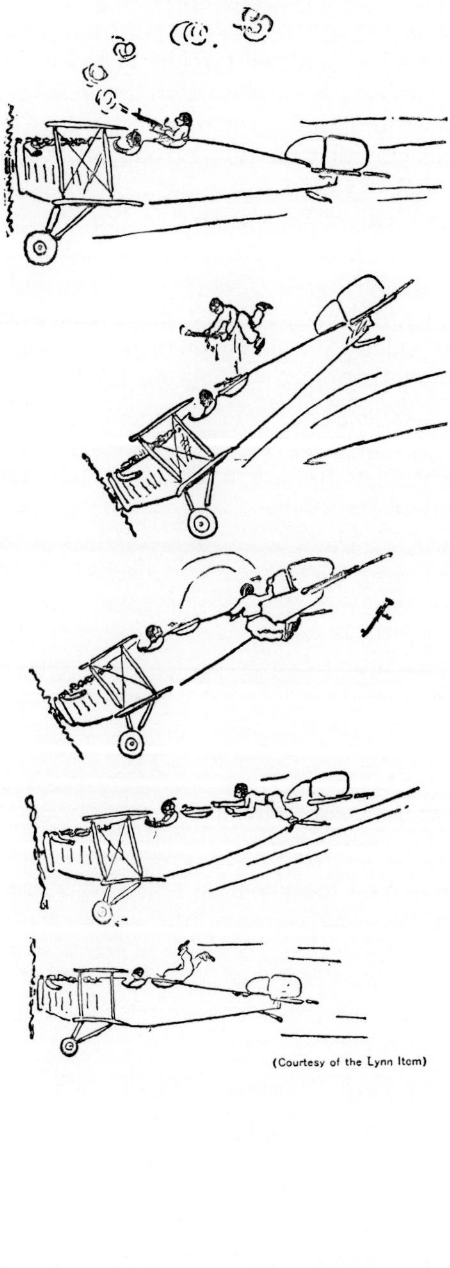

(Courtesy of the Lynn Item)

GARDINER HORSFORD FISKE

First Lieutenant, A.S., U.S.A., Twentieth Aero Squadron
First Bombardment Group

Son of Andrew and Gertrude (Horsford) Fiske, of Weston, Mass.; was born in Boston on Sept. 14, 1892. He was educated at the Noble and Greenough School, and at Harvard College, A.B., class of 1914. Before entering the U.S. Service he was for two and a half years a member of the 1st Corps of Cadets, M.V.M.

He enlisted May 30, 1917, at Weston, Mass., trained at M.I.T. from May 1 to June 23, and was transferred to Essington, Pa., June 24, 1917. He was commissioned 1st Lieut. on Oct. 31, 1917, and ordered overseas Nov. 1, continuing his training at Issoudun and Clermont-Ferrand, France, throughout the winter and spring of 1918. He was attached to the French School at Châteaudun and Chartres, G.D.E., during the summer of 1918. On Aug. 31 he was assigned to the 20th Aero Squadron, 1st Bombardment Group, and took part in 14 bombing-raids over the lines, and two patrols as biplace pursuit. Stationed at Toul and Amanty during the St.-Mihiel drive; at Maulan during the Meuse-Argonne drives.

Lieut. Fiske's account of the Squadron's "Last Raid," is embodied elsewhere in this work, as well as a description of his remarkable experience in being hurled from his plane when at an altitude of 2000 feet. Officially credited with the destruction in combat of one enemy aircraft. Acted as flight leader in five bombing raids.

He was honorably discharged at Garden City, N.Y., on Feb. 14, 1919.

Citation

France, 21st Nov., 1918

The Army Air Service Commander, First Army, cites the following officers and men for exceptional devotion to duty:

45. First Lieutenant G. H. Fiske, A.S., U.S.A., as observer of the 20th Aero Squadron, First Day Bombardment Group, participated in every raid made by the Squadron in the Argonne-Meuse sector during Oct., 1918.

By order of Colonel Milling
W. C. Sherman
Lt. Col., A.S., U.S.A.
Chief of Staff

Married, Oct. 15, 1919, Constance Morss.

THE LAST RAID

BY LIEUTENANT GARDINER FISKE

Thirty of our bombing planes executed a successful raid on Mouzon and Raucourt this morning, dropping over two tons of bombs with good effect. — American *Communiqué* of Nov. 6.

To the Headquarters of the 1st Day Bombardment Group at Maulan, south of Bar-le-Duc on the evening of Nov. 4, came the daily telephonic order from General Headquarters. It was as usual a very simple order, giving nothing beyond the bare facts of the work the Squadrons were to do the following day. This time the order said, "Stand by to bomb Mouzon at 9.45 A.M."

On receiving this order the flight leaders and deputy leaders went to their maps to locate the new objective and study photographs of the town to pick out the points of military value. In studying Mouzon it was not difficult to see what we were to do. The town lay on the east bank of the Meuse with a suburb on the west bank where the railroad station and warehouses were situated. We decided to try to cut the railroad and destroy the warehouses.

The next morning our orderlies called us early enough to see a low-lying mist over the camp. It was just dawn. We dressed amidst shouts from the barracks of "Come on, rain." This appeal to the rain god was heard every morning whatever the weather, as rain was sure preventive of bombing raids. Nevertheless, we felt that thrill which came only when we were on the alert to go over.

At 7.15 the flight leaders held their meeting in the office of the Group Commander, where the Colonel outlined the plan of the formation to be used. This morning, if the weather cleared up, we were to go over in three "V's," the 166th Squadron first, then the 20th, and lastly the 11th. We were to meet over our own field at 8000 feet, fall in behind one another in order, and climb to the final height of 13,000 to 14,000 feet during the final run to the lines. We were to bomb with the wind, which the weather report showed to be blowing toward Germany at a speed of about 30 miles an hour. This was rather a stiff wind, difficult but not impossible to operate in.

The sun appeared quickly, drying up the mist as if anxious to see us get on our way. We dressed carefully in our flying clothes, climbing into the De Havilands, and tested out our sights, machine guns, and Vérys pistols. Soon the signal "all set" was given. A Vérys pistol was fired showing one green ball, giving the signal to start the Libertys. With a roar the long line of engines started almost all at once as the mechanics swung the propellers and the process of warming up began. Then we — we were flight leaders that day in our Squadron, the 20th — began taxiing to the starting-line; number 2 followed, then number 3, and so on until the whole flight were ready in formation on the ground — all the powerful engines throbbing and the propellers turning over. Suddenly the Operations Officer, noting the Squadron ahead of us had left the field, fired a single red Vérys light from the line. We opened our throttle and moved forward, taking off into the air. As we took off, numbers 2 and 3 started forward and in their turn leapt into the air, numbers 4 and 5 followed, then the next two and finally the 9th, until all the planes were in sight.

Our next difficulty was to gather the Squadron into formation. After getting up to 1000 feet altitude, we throttled down until 2 and 3 caught up and climbed a little above and behind us. We three then continued climbing slowly until the rest gathered together and formed our "V" in a wide, loose formation.

The flight climbed together until we reached our desired altitude over the field. Taking one hour, this part of the trip is always very tiresome. One sits gazing at the altimeter, wondering if one will ever get up, the time passing so slowly. Down below the country gradually gets more and more spread out, until the forests blend into a patch of green and the rivers show only as nickled lines.

We returned over the field, looking meanwhile for the other two Squadrons. Finally down below us we saw the leaders, the 166th, starting for the lines. We fell in line behind them, passing over Bar-le-Duc and flying up the valley with the Argonne Forest on our left and Verdun on the right. As we neared the lines I signalled the planes into close formation so that by the time we crossed we were prepared to withstand an attack, the planes being stepped up and back with the "V" much smaller. One plane here firing a red light fell out with motor trouble, not being able to keep up with our speed. We all had orders to return in this contingency.

The clouds were numerous and heavy, but we could see the leading Squadron ahead as well as patches of ground in spots showing us our position. We were travelling at a terrific rate, the wind being apparently much stronger than the weather report showed. Stenay was plainly visible on our right. I thought of turning and dropping our bombs there, but as the leaders still went on I followed, thinking that they could see the objective from their position, though I could not see it from ours. As they reached the place where Mouzon was situated, they turned to the left over Raucourt, because, as we learned later, Mouzon was covered with clouds when they passed it. All this time the anti-aircraft shells were bursting around us, but our speed compared with the ground was so great that they were very inaccurate at our height of 14,000 feet. They showed, however, that we were discovered by the enemy and we could expect an attack by their planes.

As we reached Mouzon luck caused a sudden rift to appear in the clouds and the town was plainly visible. I steered the pilot, by the reins attached to his arms, for the town, swinging the formation to the right. Getting the edge of the town in the sight I gave the "all set" signal by firing off a Vérys light with seven green balls. At this point always comes a tense moment. The town passed back along the bar of the sight, reached the cross-bar and passed it. I pulled back the lever and let go our bombs. Waiting a few seconds to be sure all the Squadron had dropped theirs, I signalled to the pilot that all was well and to go home. Leaning over the side of the plane as far as possible, I tried to see the effects of the bursts, noticing one on a barracks and some flames near the railroad.

We turned now down the Meuse toward home against the wind, feeling that all was well. It had been a successful raid, and we were feeling happy about it.

Without warning a blue body with a white cross flashed up in front of us. Grasping a Vérys light, always kept prepared, I gave the "Enemy Aircraft" signal — seven red balls — and stood up at the guns ready for the attack. The first Boche passed from under our wing and came up under our tail. I gave him one volley as he passed and continued as he hung on his propeller not twenty feet from us, just behind our horizontal stabilizer. In this volley I shot away our right flipper wires so that I had to be careful in the future in shooting on the other side, as if both sides were shot away we should be forced to land. This blue fellow went down some distance, but climbed up behind us again and reopened fire, his tracers flashing all around us, but never hitting any vital part.

The other planes in the formation were having their troubles too. From the leader's place I could see one Boche in flames above the rear of the formation and one Liberty going down below for protection. This plane was smoking, but not yet in flames. Then the fight stopped just as suddenly as it began. I counted the Squadron, and slacking speed to gather the planes back into the "V," found there were seven left. We seemed to have got at least two Boches and had lost one of ours.

At this point two more German Squadrons appeared from the rear. The first thing I saw was one of our rear planes dive down suddenly into the middle of the "V" with two black-and-white-checked Fokkers after him. One of these fell out of control into a vrille; the other fell back and satisfied itself with long-distance firing; the Liberty went back to its old position. The tracers were flying by in the rear of the formation in all directions, but it was impossible to see exactly how many Boches were in the attack. One started crawling up on us from behind about twenty-five feet below. I fired bursts at him steadily, but he still came on. Having made a habit of always keeping one magazine in reserve on the gun fully loaded, I felt in the cockpit for a fresh one to replace the one just used up. There were none left. The reserve I had on the gun was now the last shot I had in the plane. As the German came nearer I fired in bursts of ten my last magazine. He turned back, luckily, as we were now helpless in case he persisted. I swung the useless tourelle back and forth pretending to point the guns at him as he hung back 400 yards behind. Finally, we seemed to crawl by Stenay and got over our lines at Dun-sur-Meuse. Here again I counted the flight. There were five left.

We arrived back at the field to await the hardest part of the whole raid. After making our report we watched the sky for the missing planes to come in. One hour passed; then two; finally we heard a month later that one plane had gone down in flames and two others had been forced to land in German territory. This was our last raid, as the rain god answered our daily supplications from Nov. 6 to Nov. 11.

NINETY-SIXTH AERO SQUADRON
FIRST DAY BOMBARDMENT GROUP

By Lieut. Arthur Hadden Alexander

The 96th had one of the most unique and checkered histories of any American Squadron at the front. The enlisted personnel, commanded by Capt. George C. Thomas, was one of the first to get to France; it was trained in French factories and airdromes, and when the American Bombing School was started at Clermont-Ferrand, in Jan., 1918, it was detailed there, and there its history really begins.

When the first group of bombing pilots had finished their training and were ready for the front, they had no planes of any kind — French, British, or American — fit to take to the front. As a result of the prospecting advertising which bombing had been given, much pressure was brought to bear in this direction, and it became necessary to get some kind of a bombing squadron to the front. After delays and changes in plan, ten planes of the Bréguet (French) type, which had been used in school for some time, went forward about the last of May.

Ten lucky (or unlucky) pilots, and ten observers, climbed into their old machines, already partly worn out, for a 200-mile trip from Clermont-Ferrand to Amanty, where the field from which they were to operate was located. At Amanty, they were joined by other pilots and observers, who had been sent out earlier to do observation work, and the great American aerial bombing offensive, which was to have had thousands of American planes at that time, according to the schedule, was launched the first part of June, with ten second-rate and partly worn-out French planes and ineffective French bombs.

After a few trips over the lines, Major Brown, then in command of the Squadron, took off on his well-known trip, famous throughout the Army. About July 10, the weather looked uncertain, but he had had orders to raid whenever it was possible. Seeing an opening in the clouds, he called out his flight, and in spite of the adverse advice of the French and British, started for Germany. The flight of six planes had no sooner gone through the opening than the clouds closed in solidly beneath them. They continued, with a high wind at their backs, until they saw an opening, through which was seen a city which they did not recognize. Turning for home, they flew for nearly two hours, but the wind against them was so strong that they made practically no progress, and finally, one by one, were forced to come down, out of gasoline, somewhere in the vicinity of the Rhine. Some tried to get away, but they were all captured, and a few days later, so the story goes, the Germans dropped a note saying — "Thanks for the six planes, but what shall we do with the Major?"

After this episode the Army operations reports read: "Army bombardment, First Day Bombardment Group, 96th Aero Squadron, planes on hand, -2; available for duty, -1." This was the standing of American aerial bombing until the latter part of July, when new planes were received from the French, and operations recommenced. During the month of Aug. the 96th operated continuously, with from one to three raids a day, whenever it was at all possible to get over, with only a few minor casualties. In Sept., how ever, came casualties that were exceeded by those in no squadron at the front. The Richthoffen circus was sent down to wipe out American bombing before it could get properly started, and they nearly succeeded in doing it. On Sept. 4, four men were badly wounded and only escaped with their lives through clever leadership on the part of the Flight Commander, who kept the formation in the sun. This was merely a start, for on Sept. 12, with the St.-Mihiel offensive, in rain and impossible weather, doing low altitude bombing, the Flight Commander was lost on one trip; four men lost from another flight; and as the days went on, one more was killed while landing in the dark. Following this a flight of four planes was completely wiped out, with eight men gone; later an observer was killed, and there were any number of flights from which the men returned only through remarkable flying and leadership. Not only were men killed and wounded, but the strain of the work and conditions in the Squadron were such that many men were unable to stand it, and when the Armistice was signed there was only one pilot who had remained with the Squadron from the time of its transference to the front in June.

ARTHUR HADDEN ALEXANDER

FIRST LIEUTENANT, A.S., U.S.A., NINETY-SIXTH AERO SQUADRON
FIRST DAY BOMBARDMENT GROUP

SON of Arthur Bengough and Stella Hadden Alexander; was born in Decatur, Ill., on Oct. 27, 1892; descendant of Henry Lewis, of the Revolutionary Army. In 1910 he graduated from Phillips Exeter Academy, where he played on the football team; and from the Univ. of Wisconsin, B.S. 1914, where he played on the 'Varsity Football team for three years, on the tennis team, and was captain of the hockey team; of Harvard University, Graduate School of Landscape Architecture, M.L.A. 1917.

He enlisted in the Aviation Section of the Signal Corps on June 13, 1917, and entered the 4th class of the Army Aviation Ground School at M.I.T. on that date. After six weeks' ground-work he was selected among ten from that class to be sent to France for flying training, and sailed on Aug. 22, 1917. He entered the French "École d'aviation militaire" at Tours, Oct. 1, where he received his preliminary flying training under the French; then was sent to the American School at Issoudun for advanced training and was commissioned 1st Lieut. Feb. 20. Upon completion of the course at Issoudun, he was returned to Tours in March as an instructor for two months and a half. On June 1, he went to the Bombing School at Clermont-Ferrand (7th Aviation Instruction Centre) and was ordered to the front, July 14, 1918, where he was detailed to the 96th Squadron, the first American Bombing Squadron to be organized, and participated in daylight bombing raids over enemy territory until wounded. On Sept. 4, while returning from a raid, and still 25 miles beyond the lines, his Squadron of 8 planes was attacked by 15 or more enemy planes and badly shot up. All managed to return safely, however, and two German planes were shot down. Lieut. Alexander was severely wounded, a bullet passing through his abdomen, but he succeeded in landing safely on his own field after fainting several times during the descent. He was awarded the D.S.C. by General Pershing with the following citation:

For extraordinary heroism in action on Sept. 4, 1918. While on a bombing expedition with other planes of his squadron, Lieut. Alexander engaged in a running fight over hostile territory with a superior number of

enemy battle planes, from Friauville to Lamorville, France. He was seriously wounded in the abdomen by a machine-gun bullet and his observer was shot through both legs. Although weak from pain and loss of blood, Lieut. Alexander piloted his plane back to his own airdrome and concealed the fact of his injury until after his observer had been cared for.

After partial recovery from his wound he was called back to duty at General Headquarters to represent the Air Service on the Board of Awards, which was composed of a man from every branch of the Service who had been wounded, decorated, and seen a year's service. This board passed on recommendations for the Congressional Medal and D.S.C. Lieut. Alexander was returned to the U.S. in Feb., 1919, and honorably discharged at Garden City, N.Y., Feb. 7, 1919.

Lieut. Alexander has described the raid of Sept. 4, over Germany, in the following extract:

We had just dropped our bombs on the railroad tracks when Boche machines began to appear from every side. The wind was such that we had to stay over there much longer than usual, which gave them a chance to come up at us. At first it was a fairly even scrap, but more and more of them kept coming on until you saw them wherever you looked. Once I looked down, and there was a gang more on the way up. We were in the back of the formation and things got hotter and hotter. They kept closing in and we gave them all we had, but it finally got to be almost impossible to keep them off because they were so many.

They closed in on us as close as 30 to 50 yards at times, and you have no idea what a sensation it is to hold to your formation and hear the Boche machine guns, from four to five planes, cracking at you, and see their tracer bullets flashing by your head and hear and feel them hitting the wings and fuselage. McLennan, my observer, kept after them all the time, tapping me on the shoulder as he wanted me to tip up to give him shots, until he finally collapsed with two bullets in one leg and one in the other. Almost at the same time a bullet went into my side. From then on the only thought I had was to get back. . . . How I got there I don't know, but we finally got back to our own field and a safe landing before I went completely under, once more proving that the power of God is more powerful than that of evil.

*STEPHEN T. HOPKINS

Second Lieutenant, A.S., U.S.A., Ninety-Sixth Aero Squadron, First Day Bombardment Group

Killed in action, Sept. 13, 1918

Son of Dr. Edward E. and Louise (Tullock) Hopkins; was born in Newtonville, Mass., March 19, 1892. He was a direct descendant of the signer of the Declaration of Independence whose name he bore. He prepared for college in the Newton schools, and graduated from Harvard College in 1914. During his high school and college career, he was prominent in athletics; he played on the 'Varsity hockey team for three years, and later on the Boston Athletic Association hockey team. He was a member of the Hasty Pudding, Institute of 1770, D.K.E., 'Varsity, Iroquois, and Porcellian clubs.

After graduation from college, he spent a year at the Harvard Business School, and then went into the Lancaster Mills, at Clinton, to learn the cotton business, where he remained two years. He was then made assistant treasurer of the Becker Milling Machine Company at Hyde Park, which position he held at the time of his enlistment.

He entered the Army Aviation School of the M.I.T. in Sept., 1917, and the following month was sent to Foggia, Italy, sailing Oct. 28; there, after seven months' training, he was commissioned 2d Lieut., May 13, 1918.

From Foggia, he went to Vendôme, France, for further training, and later to Clermont-Ferrand for practice in bombing and formation flying. At the completion of his training he was sent as a bombing pilot to the 96th Aero Squadron.

He entered active service at the front in Aug., 1918, and during the great offensive at St.-Mihiel, his plane was shot down in flames, and both he and his observer, Lieut. Bertram Williams, were killed. News that these two aviators were missing in action was received by their relations some three months before it was ascertained that they had been killed. They were buried at Charey, France.

Just before starting upon his last flight over the enemy lines Lieut. Hopkins wrote to his father:

> We have been all ready to take a trip into Germany several times only to have it called off just at the last moment. Yesterday we repeated this several times. We got up early in the morning ready to start, but the

weather was so bad that you could n't get off the ground. As you have probably read, the much heralded U.S. drive started, and we were particularly anxious to contribute our share. At last, under the most unfavorable weather conditions, our squadron leader started out alone. He did not return. We then got our formation ready and had our motors tuned up, bombs on, machine guns tested, etc. Just then a plane which was landing on our field crashed into my machine, thereby wrecking it. Thus I was deprived of my first trip over the lines. This formation returned with the exception of one machine, which, however, is safe at another aerdrome. Finally I procured a machine and was to go in the next formation. We waited around and attempted to make several starts, but each time such a storm would hit the field that we simply could n't get away. At last we started, just before dark. We went to our objective and dropped our bombs; it was dark then. I have never seen such a sight in my life. The whole country was one mass of flames, where the Germans were in retreat. You could see the flashes of the guns, and anti-aircraft occasionally broke around us. However, as it was dark, the anti-aircraft and Hun machines were scarce. It was a most remarkable day, as every time we were given an objective during the day, we would proceed there and find that the Americans had it. . . . If they can only keep it up! After we dropped our bombs, our work really only started, so far as getting on to terra-firma safely was concerned. It was pitch dark and we flew for a long time on a straight course that we knew would ultimately take us over the lines. We finally recognized a river that we knew was in France. So far so good. The next question was how to find a good field or our own field to land on. Of course, all lights are out in this country and consequently there were very few landmarks. The moon finally came out, and by the aid of this we were able to follow rivers and the shapes of certain forests, and finally, in the direction of our field, we saw some flares. Perhaps we were n't pleased! Three of the machines smashed in landing, but the teams were not hurt. I was the only one who did not damage a machine. One team did not return and I have just heard that the pilot was killed in trying to land. It was too bad as he was a fine chap from Princeton.

This letter was prefaced by the words: "Just a note before I start out for a hard day's work." From this flight Lieut. Hopkins did not return.

CHARLES R. CODMAN

First Lieutenant, A.S.A., U.S.A., Ninety-Sixth Aero Squadron, First Day Bombardment Group

Son of Russell S. and Anna K. (Crafts) Codman; was born in Boston, Mass., Feb. 22, 1893. He was educated at Groton School, Mass., and Harvard College, A.B. 1915. Prior to the declaration of war, he served with Battery A, M.V.M., one year; and with the American Ambulance Field Service for nine months.

He enlisted in April, 1917, attended the M.I.T. Ground School, and the Flying School at Essington, Pa. He was commissioned 1st Lieut. on Oct. 31, 1917, and sailed for France with the A.E.F. about Nov. 1. He trained at the U.S. Flying Schools at Issoudun and Clermont-Ferrand, France, and on the completion of his courses was assigned to the 96th Aero Squadron.

Lieut. Codman was in active service at the front from June 3 to Sept. 16, 1918. While bombing Conflans, on Sept. 16, 1918, he was in a flight of four machines attacked by 24 Fokkers. The other three machines in the formation were brought down in flames and the occupants killed. Lieut. Codman and his observer, Lieut. S. A. McDowell, of Philadelphia, were the only survivors of the flight, and McDowell was severely wounded, but not before he had brought down three enemy planes. Lieut. Codman's machine was shot down, and he being wounded was made prisoner near Conflans. He remained a prisoner in Germany until the Armistice. He escaped from Landshut prison about Nov. 8, together with James Norman Hall, Henry Lewis, and Robert Browning, all of the U.S. Air Service. They arrived in Berne, Switzerland, Nov. 19; sailed for America; and on Jan. 3, 1919, Lieut. Codman was honorably discharged at Garden City, N.Y.

Brother in Service:— Russell S. Codman, Jr., 1st Lieut., U.S.A., Dépôt Brigade, Camp Devens.

Citation

Received from the French Army Citation and Croix de Guerre with Palm; also, cited in Citation Orders No. 1, by General Headquarters, American Expeditionary Forces, for Gallantry in Action Sept. 16, 1918, while engaged in Bombing Expedition near Conflans, France.

*BERTRAM WILLIAMS

First Lieutenant, A.S.A., U.S.A., Ninety-Sixth Aero Squadron, First Day Bombardment Group

Killed in action, Sept. 13, 1918

Son of John Bertram and Olive (Swan) Williams; was born in Cambridge, Mass., on Sept. 11, 1896. He was educated at the Browne and Nichols School, Cambridge; at the Middlesex School, Concord, Mass.; and at Harvard College. At the Middlesex School, he made the second school crew in 1913, and rowed bow in the first crew in 1914. He was also a member of the dramatic and debating clubs, managed the baseball team in 1912, and the crew in 1913. He entered Harvard with honors, belonged to the Phœnix, the D.K.E., and the Owl clubs, and rowed on the freshman crew, which won the four-oared race at New London in 1914. In 1916 he was given six months' leave of absence from college to join the Morgan-Harjes Ambulance Corps, sailing for France in Feb. He was assigned to Formation No. 5, and went at once to the front near Verdun. This corps was cited for the work done under fire from March 8 to 19.

Bertram Williams returned to college in Sept. and joined the R.O.T.C. at Harvard. He was accepted for the Air Service in July, and was assigned to M.I.T. for Ground School work in Aug., 1917, graduating in Oct. Being among the "honor men" of his Squadron, he was at once ordered overseas, and sailed on Oct. 17, 1917. He wrote at sea: "We got so efficient at abandon ship drill that it was almost disappointing not to have a chance to use it." Immediately on his arrival at St.-Nazaire, he was sent to the 3d Aviation Instruction Centre at Issoudun. He stayed there until March, 1918, when he volunteered, with 25 others, for a two weeks' ground course preparatory to becoming an observer, and was ordered to Gondrecourt. From there he wrote:

> We are the first fighting observers, and ever since we volunteered for it, they have never known just what to do with us. For this reason we all wear white elephants on our identification plaques.

He was at the Aviation Instruction Centre at Tours until April, and was then sent on to Cazaux. He wrote home:

> There are four of us picked according to our grades at Tours, who are going to the School of Aerial Gunnery at Cazaux. All this may not mean much to you, but any one who has been through the French School at

Cazaux is a little bit better than any one else in the flying world over here, and I am tickled to death.

In a later letter, he said:

> When we were shooting at a silhouette of an airplane on the ground, I was lucky enough to get 28 per cent, which put me on the Tableau d'Honneur — the third American to get on it.

He was commissioned 1st Lieut. at Cazaux, in May, 1918, and ordered to Clermont-Ferrand, where he remained until Sept., when he was attached to the 96th Squadron. On Sept. 13 Lieut. Williams and his pilot, Stephen Hopkins, were in one of three planes flying over Chambley. One of the American planes was separated from the rest, and 20 German machines attacked the remaining two. Both were shot down in flames. Lieut. Williams and Lieut. Hopkins were reported "missing in action," in the middle of Sept., and later "killed in action." They were buried at Charey, France. In June they were reinterred at Thiaucourt, one of the national cemeteries. The following is quoted from a letter written by Lieut. Roth, observer in the plane which was not shot down:

> I was one of the men who were on the bombing-raid the day your son Bertram was killed, and I want to tell you with my whole heart that a man never died a braver death than your son did . . . the weather conditions were so bad during the first days of the St.-Mihiel drive that flying was almost out of the question, and yet those in command of the aviation felt that there was need for us to do what we could in order to help defeat the enemy. . . . We had lost some planes over the lines but a great many more were broken up on the flying-field because of the bad condition the ground was in. The result was that on the morning of the 13th our Squadron had only five planes in commission, and when we received notice to go out on a raid in the afternoon, these planes were made ready for the start.
>
> Our objective that day was only a little distance over the lines and none of us had any idea that we would encounter the opposition that we did. We had scarcely gotten over when we were able to see the road running from Chambley to Gorze but could observe no troops on the road and turned to our alternative objective, which was the town of Chambley, and prepared to bomb the town. Just as we were turning in order to pass over the town, the German anti-aircraft batteries began shooting at us, and the black puffs which always follow the explosion of shells gave away our position and the next instant we could see a whole flight of fast German pursuit planes, possibly around fifteen in all, diving down through the clouds at us, and the next instant they were on top of us. However we had

our work cut out for us and dropped our bombs down on the town, and tried to protect ourselves as best we could. It looked hopeless, and as for myself I never expected to get back across the lines — Lieut. Williams and his pilot, Lieut. Hopkins, Lieut. Thompson and his pilot, Lieut. Farnsworth, being of course slightly in the rear had to stand the brunt of the fighting, but the odds were so great that the attack was coming from three sides at once. Nevertheless, Lieut. Williams and Lieut. Thompson stood by their guns so bravely until they were overwhelmed and forced down, that the attack was slowed up for an instant and no doubt that instant was a great factor in carrying out the mission. I feel that when these officers in the two planes that went over on this mission, absolutely unprotected by scout planes, not only succeeded in carrying out the mission before they were killed but aided one of the other planes in returning safely to the lines, their heroism in doing all this deserves to come under the consideration of whatever Board at Washington has the awarding of the Distinguished Service Cross.

This letter from Lieut. Roth furnishes the only account of this battle which has so far been received, and its expression of the conviction of a fellow officer, in regard to the deserved award of the D.S.C., would have meant more to the men who had given their lives in this encounter than any decision of the authorities at Washington.

Lieuts. Williams and Hopkins lie near together at Thiaucourt, France, under the white crosses that they were so ready to win.

Among Lieut. Williams's effects was a bronze medal, evidently awarded for his shooting record at Cazaux.

JOHN CHARLES EARLE McLENNAN

SECOND LIEUTENANT, A.S., U.S.A., NINETY-SIXTH AERO SQUADRON, FIRST DAY BOMBARDMENT GROUP

SON of John K. and Isabella (Morrison) McLennan; was born in Newport, R.I., Aug. 9, 1891. He was educated in the public schools of Newport, R.I., and at the Univ. of Pennsylvania; he received the degree of B.S. in Electrical Engineering in 1916, from the Towne Scientific School, U.Pa. After graduation he held a position in the Philadelphia Electrical Co.

In May, 1917, he applied for a commission in the Aviation Section of the Signal Corps, and was offered a non-flying commission. This he refused, perferring to enroll in the flying section of the A.S. Signal Corps, in which he enlisted July 30, 1917, at Essington, Pa.

On Sept. 15, 1917, he entered the U.S. School of Military Aeronautics at Princeton, N.J., completing the course on Nov. 10, 1917. He was ordered overseas with the 16th Foreign Detachment of Cadets, sailing on Nov. 23. He was stationed for the winter at St.-Maixent, France, leaving there on March 12, 1918, for the 1st Corps Gunnery School at Gondrecourt. He took up Aerial gunnery at Cazaux, from March 25 to April 24, returning to St.-Maixent on completion of the course. He was commissioned 2d Lieut. A.S.(A.) May 18, 1918. On May 27 he was sent to the 7th Aviation Instruction Centre at Clermont-Ferrand, to take up bombing, completing this course about the first of July, when he joined the 96th Aero Squadron then stationed at Amanty, Meuse. He remained with the 96th Squadron during July and Aug., making frequent bombing raids over the territory between Verdun and Metz.

On Sept. 4, 1918, Lieut. McLennan and his pilot, Lieut. A. Hadden Alexander, were both severely wounded in an action with enemy planes over Conflans. With great heroism the wounded pilot was able to bring the plane safely back to the home field. McLennan was in the hospital at Châlet Guyon until Jan. 3, 1919, the Armistice meanwhile having been signed. He was sent to Gondrecourt for reassignment to duty. From there he was detailed to duty with freight trains running between the advance S.O.S. and the Army of Occupation in Germany; this duty lasting until March 5, 1919, when he was ordered back to the U.S. He was honorably discharged at Garden City, N.Y., in June, 1919.

ROY WALES HALL

FIRST LIEUTENANT A.S., U.S.A., NINETIETH AERO SQUADRON
FIRST OBSERVATION GROUP, AND NINETY-SIXTH AERO
SQUADRON, FIRST BOMBARDMENT GROUP

SON of George E. and Anna Gertrude (Bachelder) Hall, of Needham, Mass.; was born in Dorchester, Mass., Oct. 13, 1895. He was educated at the Warren Private School and English High School, where he was a member of the track team. He was 1st Lieut. in the United Boys' Brigade of America. In the summer of 1916 he attended the Plattsburg Camp.

On May 4, 1917, Lieut. Hall enlisted in Boston for the Plattsburg Officers' Training Camp; after which training he attended M.I.T. Ground School, and the School at Mineola, N.Y. He was ordered overseas, and stationed at the 3d and later at the 7th Aviation Instruction Centre, attached to the 90th Aero Squadron and the 96th Squadron, operating in the Toul sector, France. He had qualified for his commission Sept. 11, 1917, having finished his R.M.A., and was commissioned 1st Lieut. Jan. 18, 1918.

Being trained as a pursuit pilot and a bombing pilot, Lieut. Hall was first assigned to artillery observation, then to bombing, which he followed chiefly, with the 96th Squadron. He spent 22 months in Service, 16 months overseas. On Feb. 11, 1919, he was put on the list as a casual officer and in Class 2 (Reserve), at Garden City, N.Y.

Twin brother in Service —

Ray Currier Hall, Hospital Serg't., 22 months; Camp Upton, 19 months; Ambulance Service, 3 months.

JOHN E. BERRY

First Lieutenant, R.A.F., Two Hundred Tenth Squadron
Fifth Group

Son of George E. and Charlotte K. Berry; was born at Malden, Mass., Jan. 7, 1895. He was educated at the Malden High School, Brewster Academy, and at Dartmouth College. In athletics he played football and hockey.

He enlisted in the U.S.N.R. Flying Corps, in May, 1917, and attended the M.I.T. Ground School, Flight A (1). In Oct. he joined the Royal Flying Corps, Cadet Wing, at Long Branch, Toronto, Can. He trained at the School of Military Aeronautics, Toronto University; at Armour Heights, and Leaside Flying Camps, Toronto. He continued his training at the School of Aerial Gunnery, Hamilton, Ont. In May, 1918, he was commissioned 2d Lieut., R.F.C.

He sailed overseas to England, and completed his training at Cranwell Flying Camp, and Freiston No. 4 Fighting School, Lincolnshire. He was commissioned 1st Lieut., R.A.F., in Sept., 1918, and attached to Squadron 210, 5th Group, at Eringham, near Dunkirk, France. Later he moved to Cambrai, and saw active service until the end of the war. Lieut. Berry was officially credited with two Hun planes "crashed." He was demobilized at London, Eng., in March, 1919, and returned to the U.S.

*RAYMOND CLYDE TAYLOR

First Lieutenant, A.S., U.S.A., Ninety-Sixth Aero Squadron, First Day Bombardment Group

Killed in action, Sept. 16, 1918

Son of Alexander and Barbara (Annand) Taylor, of Billerica, Mass.; was born at North Sullivan, Me., on April 30, 1892. He was educated at Arlington High School, and at Tufts College, graduating (*cum laude*) in 1916. While at college he completed his training in the Mechanical Engineering Department, where he showed great initiative and constructive ability; was a member of the S.I.A. Fraternity, and the Glee Club. Upon graduation he was selected with three other young men from Arlington to attend the Plattsburg Training Camp, during the summer of 1916.

In Feb., 1917, he went to New York and volunteered for the Aviation Service. He enlisted April 1, 1917, and was sent to Miami, Fla., for instruction; then to Austin, Tex., June 3 to July 27. He trained at Rantoul, Ill., 10th Aero Squadron, July 27 to Sept. 16; at San Antonio, Tex., 136th Squadron, Sept. 16. to Oct. 10, and was then transferred to Fort Wood, N.Y., for a few days before sailing overseas. He was commissioned 1st Lieut. on Oct. 1, 1917.

He reached France about Nov. 5, 1917, and was stationed at the 3d Aviation Instruction Centre, Issoudun. On March 3, 1918, he continued his training and later served as an instructor at Tours, and from April 25 to July 10, attended the Bombing School at Clermont-Ferrand. From there he wrote on May 9:

> What have we "Great Americans" done in our year of war? I hope to get to the front by the time this letter reaches you, but there seem to be so many side-tracks and the French are quite able to fly their own planes and the British are too darned good flyers to take any chances on greenhorns, — our only hope is to borrow an old bus from somewhere. If you people can fix the heads of those individuals who have held up machine guns, so they can think straight — and fix the spies who help them — you will be doing the Allies the greatest service . . . it's a shame that many of us have been in training for over a year and we have n't had a look at the Boches yet. . . . We want guns, bullets, and planes and we want them badly.

On July 10, Lieut. Taylor joined the 96th Aero Squadron at Amanty, where he realized his desire to get to the front, returning from his first flight over the lines with four bullet holes in his plane.

This number was increased to 36 bullet holes up to the time the aviators were forbidden to paint black crosses over the holes.

While at the front Lieut. Taylor was offered the rank of Captain, if he would go back to one of the schools as instructor, to which he replied: "They need me at the front now more than anywhere else."

On Sept. 16, he made his last flight. 6 Bréguets left Amanty, but owing to motor trouble but 4 planes crossed the lines east of St.-Mihiel. On approaching Conflans, 24 enemy aircraft were sighted; these attacked them after they had dropped their bombs on their objective.

An extract describing the combat, from the report of Lieut. Charles R. Codman, follows:

> Before reaching us the enemy aircraft (Fokkers and Pfalz) divided into three groups, the first circled round our rear, the second to the southwest to cut us off at the lines, the third attacked us directly. Their fire was first concentrated upon No. 2 machine (in which was Lieut. Raymond Taylor, pilot, and Lieut. Wm. A. Stuart, observer). I think the pilot was hit by the first burst, as the machine went suddenly out of control, skidded out of the formation and, according to Lieut. McDowell, my observer, went down in flames.
>
> No. 3 machine (Lieut. Codman's) moved over to No. 2's place, with the intention of making room for No. 4, which was slightly to the left of the formation. No. 4 was attacked, however, before regaining the formation and was brought down, according to Lieut. McDowell, in flames. No. 1 machine was next attacked and the gasoline tank hit. It went down in flames. The above all took place within the space of five minutes, I should say, in the vicinity of the objective.

Lieut. Codman's machine was of a newer and faster type than the others and equipped with an *armored gasoline tank which could not explode. This enabled him to land safely.* Undoubtedly Lieut. Taylor and his observer were attacked by a dozen enemy planes, made a brave fight, and before being shot down themselves shot down one enemy plane, as testimony to this effect was given by several witnesses. The plane fell near the village of Mainville, some 10 miles from their objective, Conflans, and there Lieut. Taylor and his observer are buried in a field between Mainville and Norroy-le-Sec.

Married, Oct. 1, 1917, Dolly Anna E. l'Hatton.

Brother in Service —

Theodore M. Taylor, Motor Transportation Corps.

*SAMUEL PIERCE MANDELL, Second

First Lieutenant, A.S., U.S.A., Twentieth Aero Squadron, First Day Bombardment Group

Killed in action, Nov. 5, 1918

Son of George S. and Emily (Proctor) Mandell; was born in Boston, Mass., March 20, 1897. A special slant was given his boyhood by an out-of-door environment. His days were spent in riding, hunting, breaking colts, and playing polo. He entered Harvard College from St. Mark's in 1915. His freshman vacation he devoted to the Harvard Flying Corps, going to Ithaca, N.Y., and the next spring enlisted at Newport News, March 3, 1917, though the U.S. had not then entered the war. Here he qualified as pilot July 25, and passed on to M.I.T., Cambridge, and Mineola, N.Y., where he received his commission, Nov. 5, 1917. Thence he proceeded overseas, Dec. 15.

Landing at Glasgow, he was sent to Winchester, and almost immediately to France: Issoudun, Jan. 25 to March 20; Tours, to May 21; Clermont-Ferrand, to July 11; Châteaudun, to Aug. 18; Orly, and finally on Aug. 30 was assigned to the 20th Aero Squadron and the front.

The very first flight over enemy lines which the 20th was asked to make was to take part in the St.-Mihiel drive. In driving rain and hail, weather such as none of them had ever before been permitted to venture out in, these untried men were sent to support the American attack. That they met the crisis splendidly is recorded in the citation which the Group received, for having "shown a devotion to duty and initiative which has not been exceeded by any troops on the front."

Mandell participated in 17 raids, practically all that were made by the Squadron, and for this he was cited. On the day before his last flight, he was certified for bringing down an enemy Fokker.

His last flight — and it was the last American air raid of the war — was on Nov. 5, Mouzun being the objective. A detailed account is given elsewhere. It was in the third fight that his "ship" shot up. An aileron was put out of commission and the engine was shot dead. The "ship," then some 12,000 feet up, sank in great spiral vrilles from which its occupants managed to right it about every 1000 feet. The last recovery was less than 100 feet from the the ground. It fell within a few yards of the canal in Martincourt.

Lieut. R. W. Fulton, of N.Y., his observer, was practically unhurt; Mandell's leg was badly broken. The exact details of his other injuries are doubtful. The Germans marched Fulton away, and left the wounded pilot propped against his plane.

The rest of the story is gleaned from the inhabitants of the town. About 4 o'clock in the afternoon, a German captain of infantry came to the bank, took a rifle from one of the guards, and deliberately fired a number of shots into the helpless American.

It was the 17th before a detachment from the 5th Marines, in passing through the town, were notified of the dead young aviator. Reverently they buried him where he fell. Shortly afterward, the Meuse overflowed. It was thus that news came to Lieut. Petit, of the 58th Field Artillery, who had known Mandell at home as a fellow sportsman. Petit immediately arranged for a reinterment in a little country churchyard on the hill nearly opposite. Later, the body was again transferred to the little U.S. military cemetery between Beaumont and Letanne.

Citations

(*General Orders, No.* 27) *November* 17, 1918

First Lieutenants S. P. Mandell, John T. Willis, Jr., and Gardner H. Fiske and Second Lieutenant L. P. Koepfgen, 20th Aero Squadron, First Day Bombardment Group are hereby credited with the distinction, in combat, of an enemy Fokker, in the region southwest of Montmédy at 12,000 feet altitude, on November 4, 1918 at 15.25 o'clock.

By order of Col. MILLING
U. C. SHERMAN
Lieut. Col. A.S., U.S.A., Chief of Staff

(*General Orders, No.* 29) *November* 21, 1918

Extract

The Army Air Service Commander First Army cites the following officers and men for exceptional devotion to duty.

First Lieutenant S. P. Mandell, A.S., U.S.A., as Pilot of the 20th Aero Squadron, First Day Bombardment Group, participated in every raid made by the squadron in the Argonne-Meuse sector during October, 1918.

By order of Col. MILLING
U. C. SHERMAN
Lieut. Col. A.S., U.S.A., Chief of Staff

DONALD D. WARNER

First Lieutenant, A.S., U.S.A., Ninety-Sixth Aero Squadron
First Day Bombardment Group

Son of Clyde Longyear and Caroline Eunice Warner, of Swampscott, Mass., was born in Rochester, N.Y., Feb. 25, 1895. He graduated from the English High School in 1914, and attended M.I.T., class of 1918, three years; leaving to enlist at the end of his junior year, July 16, 1917, at Cambridge.

He received ground school training at M.I.T., graduating in Oct., 1917, and was sent immediately with others of his class overseas, sailing Nov. 2, 1917. He trained as a bomber at Clermont-Ferrand, France, and at the Aerial Gunnery School, Cazaux, France. Finishing his training in April, 1918, he was at once ordered to the front, where he was commissioned 1st Lieut., May 18, 1918, U.S., A.S., and was later attached to the 96th Aero Squadron, 1st American Bombardment Group.

Lieut. Warner participated in frequent bombing raids, and did notable service until Sept. 4, 1918, when he was wounded in action very severely. For his bravery at this time he was recommended for advanced flying rating by the War Department, on the date of Sept. 4, 1918, and was awarded the Distinguished Service Cross on Jan. 18, 1919. The ceremony was performed on the steps of the U.S. Army General Hospital, No. 10, Parker Hill Avenue, Roxbury, Mass., by Colonel Joseph Taylor Clarke, Commandant, while the medical department of that institution, 600 men and 50 officers, stood at attention.

Citation

D.S.C.

While on a bombing expedition with other planes of his squadron, he engaged in a running fight over hostile territory with a superior number of enemy battle planes from Friauville to Lamorville, France. During the combat he was severely wounded, his right thigh being shattered. In spite of his injuries he continued to operate his machine guns until the hostile formation had been driven off and one plane shot down burning.

GILBERT STANLEY

First Lieutenant, A.S., U.S.A., Ninety-Sixth Aero Squadron
First Day Bombardment Group

Son of William and Lila Courtney (Wetmore) Stanley, of Great Barrington, Mass.; was born Jan. 14, 1897, at Pittsfield, Mass.; educated at the Berkshire School, Sheffield, Conn., and at Yale College, where he spent two years.

He enlisted on June 10, 1917, at New York. He graduated from the Cornell Ground School, in the class of Oct. 13, 1917, and sailed for France as a cadet, Oct. 21, 1917. He was employed at first in building the 3d Aviation Instruction Centre at Issoudun. About March 1 he was assigned to St.-Maixent, and April 15 to his first flying school at Tours. He received his brevet and his commission as 1st Lieut. on June 7, 1918. In Sept. he was sent to Issoudun, for further training, and later transferred to Clermont-Ferrand. He finished the course in bombing Oct. 1, 1918 and then joined the 96th Aero Squadron, 1st Day Bombardment Group.

On Oct. 29, with his observer, Lieut. Folger, he was officially credited with being wounded in action by enemy aircraft, and with the distinction in combat of a Fokker. Though pursued by enemy machines, they succeeded in reaching their own lines just outside Verdun. Lieut. Stanley returned to the U.S., Feb. 20, 1919.

Brothers in Service —

Clarence Stanley Ensign, U.S. Naval Aviation.
Leonard Stanley 1st Lieut., A.S., U.S.A.,

CHARLES E. TROWBRIDGE

FIRST LIEUTENANT, A.S., U.S.A., NINETY-SIXTH AERO SQUADRON
FIRST DAY BOMBARDMENT GROUP

SON of Edward R. and Alice (Eastman) Trowbridge; was born at Providence, R.I., June 9, 1895. He was educated at Hotchkiss School, Lakeville, Conn., 1913; and Sheffield Scientific School, Yale, Ph.B. 1917.

He enlisted on April 18, 1917, at Mineola, N.Y., with rank of Sergeant, A.S., S.E.R.C. He studied at Mineola, qualifying as R.M.A. on June 28, 1917. On July 10 he was commissioned 1st Lieut. From July 15 to Aug. 20 he was stationed with the 8th Aero Squadron at Mt. Clemens, Mich.; from Aug. 22 to Sept. 19 with the 44th Aero Squadron at Dayton, O., as supply officer. He was in command of the 13th Aero Squadron from Sept. 20, 1917, to Jan. 26, 1918, during which time the Squadron was moved from Dayton to Garden City, N.Y.; was outfitted, and sailed for France on Dec. 4, 1917. Lieut. Trowbridge was in command of the 15th Foreign Detachment of "Flying Cadets" for one month at St.-Maixent, France. He then received advanced training at the 7th Aviation Instruction Centre, Clermont-Ferrand; and was Instructor there from May to Nov. He was attached to the 96th Aero Squadron in the Argonne-Meuse sector in Nov., 1918. Lieut. Trowbridge was honorably discharged at the Air Dépôt, Garden City, N.Y., on Feb. 15, 1919.

FRANCIS W. COWLES

First Lieutenant, A.S., U.S.A., Ninety-Sixth Aero Squadron
First Day Bombardment Group

Son of Walter G. and Nellie F. Cowles, of Hartford, Conn.; was born at Abilene, Kan., on Oct. 28, 1889. He was educated at the Hartford public schools; Conn. Literary Institute, Sheffield, Conn.; Allen School, West Newton, Mass.; and U.S. Naval Academy, Annapolis, Md.

He enlisted at Plattsburg, N.Y., on May 15, 1917. He trained at Plattsburg, at M.I.T. Ground School, at the flying fields in Mineola, N.Y., and at Kelly Field, Tex. He was commissioned 1st Lieut. in Sept., 1917, and sailed overseas in command of the 117th Aero Squadron on Dec. 16, 1917. He was stationed at Issoudun, where he was in command of one of the fields, and at Clermont-Ferrand. He was assigned to the 96th Aero Squadron, and participated in several bombing raids over and around Verdun and St.-Mihiel. He was a trained and experienced bomber; and while awaiting planes for his especial work he did much ferrying of new planes from Paris to the battle-lines. He developed considerable aptitude for cross-country work in strange places, and was ordered to take a special course in aerial navigation in England, but owing to the Armistice the order was revoked. He was discharged at his own request on Feb. 1, 1919.

Brother in Service —

Donald B. Cowles, 1st Lieut., U.S. Marine Corps, Aviation Force; died in Service.

*DONALD B. COWLES

First Lieutenant, U.S. Marine Corps, Squadron D
First Aviation Force

Died of pneumonia, Oct. 1, 1918

Son of Walter G. and Nellie F. Cowles; was born at Hartford, Conn., July 26, 1895. He was educated in the public schools of Hartford; at Holderness School, Plymouth, N.H.; and at N.Y. Military School, where he graduated with military honors.

He enlisted on July 5, 1917, at Winthrop, Md.; he was attached to the Winthrop Rifle Range, and trained at Quantico, Md., Officers' School. He was then chosen as one of the First Aviation Force of the Marine Corps, and trained as an aviator at Garden City, N.Y.; Philadelphia Navy Yard; and Miami, Fla., where he became an instructor in advanced flying and acrobacy. He was commissioned 2d Lieut. on June 22, 1917, and 1st Lieut. on July 1, 1918. He sailed overseas Sept. 16, 1918. Two days after landing at Liverpool he died in that city, of pneumonia, on Oct. 1, 1918; he was buried at Hartford, Conn.

Brother in Service —

Francis W. Cowles, 1st Lieut., A.S., U.S.A., 96th Aero Squadron.

*BRAYTON NICHOLS

Second Lieutenant, One Hundred Sixty-Sixth Aero Squadron, First Day Bombardment Group

Killed in airplane accident, April 2, 1919

Son of Dr. Charles L. and Mary J. (Brayton) Nichols; was born in Worcester, Mass., on Dec. 29, 1892. He attended a private school in Worcester, spent two years in school at Lauzanne, Switzerland, and then fitted at Pomfret School, for Harvard College, graduating in 1915. While in college he enlisted in Battery A, M.V.M., and in 1916 went as a private in this battery, 1st Mass. F.A., N.G., to the Mexican Border, being stationed at Fort Bliss, El Paso, Tex., from June 10 to Oct. 17. On his return he entered Tufts Medical School, where he studied until the U.S. declared war on Germany. He then went to the Plattsburg Officers' Training Camp. He there elected Aviation, and in Aug. took a special course at Newport News, Va., at the Curtiss Aviation School, receiving a commission as Pilot. From Oct. to Dec. he attended the Ground School at M.I.T. and was then sent to Ellington Field, Houston, Tex., where he remained until June, 1918. There he was commissioned 2d Lieut. in March, 1918. From July 11 to Sept. he was at the finishing school at Fort Worth, Tex., and then went overseas to France. He stayed at the Bombing School at Clermont-Ferrand for five weeks and was then assigned to the 166th Aero Squadron at the front. After the signing of the Armistice the Squadron was moved forward with the Army of Occupation, being first assigned quarters at Joppécourt, then at Luxembourg, and later at Trèves, Germany, where it remained until its return to the U.S. in April, 1919. Their time was spent in single flight, in practice formation, and in aerial photography, in order to be prepared for further action if the peace negotiations failed. During a regular formation flight, on April 2, an air collision occurred involving four of the machines, three of which fell to the ground, three men being killed, and one drowned in the Moselle River. Lieut. Nichols was killed in this accident at Kordel, a few miles from Trèves, and was buried at the Stadt Cemetery at Trèves with his companions.

Brother in Service: Charles L. Nichols, Jr., private, 34th Machine Gun Squadron, 76th Division, Camp Devens.

HENRY BRIGGS

First Lieutenant, A.S.A., U.S.A., Ninety-Sixth Aero Squadron, First Day Bombardment Group

Son of Charles P. and Gertrude (Russell) Briggs of Lexington, Mass.; was born in Lexington on Jan. 26, 1896. He was educated at the Lexington High School, and at Harvard College, class of 1918. He attended the Officers' Training Camp at Plattsburg, in 1916, and belonged to the Harvard R.O.T.C.

He enlisted in the Air Service at Cambridge, Mass., on July 7, 1917, and was assigned to the Ground School at M.I.T., where he remained from Aug. 13 to Oct. 6, 1917. He was then ordered to Mineola, N.Y., where he was stationed from Oct. 14, to Oct. 27. He proceeded overseas, arriving in Liverpool on Nov. 10.

He continued his training in France: at Issoudun from Nov. 17, 1917, to Jan. 8, 1918; at the Aerial Gunnery School, Cazaux, from Jan. 12 to Feb. 7; at Issoudun, from March 6 to April 1; at Tours (preliminary training) from April 2 to July 3; at Issoudun (secondary training) from July 15 to Sept. 6; and at Clermont-Ferrand (final training as bomber) from Sept. 7 to Oct. 1. He was assigned to the 96th Aero Squadron, 1st Day Bombardment Group, at Maulan on Oct. 9, 1918. With his observer, Howard C. Binley, he bombed Villers-devant-Dun, Bayonville, Brequency, Damvillers, Tailly, and Stenay. On three of these trips his plane was struck. His total time spent in bombing was 760 minutes.

He was commissioned 1st Lieut. on May 13, 1918. He was discharged from the Air Service at the Air Service Dépôt, Garden City, N.Y., on Feb. 3, 1919.

Citation Extract

. . . .

15. First Lieutenant H. Briggs, W. H. Moreland, and H. C. Binley and Second Lieutenant W. R. Maynard, 96th Aero Squadron, 1st Day Bombardment Group, are hereby credited with the destruction in combat of an enemy Fokker in the region between Verdun and Damvillers, at 3600 metres altitude, on October 29th, 1918, at 1.20 o'clock.

. . . .

Brother in Service —

Russell Briggs, Cadet, A.S.A., U.S.A.

RUSSELL BRIGGS

Cadet, A.S., U.S.A.

Son of Charles P. and Gertrude (Russell) Briggs, of Lexington, Mass.; was born in Lexington on Aug. 14, 1894. He was educated at the Berkshire School, from which he graduated in 1914, and at Harvard College, graduating in 1918. He belonged to the Harvard R.O.T.C. He enlisted in Boston on Jan. 5, 1918, and was sent to Kelly Field, San Antonio, Tex. He was honorably discharged from the Service at Kelly Field, on Nov. 29, 1918.

(Portrait on opposite page.)

Brother in Service —
Henry Briggs, 1st Lieut., A.S.A., U.S.A., 96th Aero Squadron.

DOUGLAS R. BUCHANAN

First Lieutenant, A.S., U.S.A., Ninety-Sixth Aero Squadron, First Day Bombardment Group

Son of Mr. and Mrs. James B. Buchanan, of North Adams, Mass.; was born at Lowell, Mass., Aug. 12, 1896. He was educated at the Lowell High School, and at the Mass. Institute of Technology. He was a member of the Lowell High track team, and of the 'Varsity track team at M.I.T. At the end of his junior year, he enlisted at Boston, May 18, 1917, and entered the M.I.T. Ground School, where he completed the course, and was then sent to Mineola, N.Y., for further training. He was ordered overseas to France, and trained at Issoudun, and at Clermont-Ferrand. He was commissioned 1st Lieut. Nov. 2, 1917. He was first attached to the 90th Squadron and then to the 96th. Lieut. Buchanan was sent to Italy, and later returned to Issoudun, where he was just completing chasse training when the Armistice was signed. He returned to the U.S. and was honorably discharged at Garden City, N.Y., March 21, 1919.

RAYMOND S. COWARD

SECOND LIEUTENANT, A.S., U.S.A., FIRST AERO SQUADRON

SON of George F. and Mary Stewart (McLeod) Coward; was born in Cambridge, Mass., on June 8, 1895. He was educated at the Cambridge Latin School, and at M.I.T., class of 1918 (course uncompleted). There he was on the track and hockey teams in 1916–17. Previous to enlistment he trained one year with the M.I.T. Cadets.

He enlisted on April 28, 1917, at the Officers' Training Camp, at Plattsburg, which he attended for three months. From Aug. 14, 1917, to March 4, 1918, he trained with S.M.A., M.I.T. and with the Detachment of Flying Cadets, at Kelly Field, No. 2, San Antonio, Tex. He was commissioned 2d Lieut., A.S., Signal R.C. on March 4, 1918. From March 4 to July, 1918, he continued training at Camp Dick, Dallas, Tex. and at Fort Sill, Okla.

Lieut. Coward was ordered overseas in July, 1918, with the Aviation Section (unattached). Later he was transferred to the 1st Aero Squadron, with which he saw active service until the signing of the Armistice. He was for seven weeks in the Argonne sector, on observation duty; and took part in the fight at Argonne Forest. Later, he made flights over many of the contested battle-fields, including Verdun and the French trenches in the Champagne sector.

Lieut. Coward was with the Army of Occupation at Weissenthurm, Germany, with the 1st Aero Squadron, 3d Army.

Brother in Service —

Warren F. Coward, Private, U.S.A., Ordnance Department.

*WILLIAM KEY BOND EMERSON, Jr.

SECOND LIEUTENANT, A.S., U.S.A., ESCADRILLE C 21, AND TWELFTH AERO SQUADRON

Killed in action, May 14, 1918

SON of William Key Bond and Maria Holmes (Furman) Emerson; was born in New York City, April 9, 1894. He graduated from Middlesex School, Concord, Mass., in 1912, and entered Harvard College with the class of 1916. He left college in his sophomore year to join the American Ambulance Field Service, and served with the Unit in France for six months, in 1915; but returned to graduate with his class at Harvard in June, 1916.

In 1917 he again joined the American Ambulance Field Service, and went this time to Serbia, attached to the Army of the Orient. He received the Croix de Guerre with one Star, for "conspicuous gallantry in rescuing wounded under fire, near Monastir, in Aug., 1917."

Returning to France he was commissioned 2d Lieut. He attended the French Officers' Artillery School at Valdahon; and after graduating in Feb., 1918, he was attached for a short time to the 15th Field Artillery, U.S.A., then to the French Escadrille C 21. He was transferred from the French Service to the 12th Aero Squadron, U.S.A. On the afternoon of May 14, 1918, Lieut. Emerson was acting as artillery observer, with Lieut. Cyril M. Angell, of Attleboro, Mass., as pilot; and they were flying over the German lines north of Toul. They disappeared into low-lying clouds, and were next seen falling within the American lines, probably hit by an anti-aircraft shell, though there is no positive proof of this. Both aviators were killed. Lieut. Emerson was buried in the cemetery of the 104th Infantry, U.S.A., at Vignot, France, north of Toul.

He was the first Field Artillery Officer to be killed in action in the war while flying for the U.S. Army. In recognition of this fact the Aviation Field at Camp Jackson, S.C., has been named "Emerson Field," by the War Department.

*CYRIL M. ANGELL

SECOND LIEUTENANT, A.S., U.S.A., TWELFTH AERO SQUADRON

Killed in action, May 14, 1918

SON of Thomas H. and Charlotte Angell, of Attleboro, Mass.; was born in Fall River, Mass., April 9, 1895. He attended the Newport High School, and graduated from the Fall River High School, and from M.I.T.

He enlisted at Champaign, Ill., in Aug., 1917, and trained at the Univ. of Ill. School of Military Aeronautics. He was then attached to the Royal Flying Corps, Squadron 83, training at Camp Mohawk, Deseronto, Can.; and later the R.F.C. School of Aerial Gunnery, Hicks, Tex. He was commissioned 2d Lieut. in Aug., 1917.

Lieut. Angell received overseas orders, and was stationed in France, first with the 147th Aero Squadron, A.E.F.; then with the 12th Aero Squadron, A.E.F. He was killed in action at Vignot, France, on May 14, 1918.

Lieut. Angell was flying as pilot, accompanied by Lieut. W. K. B. Emerson, Jr., as artillery observer. They went up in the afternoon of May 14, 1918, flying over the German lines, and were lost to sight until those watching for them saw them fall inside of the American lines, presumably shot down by the enemy. Both pilot and observer were killed. Lieut. Angell was buried in the cemetery of the 104th Infantry, U.S.A., at Vignot, France, north of Toul.

BARTLETT BEAMAN

FIRST LIEUTENANT, A.S.A., U.S.A., TWELFTH AERO SQUADRON

SON of Harry Clayton and Jennie (Bartlett) Beaman; was born in Princeton, Mass., on July 20, 1890. He was educated at Phillips Andover Academy, and at Harvard College, from which he graduated in 1913. He was on his class baseball nine at college.

On May 10, 1917, he attended the Officers' Training Camp at Plattsburg, and was transferred from there in July to the Ground School at M.I.T., where he graduated in Oct., 1917. He was sent overseas on Nov. 2, 1917, and received further training at Tours, 2d Aviation Instruction Centre, and at Issoudun, 3d A.I.C. He was commissioned 1st Lieut. May 16, 1918. For a considerable time he acted as "ferry pilot," taking new machines to the front.

He joined the 12th Squadron toward the end of the Argonne offensive, and was in active service as observation and photographic pilot up to the time of the signing of the Armistice, when he was assigned to the Army of Occupation at Trèves and Coblenz. When the 12th Squadron was detailed home he was detached for duty with the 4th Corps, and attached to Headquarters Air Service at Zinzig.

He sailed from Marseilles on June 10, and was honorably discharged July 15, 1919.

MAHLON PHILIP BRYAN

SECOND LIEUTENANT, A.S., U.S.A., TWELFTH AND FIRST AERO SQUADRONS, FIRST OBSERVATION GROUP

SON of Mahlon R. and Bertha L. (Schrack) Bryan, of Brookline, Mass.; was born at Camden, N.J., Aug. 9, 1895. He attended the Hackley School, Tarrytown-on-Hudson, and entered Harvard College with the class of 1919. He served for nine months with the American Ambulance Field Service, Section VIII, in 1916–17.

On returning to America, he enlisted at M.I.T., Cambridge, Mass., on July 23, 1917. He reported for duty on Sept. 5 at Fort Wood, N.Y., and was attached to a company of 100 which was sent to Toronto, Can., to train with the Royal Flying Corps. After completing the ground-school work in Toronto in Nov. he was sent with the Canadians to Fort Worth, Tex. There he was attached to the 27th Aero Squadron, one of the first American squadrons to be organized. After he had finished the required tests and had completed the gunnery course, he was commissioned 2d Lieut. Feb. 5, 1918, and placed on active duty. Almost immediately he received his overseas orders, and sailed from New York for Liverpool. There he joined the 27th Squadron which had sailed a few weeks previously; he went with this Squadron to Issoudun, France, for higher training. After he had passed through Field No. 7 at Issoudun, he, with four other pilots, was transferred to the 12th Aero Squadron which was already in the zone of advance, ready for work over the front. He reported to the new Squadron at Amanty and remained with it until the end of the year. In June the Squadron was detached from the 1st Corps Observation Group and temporarily sent to work over the Lunéville sector. On July 1, 1918, the Squadron rejoined the Group near Château-Thierry and participated in the general advance. Subsequently Lieut. Bryan's Squadron removed to Toul, where it stayed through the St.-Mihiel offensive, and later served throughout the Argonne-Meuse drive. After the signing of the Armistice the Squadron became part of the Army of Occupation in Luxembourg and Germany.

Lieut. Bryan left Squadron 1 at Trèves, Germany, on Dec. 29, 1918, for transfer to the United States, arrived in America on March 3, 1919, and was honorably discharged at Mineola, N.Y.

HENRY WILLIAM DWIGHT

Second Lieutenant, A.S., U.S.A., Twelfth Aero Squadron
First Observation Group

Son of Henry W. and Caroline M. Dwight, of Cambridge, Mass.; was born at Brookline, Mass., Jan. 12, 1896. He was educated at Phillips Andover Academy, class of 1914, and at Williams College, class of 1918. He was on the track team at Andover and at Williams.

He enlisted at Boston, on April 10, 1917, U.S.N.R.F., and was transferred to Army Aviation on Aug. 23, 1917. He attended the Ground School, M.I.T., from Sept. 29 to Nov. 20, 1917; was attached to R.F.C., Can., for further training, which he received at Fort Worth Field, Nov. 27, 1917, to March 7, 1918. He was commissioned 2d Lieut., A.S., U.S.A., on March 7, 1918, and was assigned to the 184th Aero Squadron. He sailed overseas on June 29, 1918, landed in England July 7, and was sent to France July 10, with casual officers; attached to the 3d Aviation Instruction Centre, July 17 to Aug. 10, 1918; he attended the School of Aerial Gunnery at St.-Jean-des-Monts, from Aug. 10 to Aug. 25; was made Staff Pilot, 2d Aviation Instruction Centre, Aug. 25, 1918, serving until Oct. 9, 1918. He served with the 12th Aero Squadron, 1st Corps Observation Group, from Oct. 10 to Nov. 22, 1918, and took part in the Argonne-Meuse offensive from Oct. 10 to Nov. 11. He was attached to the 12th Aero Squadron, 4th Corps Observation Group, Army of Occupation, from Nov. 22, 1918, to Feb. 11, 1919, stationed at Trèves and Coblenz, Germany; served as Casual Officer at Bordeaux Embarkation Camp from Feb. 22 to April 13, 1919. He sailed for America; landed at Hoboken, May 3, 1919, and was honorably discharged from the U.S. Army at Mitchel Field, Garden City, N.Y., on May 5, 1919.

Brother in Service —

Winslow Dwight, Sergeant in Tank Corps, A.E.F.

*SIDNEY W. BEAUCLERK, Jr.

First Lieutenant, A.S., U.S.A., Twelfth Aero Squadron
First Observation Group

Killed in action, Oct. 29, 1918

Son of William Preston and Jennie M. (Hayward) Beauclerk; was born at Irasburg, Vt., Oct. 10, 1895. He prepared for college at the public schools of Concord, N.H., and entered Syracuse University in the class of 1919. In Aug., 1916, he attended the Officers' Training Camp at Plattsburg. He enlisted May 11, 1917, and went to Madison Barracks, Watertown, N.Y. On July 18, 1917, he entered the U.S. Aviation Ground School at Ithaca, N.Y., and on completion of his course there was sent overseas to Foggia, Italy, Sept. 25, 1917.

He received his pilot's license in Italy; was commissioned 1st Lieut. on March 22, 1918, and was sent to France for further training at Tours and Issoudun. He was assigned to the 12th Aero Squadron Sept. 8, 1918, and took part in the St.-Mihiel drive, being later transferred to the Argonne sector.

His excellent work performed in the St.-Mihiel attack proved him one of the best men in the Squadron and he received high praise from his commanding officers in the Argonne.

On Oct. 29 he was sent up with a formation of six planes whose mission was to photograph a sector over which the infantry must advance the next morning. The formation was attacked by overwhelming numbers, but in spite of this the mission succeeded, through the heroism of Lieut. Beauclerk, who sacrificed his own plane to save that containing the pictures necessary for the guidance of the infantry. By taking the bullets intended for the photographic plane, he doubtless saved many lives in the impending advance.

He fought to the last, and when he came down behind the German lines, mortally wounded, he landed his machine in such a way as to save his observer's life.

When on the following morning the infantry made its famous attack, which had a direct bearing on the end of the war, they found the grave of Lieut. Beauclerk, who had been buried with military honors by the enemy at Champigneulle, five miles east of Grand Pré. Upon a cross these words were inscribed, "Here lies an American flyer, Lieut. S. W. Beauclerk, Jr., killed Oct. 29, 1918."

STEPHEN HENLEY NOYES

MAJOR, J.M.A., A.S., U.S.A., CORPS OBSERVATION GROUP
FIRST ARMY

SON of Lieut. Boutelle Noyes, U.S.N., and Charlotte (Luce) Noyes; was born at Newport, R.I., Nov. 26, 1881. He was educated at St. Mark's School, Southboro, Mass., and at Harvard College, A.B. 1903, Scientific School, B.S. 1905. He played quarter-back on the 'Varsity team in 1905; prior to the war he was a member of Battery A, M.V.M.

Previous to enlistment he took a preparatory course in a private flying school at Essington, Pa., reporting for duty at Newport News on Feb. 5, 1917. From then until April 14 he trained at the Curtiss Flying School. While awaiting overseas orders he was attached to the 1st Aero Squadron, stationed at Columbus, N.M. He was commissioned 1st Lieut. May 10, 1917, and sailed overseas Aug. 12, 1917. He trained in France at Avord and at Cazaux; was attached to the 1st Aero Squadron, from Sept. 1, 1917, to June 30, 1918, acting as Flight Commander. He first flew over the lines on April 5, 1918.

From July 1 to Oct. 25 he commanded the 12th Aero Squadron. He was commissioned Capt. on Aug. 1, 1918. His Squadron served in every engagement in which our troops participated — Seicheprey, Château-Thierry, Fismes, St.-Mihiel, and the Argonne. He won the Croix de Guerre near Châtel Chéhéry, July 6, 1918, and the Distinguished Service Cross in the Argonne, Oct. 16, 1918.

From Oct. 26 to Dec. 1, 1918, he commanded the 5th Corps Observation Group; and from Dec. 1 to April 16, 1919, he commanded the Corps Observation Group, 1st Army. He was appointed Major, J.M.A., April 23, 1919. He was honorably discharged at Mitchel Field, N.Y., on May 27, 1919.

Citations

Croix de Guerre (*translation*)

Pilot of the first rank, cool and brave, model of duty for his Squadron. On July 6, 1918, attacked first by an enemy patrol, he dispersed them by his brave manœuvres, and permitted his observer to take the desired photographs. Attacked a second time, he destroyed one of his adversaries in a severe combat; ended his flight by a reconnaissance at the height of 500 metres over the German lines.

D.S.C.

For extraordinary heroism in action near Châtel Chéhéry, France, Oct. 16, 1918. Capt. Noyes volunteered under the most adverse weather conditions to stake the advance lines of the 82d Division. Disregarding the fact that darkness would set in before he and his observer could complete their mission, and at the extremely low altitude of 150 feet, Capt. Noyes proceeded, amid heavy aircraft and ground machine-gun fire, until the necessary information was secured. On the return, due to darkness, he was forced to land on a shell-torn field, and proceeded on foot to Headquarters with valuable information.

CARLE E. ROLLINS

Second Lieutenant, A.S.A., U.S.A., Thirty-Third Aero Squadron

Son of Frank E. and Mabel C. Rollins; was born in Dover, N.H., Oct. 30, 1890. He was educated at the Dover High School, and at Dartmouth College. At Dartmouth he played baseball and football. He belonged to the Business Men's Military Association of New York City. He enlisted in Chicago, Ill., June 30, 1917, and was assigned to the Ground School at the University of Illinois. He was ordered overseas, and received his preliminary flying training at the French school at Châteauroux, from which he was transferred for advanced training to the 3d A.I.C. at Issoudun, France. He was subsequently assigned to the 33d Aero Squadron, and detailed to Issoudun as Flying Instructor at the 3d A.I.C. He was commissioned 2d Lieut. on May 18, 1918.

Father in Service: Frank E. Rollins, Capt., N.H. National Guard, during the Spanish War; retired rank, Lieut.-Col., N.H.N.G.; at present Major, N.H. State Guard.

WILLBURT EDWARD KINSLEY

Second Lieutenant, A.S.A., U.S.A., Ninetieth Aero Squadron, Third Observation Group, D.S.C.

Son of Mr. and Mrs. Charles E. Kinsley, of Winchester, Mass.; was born Sept. 12, 1891, at Somerville, Mass.; educated at Winchester High School and the Rindge Manual Training School, Cambridge.

He enlisted at Ithaca, N.Y., on July 9, 1917, in the U.S. Air Service. He was trained at Cornell Ground School; Elementary Flying School at Selfridge Field, Mt. Clemens, Mich.; and at Gerstner Field, Lake Charles, La. (advanced flying). He was commissioned 2d Lieut. Chasse Pilot, at the Gerstner Field, on Feb. 8, 1918. He sailed overseas in Feb., 1918, and received advanced training at Issoudun, France, and Cazaux Gunnery School. He was appointed to the 90th Aero Squadron, 3d Observation Group, 1st Army, July 1, 1918, at Ourches. He made his first flight over the lines on July 3, 1918. The Squadron was stationed at Souilly and Béthainville during the Argonne-Meuse offensive, and at Ourches during the St.-Mihiel offensive. Up to the time of the St.-Mihiel offensive Lieut. Kinsley's work consisted of reconnaissances and observations. He performed infantry liaison work in the Toul sector and east of the Meuse River, taking part daily in the St.-Mihiel offensive. His record shows 78 hours' total flying over the German lines. He received official credit for two German planes shot down in the Argonne drive east of Cunel. He took part in 17 individual combats, at St.-Mihiel, Argonne, Meuse, and Verdun. He was recommended by his C.O. for promotion. He was honorably discharged at Garden City, N.Y., on Feb. 13, 1919.

Extracts from his citations and from letters written by Lieut. Kinsley's two Commanding Officers follow:

For extraordinary heroism in action east of Cunel, Verdun sector, France, 7th Oct., 1918. While staking the advanced lines of the 80th Division he was attacked by eight enemy machines (Fokker type) which dived from a near-by cloudbank. Although attacked simultaneously by the enemy planes he placed his airplane in such a position that his observer, 2d Lieut. William O. Lowe, S.M.S., was able to shoot down and crash one enemy plane and disable a second so badly that it was forced to land a few kilometres inside the German lines. Later, on the same mission, he was attacked again by a patrol of five enemy planes, scout machines, and in a running fight he drove these off and successfully completed his mission.

WILLBURT EDWARD KINSLEY

France, Dec. 18, 1918

The Air Service Commander, First Army, cites the following named officer for exceptional devotion to duty: 2d Lieut. Willburt Edward Kinsley, Air Service, U.S.A., Pilot, 90th Aero Squadron, by his spirit, initiative, and ability, was an inspiration to service among officers and men. He served with distinction for five months at the front.

Lieut. Kinsley has served under me for the past five months and has proved himself a capable officer and a pilot of great skill and courage. He has always been one of the first to volunteer for the most difficult and dangerous missions. He flew in the worst possible kind of weather in both the St.-Mihiel and Verdun-Argonne-Meuse offensives and has been officially credited with the destruction of two enemy planes in aerial combat. For extraordinary heroism he has been recommended for and is shortly to receive the Distinguished Service Cross. He has also been recommended for the Distinguished Service Medal. [Signed, Captain W. J. Schauffler, Jr., A.S., U.S.A., 3d Corps, Commanding Observation Group, Nov. 30, 1918.]

As one of the oldest and most experienced pilots of this command, Lieut. Kinsley has, by his coolness and skill as a pilot on active fronts, been a source of great inspiration to pilots and observers joining the Squadron, and has thus contributed, in an unusual degree, to the esprit which has made possible the Squadron's successful participation in the St.-Mihiel and Verdun offensives. He has, on many occasions, demonstrated his ability both in aerial combat and as an observation pilot, and after a particularly dangerous and brilliant mission he was recommended for and is shortly to receive the Distinguished Service Cross. Because of the unusual consistency of his work he has also been recommended for the Distinguished Service Medal. [Signed, Norris Pierson, 1st Lieut., A.S., U.S.A., Commanding 90th Squadron.]

PHILIP RODNEY BABCOCK

CAPTAIN, U.S.A., A.S., COMMANDING EIGHTY-EIGHTH AERO SQUADRON, FIRST, THIRD, AND FIFTH OBSERVATION GROUPS

SON of Frederic L. and Susan (Fowler) Babcock, of Lynn, Mass.; was born at Lyme, Conn., Aug. 12, 1893. He graduated from the English High School at Lynn, where he was captain of the track team, 1911–12, and from the Mass. Agricultural College at Amherst, in 1916.

He entered the U.S. Service, May 12, 1917, at the Officers' Training Camp, Plattsburg, having previously attended the Plattsburg Camp in 1916. On June 17, 1917, he was sent to the Aviation Ground School, M.I.T., continuing his training at Mineola, N.Y., July 30 to Nov. 2. He was commissioned 1st Lieut. Nov. 2, 1917; sailed overseas and trained at Issoudun, France, Dec. 2 to Feb. 20, 1918; he was assigned to the 88th Aero Squadron, 1st Observation Group, Feb. 22, 1918, and stationed at Amanty, France. He moved to the front May 28, station Ourches (Toul sector); moved to Château-Thierry sector July 6, stations Franchéville, Ferme de Graves, Goureaucourt; moved to St.-Mihiel sector Sept. 10, station Souilly; moved to Meuse-Argonne sector, Sept. 15, stations Pretz-en-Argonne, Souilly, Béthainville, until Nov. 11, 1918. Army of Occupation Dec. 5, 1918, stations Villers-les-Chèvre and Trèves, Germany, where he was on duty with the 7th Army Corps.

Capt. Babcock took part in the following battles: Champagne, Marne defensive, Aisne-Marne offensive, Oise-Aisne, St.-Mihiel, and Meuse-Argonne, besides participating in other affairs at the Toul sector, Château-Thierry sector, Fismes sector, and Verdun sector.

He was Flight Commander Aug. 5, 1918; commissioned Capt., U.S.A., A.S., Oct. 15, 1918; and 88th Squadron Commander March 7, 1919.

Citations

D.S.C.

For extraordinary heroism in action near Fismes, France, 11 Aug., 1918. Under the protection of three pursuit planes, each carrying a pilot and observer, Lieuts. Bernheimer and Jordan, in charge of a photo plane, carried out successfully a hazardous photographic mission over the enemy's lines to the river Aisne. The four American ships were attacked by twelve enemy battle-planes. Lieut. Bernheimer, by coolly and skilfully manœu-

vring his ship, and Lieut. Jordan, by accurate operation of his machine gun, in spite of wounds in the shoulder and leg, aided materially in the victory which came to the American ships, and returned safely with 36 valuable photographs.

The pursuit plane operated by Lieuts. Hitchcock and Burns was disabled while these two officers were fighting effectively. Lieut. Burns was mortally wounded and his body jammed the controls. After a headlong fall of 2500 metres, Lieut. Hitchcock succeeded in regaining control of his plane and piloted it back to his airdrome.

Lieuts. McClendon and Plummer were shot down and killed after a vigorous combat with five of the enemy's planes.

Lieuts. Babcock and Palmer, by gallant and skilful fighting, aided in driving off the German planes and were materially responsible for the successful execution of the photographic mission.

Croix de Guerre

Lieutenant Pilot P. R. Babcock, of the American 88th Squadron

The 19th of July, 1918, having had his plane seriously hit in an infantry contact patrol, did not return until his mission was completed, with a machine riddled with bullets. The 24th of July, 1918, engaged in combat with several enemy planes which he outdistanced, received more than thirty bullets in his machine, and returned to the landing-field of his Squadron more than forty kilometres away.

Recommendation for appointment as Squadron Commander

Capt. Philip R. Babcock, A.S. (Pilot)

Flight Commander, with more than 100 hours' flying time over the lines. Has served with great credit to organization since his assignment to same, Feb. 22, 1918. Has been awarded the D.S.C. and the French Croix de Guerre for conspicuous bravery in action.

Capt. Babcock has acted as second in command of his organization for the past three months, and during the absence of the Commanding Officer has served as such very creditably.

*CHARLES W. PLUMMER

SECOND LIEUTENANT, A.S.A., U.S.A., OBSERVER, ONE HUNDRED FIRST FIELD ARTILLERY

ATTACHED TO EIGHTY-EIGHTH AERO SQUADRON

Killed in action, Aug. 11, 1918

SON of Henry M. and Alice (Hussey) Plummer; was born at New Bedford, Mass., May 25, 1890. He prepared for college at the Morristown School, N.J., and graduated from Harvard College in 1914. Prior to the declaration of war he was a member of Battery A, 1st Mass. Regiment, F.A., N.G., and went with that organization to the Mexican Border in 1916.

When war was declared he volunteered, and was commissioned 2d Lieut. in the spring of 1917. He went with Battery A to Camp Curtis Guild, Boxford, Mass., and after a month's training, sailed overseas, Sept. 10, 1917, with the 101st Regiment, F.A. Soon after reaching France he joined the Division of Aeronautics, trained as an observer at the various French camps, and was attached to the 88th Aero Squadron.

The following extract is from the report sent by Lieut. Plummer after an engagement for participation in which he received the Croix de Guerre:

July 24, 1918 *Near Beuvardes*

Observation at 800 *M*. 7–18–15 P.M.

Two monoplace planes appeared from the north, circled to the east and above us. I kept an eye on them, and could distinctly see the French colors on their tails.

A few moments later two German planes appeared, while we were over the Beuvardes Wood. I fired 25 rounds at these.

At this time we were under heavy anti-aircraft gun-fire, the pieces cutting the wings and fuselage, besides cutting several guy wires. My goggles were shot away.

On inspection I found that many machine-gun bullets had pierced the wings and fuselage; the majority of these came from behind and from above. There were only the first two planes of which I have spoken which could have done this.

On Aug. 11, 1918, while flying a protection plane near Fismes, Lieut. Plummer was attacked by five enemy planes. In vigorous fighting he succeeded in downing two planes before his own pilot, Lieut. McClendon, was killed. Before Lieut. Plummer was able to regain control of the machine, however, it crashed to earth killing him instantly.

Lieut. Louis G. Bernheimer wrote to Lieut. Plummer's family:

> It was a difficult mission inside the German lines. His duty was to protect my plane. We had taken our photographs and were crossing the lines for home when we were attacked. He fought off five planes. We think he brought two of them down before he was killed. You will be proud of him — he died gloriously.

Capt. P. R. Babcock, Commander of the 88th Squadron, wrote:

> I was piloting one of the planes in our formation and was the only one who saw Lieut. Plummer's plane go down. I assure you he was fighting gallantly to the very last, firing burst after burst of machine-gun bullets into five enemy planes that so closely pursued him.

Lieut. Plummer and his pilot were buried at Chiery, France, on a knoll overlooking the valley. Chaplain John H. Lewis officiated at an impressive service, attended by the French and American officers. As is customary for aviators, his grave was marked with a propeller blade instead of a cross.

Citations

D.S.C.

Second Lieutenant CHARLES W. PLUMMER (deceased), Observer, 101st F.A.: Distinguished himself by extraordinary heroism in connection with military operations against an armed enemy of the United States at Fismes, France, on 11 August, 1918, and in recognition of his gallant conduct I have awarded him, in the name of the President, the Distinguished Service Cross. Awarded on 16 October, 1918.

(*Signed*) JOHN J. PERSHING
Commander-in-Chief

Croix de Guerre

The Marshal of France, Commander-in-Chief of the French Armies of the East, cites in the order of the Army Corps Lieut. CHARLES W. PLUMMER, Observer in American Escadrille 88: July 24, 1918, while protecting a group of aviators over the enemy lines, he engaged in a combat with several German planes. During the combat he received more than 30 bullets in his plane, but continued to fire and succeeded in beating off his adversaries.

(*Signed*) PÉTAIN

JOHN HOLME LAMBERT

CAPTAIN, A.S., U.S.A., FLIGHT COMMANDER, NINETY-FIRST AERO SQUADRON, PILOT, OBSERVATION GROUP

SON of Harry Lambert (deceased) and Marion Booth (Lambert) Kelley, of New York; was born March 19, 1897, at Salem, N.J. He was educated at Germantown Academy, Philadelphia; Phillips Exeter Academy, class of 1915; and Harvard College, class of 1920, leaving in the middle of his freshman year to drive an ambulance in France. He served with the American Ambulance Field Service from Feb. 19 to Aug. 21, 1917, at Verdun and in the Champagne.

In Sept., 1917, he enlisted in the Aviation Section of the U.S. Army, at Paris, and trained at Tours, Issoudun, and Gondrecourt, France. He was commissioned 1st Lieut. on Dec. 1, 1917, and was attached to the 91st Aero Squadron, as a pilot in the Observation Group. Lieut. Lambert was awarded the Distinguished Service Cross (Dec., 1918) for "extraordinary heroism" in action near Stenay, France, Oct. 30, 1918.

He was commissioned Captain, March 19, 1919, and appointed Flight Commander. He was sent with the Army of Occupation to Coblenz, Germany. On March 18, 1919, he was awarded the Croix de Guerre, with Palm, for ambulance service; also a medal and citation from the French Government. An additional citation from Gen. Pershing entitled him to an Oak Leaf with the D.S.C.

D.S.C.

While on a photographic mission in the vicinity of Stenay, his work being seriously interfered with by the fire of a formation of enemy airplanes, Lieutenant Lambert temporarily discontinued his mission, attacked the formation and dispersed it, destroying one airplane and seriously damaging another. He then returned to his objective, completed his mission, and returned with information of great value.

Additional Citation

First Lieutenant JOHN H. LAMBERT, Pilot, 91st Aero Squadron, for distinguished and exceptional gallantry over Metz, Alsace, on 15 August, 1918, in the operations of the American Expeditionary Forces. In testimony thereof, and as an expression of appreciation of his valor, I award him this citation. Awarded on 27 March, 1919.

JOHN J. PERSHING
Commander-in-Chief

HORACE MOSS GUILBERT

First Lieutenant, A.S.A., U.S.A., Ninety-First Aero Squadron, First Observation Group

Son of Mr. and Mrs. Edmund Guilbert, of Boston, Mass.; was born at New Berlin, N.Y., Nov. 1, 1892. He was educated at the Gunnery School, Washington, Conn.; St. Paul's School, Concord, N.H.; and Yale College.

He enlisted in June, 1917, trained at M.I.T. Ground School, and at Hempstead Field, Mineola, N.Y. He sailed overseas and was trained at Issoudun, Amanty, Gondrecourt, and Commercy. He was commissioned 1st Lieut. in Oct., 1917. He acted as pilot in the 91st Aero Squadron, Observation Service. He took part in the St.-Mihiel drive; was later injured, and was for six weeks with the Aeronautic Division of the 4th French Army as Liaison Officer.

In Jan., 1919, he received the Croix de Guerre, with Palm, for bringing back valuable information in July, 1918, when he and one other observation plane were attacked by six enemy planes.

Lieut. Guilbert has written the following account of the work of his Squadron:

Under the command of Major, now Lieutenant-Colonel, John W. Reynolds, it was the first American Army Observation Squadron to begin work over the lines, operating over the Toul sector under the 8th French Army from the middle of June until the formation of the 1st American Army. When that was organized, shortly before the St.-Mihiel drive, the Squadron became part of the 1st Army Observation Group, of which Major Reynolds took command, Capt. Everett R. Cook, one of the original pilots of the Squadron, succeeding to the command of the 91st Squadron.

The Squadron did effective work in the St.-Mihiel operations, but it was in the attack on the Argonne-Meuse front that it was put to the test. The Germans massed their air service units in an effort to nullify the work of ours, and hardly a mission was performed without at least one combat, two or three of our planes sometimes fighting off 14 or more of the enemy. Though only an observation squadron, and in no sense an attacking or pursuit squadron, the 91st is credited officially with the destruction of 22 enemy planes, in over 140 combats. In its work over the Toul sector the Squadron lost 5 planes, on the Argonne-Meuse front, 4, with the loss of 11 pilots and observers killed in action, 12 wounded, and 9 made prisoners. Nineteen of the officers in, or formerly in, the 91st have received the Distinguished Service Cross, five the Croix de Guerre with a Palm, and five have been promoted to the command of squadrons.

WILLIAM WALLACE FOSTER

First Lieutenant, A.S.A., U.S.A., Eighty-Eighth Aero Squadron, First Observation Group

Born in Boston, Dec. 29, 1894.

He enlisted in Paris in June, 1917, with the Norton-Harjes Ambulance Unit, Section 63, R.C.A. In July and Aug., 1917, he served with the Section Sanitaire, Automobile 63, behind Verdun during the great drive. He was transferred from the French to the American forces in Sept., enlisting for aviation training. He was trained at Tours and Issoudun, and was commissioned 1st Lieut. Nov. 23, 1917, with active orders on Jan. 10, 1918; being assigned to 88th Squadron and 1st Aero Squadron, 1st Observation Group. He was flying over the front lines from May to Aug., 1918, including the engagement at Château-Thierry. On Oct. 28, 1918, he was assigned Commanding Officer of Flight C, 351st Aero Squadron, at 1st Artillery Observation School, near Rennes, France. He was honorably discharged on Feb. 14, 1919, at Hoboken, N.J.

W. LAWSON LOCKHART

First Lieutenant, A.S.A., U.S.A., Twelfth Aero Squadron
First Observation Group

Son of Joseph S. and Eva A. Lockhart; was born in Cambridge, Mass., on Oct. 12, 1896. He was educated at the Lycée de Vesoul, Haute Seine, France; at Acadia University, N.S.; and at the Mass. Institute of Technology.

He enlisted in June, 1917, at the Harvard R.O.T.C., and in Aug. was transferred to the Air Service. After an eight weeks' course at the Ground School, M.I.T., he was sent to Camp Mohawk, Ontario, Can., to join Squadron 84. He was subsequently ordered to Fort Worth, Tex., to finish his flying course, and then assigned to the School of Gunnery at Camp Hicks. He received his commission as 2d Lieut. Jan. 16, 1918, and on Jan. 29 was assigned to the 139th Squadron as Flying Officer. He sailed overseas about Feb. 22, 1918.

At the end of March he was in service at the front with the 12th Squadron to which he was attached. After recovering from an operation for appendicitis at Base Hospital No. 1, he was assigned to the 166th and the 168th Squadrons, early in July, 1918, as Flight Commander. He received the citation for the Croix de Guerre for excellent work, and was commissioned 1st Lieut., A.S.A., on Oct. 10, 1918; he was second on a list of men recommended for Captaincy. Lieut. Lockhart is a member of the Aero Club of America. He was honorably discharged from the service at Garden City, N.Y., in Feb., 1919.

GEORGE C. KENNEY

CAPTAIN, A.S., U.S.A., NINETY-FIRST AERO SQUADRON
FIRST OBSERVATION GROUP

BORN at Yarmouth, N.S., Aug. 6, 1889. He was educated at the Brookline High School, and at the Mass. Institute of Technology, class of 1911.

He enlisted on June 2, 1917, at M.I.T.; trained there at the Ground School during June and July, and at Mineola, N.Y., from Aug. to Nov., 1917. He was commissioned 1st Lieut. Nov. 5, 1917. He sailed overseas on Nov. 14, 1917, and continued his training at Issoudun, France, from Dec. 15, 1917, to Feb., 1918. He was assigned to the 91st Aero Squadron on Feb. 22, and worked over the lines under orders from the French 8th Army from May 24, 1918, to Aug. 10, 1918. From that time until Nov. 11 he served with the American 1st Army, taking part in the St.-Mihiel and Meuse-Argonne operations. From Nov. 11, 1918, to April 16, 1919, his Squadron served with the American Army of Occupation. On March 18, 1919, he was commissioned Captain, and is still in the service.

D.S.C.

First Lieutenant GEORGE C. KENNEY, A.S., Pilot, 91st Aero Squadron, distinguished himself by extraordinary heroism, in connection with military operations against an armed enemy of the United States at Jametz, France, on 9 Oct., 1918, and in recognition of his gallant conduct, I have awarded him, in the name of the President, the Distinguished Service Cross. Awarded on 25 November, 1918.

JOHN J. PERSHING, *Commander-in-Chief*

First Lieutenant GEORGE C. KENNEY, Pilot, 91st Aero Squadron, for distinguished and exceptional gallantry at St.-Mihiel on 15 Sept., 1918, in the operations of the American Expeditionary Forces. In testimony thereof, and as an expression of appreciation of his valor, I award this citation. Awarded on 27 March, 1919.

JOHN J. PERSHING, *Commander-in-Chief*

Brother in Service —

Arthur I. Kenney, 2d Officer, U.S. Army Transport Kentuckian.

Sister in Service —

Gertrude L., nurse, Army Nurses Corps, stationed at Base Hospital No. 78, Toul, France.

*EDWARD LAURISTON BULLARD

Second Lieutenant, A.S., U.S.A., Ninetieth Aero Squadron

Killed in accident, April 8, 1919

Son of Frederic Lauriston and Clara Elizabeth (Keil) Bullard, of Revere, Mass.; was born at Dayton, O., on Sept. 17, 1895. He spent three years at Phillips Exeter Academy, graduating in 1916. He entered the U.S. Service May 12, 1917. After one year at Cornell University, he was several months in a provisional regiment at Madison Barracks. He volunteered for the Air Service on Aug. 1, 1918, and was trained at M.I.T. and at Princeton University School of Military Aviation. He learned to fly in Texas and Oklahoma and was commissioned 2d Lieut. May 15, 1918. Sailing from Hoboken on Sept. 26, he trained at Issoudun and Romorantin and reached the Argonne front just ten days before the Armistice. He was detached from the 90th Squadron on Jan. 21, 1919, and spent three months at the First Air Dépôt at Colombey-les-Belles, mostly in the ferry service. After having flown many hours both in America and in France and having navigated airships of many types, Lieut. Bullard, five months after the Armistice, came to his death "in the line of duty" in a motor-car accident near Toul. On April 7 he sustained fatal injuries when a wheel collapsed and his automobile was overturned. He died the next morning. A Board of Inquiry pronounced the machine defective. He was buried on April 9 in the little military cemetery near Colombey-les-Belles. He had been recommended for a 1st Lieutenancy.

He possessed marked literary ability. Describing his first Renault flight, he wrote:

> I plugged along by my lonesome and tried to pretend I was enjoying myself in a strange ship, over a strange country, going to a strange field, in a thick haze which was fast deepening into twilight, and against a stiff gale which was colder than anything I had ever felt before.

It has been learned that certain Red Cross workers, in personal letters to their own families, said of him that in addition to his remarkable physical qualifications, he was gifted with a brilliant mind, and had an unusually keen sense of humor and justice.

Brother in Service —
Frederic Keil Bullard, 1st Lieut., U.S.A., F.A.

GERARD HASTINGS HUGHES

First Lieutenant, A.S.A., U.S.A., Two Hundred Fifty-Eighth Aero Squadron, First Army

Son of William G. and Lucy C. Hughes, of Ossipee, N.H.; was born at Boerne, Tex., on Jan. 15, 1895. He was educated at Milton Academy, graduating 1912, and at Harvard College, graduating 1916. He attended the Officers' Training Camp at Plattsburg in 1916, and the Harvard R.O.T.C. On April 6, 1917, he enlisted at Boston as Sgt. S.E.R.C., and was ordered to Mineola, N.Y., for training in flying, April 12, 1917. He passed final tests, R.M.A., July 11, and was ordered to Chanute Field, Rantoul, Ill.; assigned to duty as Officer in Charge of Flying. He was commissioned 1st Lieut., A.S., S.C., on July 26, 1917.

On Dec. 15, 1917, he was ordered to Rich Field, Waco, Tex., where he remained as Asst. O.I.C.F. and Flying Instructor from Dec. 20 to Aug. 25, 1918. He was ordered overseas for training as pilot and sailed for England Sept. 8, 1918. He trained at Issoudun from Oct. 1 to 31, and at St.-Jean-des-Monts, American Gunnery School, from Nov. 1 to 8. He arrived at Toul Nov. 11, 1918, and was assigned to the 4th Pursuit Group. Two days later he was attached to the 258th Squadron. He returned to New York Jan. 31, 1919, and was honorably discharged at Garden City, N.Y., on Feb. 5, 1919.

While stationed in Texas, Lieut. Hughes was one of five members of the escort chosen to fly over the train in which Miss Margaret Wilson was travelling; receiving later from her a letter of appreciation of the escort's remarkable flying. Of this group, containing men of unusual skill and experience, three have since been killed in accidents.

Brother in Service —

George F. Hughes, Capt., A.S.A., U.S.A.

GEORGE F. HUGHES

CAPTAIN, A.S.A., U.S.A., TWELFTH SQUADRON, FIRST OBSERVATION GROUP; COMMANDING OFFICER, TWO HUNDRED FIFTY-EIGHTH AERO SQUADRON

SON of William G. and Lucy C. Hughes, of Ossipee, N.H.; was born at Milton, Mass., Sept. 8, 1892. He attended Milton Academy, and entered Harvard College, class of 1918.

He left Harvard to enlist with the Air Service in Boston on April 3, 1917. He was stationed at Mineola, N.Y., as Sgt., E.R.C., from April 12 to July 6, 1917. He was commissioned 1st Lieut. on July 20, 1917, and ordered to Wilbur Wright Field, Dayton, O., as Flying Instructor.

On Nov. 1 he was ordered overseas in command of the 12th Aero Squadron, and from Nov. 1 to 30 remained at Garden City, N.Y., awaiting embarkation orders.

He sailed on Dec. 4, 1917, and was stationed at St.-Maixent, France, until Jan. 14, 1918; on Jan. 16 he was transferred to the Staff Field, Chaumont, Headquarters A.E.F., where he remained with the 12th Aero Squadron until Jan. 31, when he was relieved of the command of the Squadron by Major Harry M. Brown, and the Squadron ordered to Amanty to assist the 1st Aero Squadron.

On May 1, 1918, the Squadron was ordered to active duty on the front to coöperate with the 1st Aero Squadron in the Seicheprey sector. From July 1 to July 25 Lieut. Hughes was stationed in the Château-Thierry sector.

On July 25 he was relieved from duty with the 12th Aero Squadron, and ordered to duty with the 2d Army Corps, B.E.F., in command of the 183d Flight Detachment. On Aug. 1, 1918, he was commissioned Capt.

On Sept. 10 the 183d Detachment was incorporated in the 258th Aero Squadron, attached to the French 7th Army; and from Sept. 10 to Nov. 14 Capt. Hughes was Commanding Officer of the 258th Squadron. From Nov. 15 to Dec. 15 he was ill in Base Hospital 82 at Toul. On his return to the U.S., he was honorably discharged at Garden City, N.Y., on Feb. 5, 1919.

Brother in Service —

Gerard Hastings Hughes, 1st Lieut., A.S.A., U.S.A.

Citation

November 11, 1918

For gallantry in action, the General Commanding cites the following officers:

Captain W. H. SAUNDERS, Observer, 12th Aero Squadron
First Lieut. G. F. HUGHES

These officers flew in an A.R. Airplane for more than two hours in the vicinity of Le Bois de Gargantua, performing adjustments of artillery fire despite an exceptionally heavy concentration of Hun anti-aircraft artillery fire. After completing *réglages* for two batteries and while conducting fire for amelioration for a third, they were brought down by shell fragments stopping their motor. In attempting to land inside the American lines, the plane was smashed.

. . . .

By command of Brigadier-General WILLIAM MITCHELL

SUMNER CARLISLE

LIEUTENANT, A.S., U.S.A., NINETY-FIRST AERO SQUADRON
FIRST OBSERVATION GROUP

SON of Abbott L. and Nancy Fifield (Dudley) Carlisle; was born at Exeter, N.H., June 14, 1892. He was educated at Exeter High School; at Phillips Exeter Academy; and at the N.H. State College. He was a member of his class football team. He had three years' military training while at college, and joined the first Plattsburg Camp in 1916, enlisting there on May 13, 1916.

He trained at M.I.T. Ground School; then at Fort Worth, Tex. He sailed overseas on Oct. 17, 1917, and was stationed at the Aviation Camp, Issoudun, France. He was sent to Campo Aveste, Italy, about the middle of Feb., 1918; returned to France in July. In Aug. he was sent to the front, where he was wounded by a shell which sent him to hospital. About Sept. 11 he was discharged from hospital, and was accepted as a pilot on Sept. 26. From then till the close of the war he saw much active service, being attached to the 91st Aero Squadron, which was in many engagements and won much glory. An Italian Salutation was granted him before leaving Italy. He was shot down twice. During the last week of the war he was flying with two other machines when they were trapped by 14 Boches. Lieut. Carlisle was the only member of the American party to return, and his own observer was killed.

Since the close of the war Lieut. Carlisle has been with the American Army of Occupation at Coblenz.

*GILBERT NELSON JEROME

First Lieutenant, A.S., U.S.A., Escadrille Spad 90
Eighth French Army

Killed in action, July 11, 1918

Was born Nov. 15, 1889, at New Haven, Conn. He attended the public schools of New Haven; graduated from Yale Sheffield Scientific School, in 1910, and from Springfield Y.M.C.A. College in 1914, winning honors both in school and college, and the freshman first prize in French at Yale.

He was deeply interested in the Boy Scout Movement, and was Scout Executive, for New Haven, from Aug., 1915, to June, 1917, when he resigned to enter the U.S. Aviation Service. His work among the boys was remarkably successful, and his name is loved and honored by them. After his death a "Gilbert N. Jerome Lecture Course for Scout Leaders" was established in his memory.

He enlisted in June, 1917, and attended the Ground School of the M.I.T., completing his course with honors. He was sent overseas in Sept., 1917, and trained at the flying schools near Bourges and Brest. On Feb. 14, 1918, he was commissioned 1st Lieut., and assigned the duty of "ferrying" planes from various points around France.

Early in June, 1918, Lieut. Jerome wrote:

> Having finished my training, I am now in the process of being assimilated with the ten others into French chasse escadrilles, fighting squadrons. Although none of my special pals came into this detachment there is a very congenial crowd; Quentin Roosevelt is one. . . . We expect soon to be sent to the front, and will handle the most desirable type of machine. It handles wonderfully in the air, but the speed is simply terrific, and it is called a "Spad."

Again he wrote:

> I am now at the front going over the lines every day. This afternoon I went to protect a photographing machine. We met no hostile planes, but were liberally "strafed" by anti-aircraft. It is very odd to watch the black balls of smoke suddenly appear in space out of nothing, and realize that they are meant for you.

Later in June Lieut. Jerome was assigned, with Lieut. Ross J. Hoffman, of Philadelphia, to a French escadrille, stationed near Nancy. Here he met his death from a German anti-aircraft gun, on July 11, while patrolling the French lines. He fell near Verdenal,

within the enemy lines, and he was buried by the French people of Blamont, Meuthe-et-Moselle, in a German military cemetery, with military honors by the enemy.

Lieut. Jerome was among the 16 chosen from 800 contestants for the 1000-franc prize offered by the "N.Y. Herald" in Paris. His poem which follows was ranked 7 on the list.

THE AIRPLANE

What strange device is this;
  This thing of metal, wood, and cloth,
So cunningly contrived, and gay with colors bright,
  Standing alone out on the grassy plain?
Inert and lifeless on its wheels and skid,
  Flaunting its glitter to the sun and sky,
It seems some giant's toy rather than
The latest product of the mind of man.

. . . .

And now one comes and grasps the twisted wood,
  And with a sudden swing exerts his strength,
His puny human force, there in the face
  Of that brute thing, that mass of steel and brass,
When, lo, a miracle is wrought! Pulsating life
  Is born, and from the heart of it
Bursts forth a mighty roar, a storm of sound,
So that the framework shakes and trembles on the ground.

Then, bounding from their hands like some wild thing
  Seeking escape from bonds intolerable,
It courses o'er the ground and leaps into the air,
  Spurning the lowly earth. Up, up, into the blue
It beats its forward way, until the mighty roar
  Fades with the height into a distant drone,
A ceaseless hum, as if some monstrous bee,
Warmed by the summer sun, was flying free.

Thus, godlike, alone, the human being,
  Loose from the fetters that for ages long
Have bound his kind to earth, rushes through space
  And with a touch controls the soaring planes;
Bends to his will the pent-up power that beats
  With frenzied force against the steely walls,
Hurling each piston back until the screw
Cuts the clear air in wisps of vibrant blue.

GILBERT NELSON JEROME

Such is the miracle of flight; the latest proof
  That smouldering deep within the soul of man,
Half-buried ofttimes by the clods which mark
  Him still a beast, there lurks the sacred flame,
The will to shape this star dust at his feet
  To serve his end, lifting himself thereby until,
Freed from his heritage of passion, fear, and strife,
He mounts to better things, to richer, fuller life.

POEM BY LIEUTENANT JEROME

Written after the death of a comrade

It cannot be, I say it cannot be;
  'T is but a moment since he stood
Here in our little group
  And smiled and spoke.
A moment's flight, and then
  He passes through the gate
That bars our view,
  Leaving us desolate.

It cannot be, I say it cannot be,
  That he who moved among us,
Winning us all by deeds and words
  Of quiet friendliness,
Has lived his few short years
  Only to slip away
Into the vanished past,
  A sad sweet memory.

It cannot be, I say it cannot be;
  Such friends can never die.
He lives beyond the gate;
  And when our turn shall come
To step across the threshold
  Into a world more fair,
He will be first of those
  Who meet and greet us there.

WILLIS STETSON FITCH

First Lieutenant, A.S., U.S.A., Tenth Aero Squadron
Caproni, Fourteenth Group

Son of Arthur E. and Gertrude (Stetson) Fitch; was born at Medford, Mass., June 10, 1896. He was educated at Medford High School, and Dartmouth College, B.S. 1917. He was coach of the Dartmouth 1920 hockey team.

He attended Plattsburg Training Camp in 1916, and was instructor of the Dartmouth Training Regiment in 1916–17. From May 12 to June 19, 1917, he attended the first R.O.T.C. at Plattsburg; from June 19 to July 28 the M.I.T. School of M.A. at Cambridge. He sailed for Italy with the 8th A.I.C., A.E.F., in Sept., 1917, and remained in that Service at Foggia, Italy, until June 15, 1918. He was commissioned 1st Lieut. on Feb. 21, 1918. From June 19, 1918, to Nov. 14, 1918, he was attached to the 10th Squadron Caproni, 14th Group, Italian War Zone. He participated in day and night bombing at the front, notably in the raid on the Austrian port of Pola. In Sept., 1918, he was decorated by the Italian Government for his exploits.

He was later in a bombing raid that was intercepted before it reached its objective. However, Lieut. Fitch succeeded in dropping his bombs on two of the enemy aviation camps, and then started back for the Italian lines. While still about 13 miles within enemy territory, five Austrian scout planes overtook him from the rear. Lieut. Fitch, who was acting as pilot, dived in order to obtain the maximum speed, and then pursued a zigzag course in the race for the Italian lines. Meanwhile his machine-gunner continued to fire at the pursuers, bringing down one of the Austrians. The other four Austrian airmen attacked in turn; but the fire from the American frustrated them. Finally Lieut. Fitch's escort, from whom he had been separated, saw his predicament and returned, driving away the enemy.

Lieut. Fitch was honorably discharged at Garden City, N.Y., on Dec. 28, 1918.

With the Decoration from the Italian Government came a report, of which the following is a translation:

Lieutenant Willis Fitch, U.S.A., was part of this escadrille from June 20 to Nov. 14, 1918. He is an officer of a serious and well-disciplined char-

acter, and fulfilled his special duty with zeal and intelligence. He is of a loyal, open nature. Even when off duty he always conducted himself correctly. He won the esteem of his superiors and the affection of his colleagues and inferiors. A skilful pilot, full of enthusiasm, he took part, with his whole soul, in the actions; he carried out eleven (11) bombardments, fulfilling conscientiously the various difficult tasks confided to him, distinguishing himself by his calmness and surety, even in the most trying moments. On account of the admirable way in which he conducted himself while flying over the enemy lines, he was decorated with the Cross for Martial Merit and proposed for the bronze medal for Military Valor.

(*Signed*) *The Captain Commanding Escadrille*
BUTTINI

(*Countersigned*) *Major Commanding the Group*
RUSSI

The work of this young and valorous pilot was always such as to evidence his faith in the cause for which his great country took up arms.

(*Signed*) *Chief of the Air Service*
LA POLLA

CLARK ROBINSON

SECOND LIEUTENANT, A.S.A,, U.S.A., EIGHTH AERO SQUADRON

SON of Frank A. and Grace (Clark) Robinson; was born in Bangor, Me., Aug. 11, 1894. He attended the public schools of Bangor, Me., and graduated from the Mass. Institute of Technology in 1916, where he took a prize of $200 for the best two years' work in Architecture.

He joined the Plattsburg Camp in Jan., 1917. He was trained at Ellington Field, Houston, Tex., and at the Post Field, Fort Sill, Okla. Subsequently he was transferred to Camp Dick, Dallas, Tex. He was assigned to the 8th Aero Squadron, Army Aviation, and sailed overseas in Aug., 1918.

During an engagement over the German lines he was shot down, and his observer was injured. They were both taken prisoner, but managed after five days to escape with some French soldiers. Lieut. Robinson was able to take out valuable information from Germany, for which he was especially commended by the General and Chief of the Air Service. While he was in Germany he was reported "missing in action," and his effects were later returned to him marked "Lieut. Clark Robinson, deceased."

At last accounts Lieut. Robinson was stationed at Bordeaux, where he was architect of the new "Victory" theatre just erected there, and had also done the designing of curtains, stage settings, etc.

Brothers in Service —

Albert E. Robinson, Sgt., U.S.A., 140th Infantry, 35th Div.

Paul Robinson, 2d Lieut., A.S., U.S.A., Carlstrom Field, Arcadia, Fla.

Sister in Service —

Katharine G. Robinson, Reconstruction Aid, Base Hospital, Camp Upton, N.Y.

Father in Service —

Frank A. Robinson (deceased), Major, National Guard, State of Maine.

RAYMOND PEACOCK BALDWIN

FIRST LIEUTENANT, FIRST ITALIAN CAPRONI SQUADRON
FOURTH AIRPLANE GROUP, ITALIAN WAR ZONE

WAS born at Brookline, Mass., Nov. 3, 1895. He prepared for college at the Volkmann School, where he was prominent in athletics, and in his senior year captain of the track team. He graduated from Harvard College in 1916, and was attending the Law School when he entered the U.S. Aviation Service, April 29, 1917.

During the summer of 1916 he drove an ambulance in France with the Morgan-Harjes Unit.

He received his early aviation training at the Ground School, M.I.T., going from there overseas to continue his training at Foggia, Italy. He was commissioned 1st Lieut. Jan. 12, 1918, and attached to the 1st Italian Caproni Squadron, 4th Airplane Group, Italian War Zone, June 18, 1918.

While returning from a bombing expedition Lieut. Baldwin's Italian pilot discovered that a new bridge had been thrown across a river, which he determined to photograph. He turned the controls over to his companion, telling him to take the machine down as low as possible, and Baldwin immediately nosed the plane over and got far below the barrage and anti-aircraft guns, guiding the machine so skilfully that an excellent photograph was taken. Within a few hours the place was identified and the bridge shelled by the Italian artillery.

Lieut. Baldwin took part in a daylight air raid on the Austrian Naval Base, at Pola, in the Adriatic. The expedition started at daybreak, and over 60 planes took part attacking in coöperation with two fleets of destroyers. It was a 110-kilometre flight straight across the Adriatic and only two or three Americans were allowed to take part. The raid was a success and the objectives were bombed and all the planes returned in safety, despite the fire directed at them by land batteries and ships in the harbor.

On July 4, 1918, Lieut. Baldwin was one of five American aviators decorated with the Italian War Cross by King Victor Emmanuel.

After acting as instructor on the Italian front Lieut. Baldwin was ordered to England, Aug. 13, 1918, as Commanding Officer of the 140th Squadron.

He was honorably discharged at Garden City, N.Y., Jan. 2, 1919.

LAWRENCE I. PEAK

FIRST LIEUTENANT, A.S., U.S.A., ESCADRE 12, G.B. 6
ESCADRILLE 66

SON of Walter Irvin and Eva Grace (Swan) Peak, of Somerville, Mass.; was born in Medford, Mass., on Jan. 2, 1893. He graduated from the Mechanic Arts High School, Boston, in 1910.

He enlisted at Somerville on July 13, 1917, and was assigned to the Ground School, M.I.T., for training, Aug. 20, 1917. After a short course there he was chosen from among the honor graduates (class of Oct. 13, 1917) to be sent abroad for pilot's training in the European schools. He was ordered to Mineola, N.Y., on Oct. 16 and sailed from New York on Oct. 26. When he arrived in France it was to find there were no facilities for advanced training. After waiting four months he volunteered as an observer in response to an urgent appeal for men for that work.

After a course at Cazaux, and the American School at Clermont-Ferrand, he was rated as an Aerial Observer, Gunner and Bomber, under both French and American systems. On May 18, 1918, he was commissioned 1st Lieut. and on June 15 was one of 16 American aviators chosen for further training with the French, the idea being to have men with actual battle experience to lead American squadrons as they were formed.

From June 15 to Oct. 23, 1918, he was attached to the French Independent Air Force as a member of Escadrille B.R. 66, G.B. 6 (Day Bombardment), Commander Vuillemin. This was one of the escadrilles which made the first reprisal raid on Germany in response to German raids on French towns; it was also a part of the famous Escadre 12.

While a member of Escadrille B.R. 66, Lieut. Peak took part in the Château-Thierry offensive, and in July covered the sector from Château-Thierry to Reims. In Aug., 1918, he was in Picardy, covering the sector from Amiens to Soissons and along the Chemin des Dames. In Sept. the escadrille was chosen as one of those to help the Americans in their St.-Mihiel attack in a sector extending from Verdun to Nancy; in Oct. he served in Champagne with the French, covering the sector from Verdun to Reims.

Escadrille B.R. 66 took part in practically every attack made by the French in these regions from July to Nov. and was awarded

the *Fourragère* colors and the Médaille Militaire (4 citations). In addition to having the French Brevet, Lieut. Peak has the distinction of being one of the two Americans who performed the necessary work to entitle them to the escadrille insignia, the "Épervier." On Aug. 11, 1918, after a series of raids, Lieut. Peak brought down his first official Boche, and on Aug. 17 was cited for the Croix de Guerre.

He was withdrawn from the French in Oct., 1918, and sent to Issoudun. After the Armistice because of his familiarity with the French language and customs, he was ordered to work with the Rents, Requisitions, and Claims Service, where he has been employed in settling large Aviation claims.

Citation

Croix de Guerre

Commander Vuillemin, Squadron 12, cites that Lieutenant LAWRENCE PEAK, an American Observation Officer of the highest order, arrived in the midst of the battle and immediately went into the fight, where he bore himself brilliantly, attacking fiercely the enemy troops by bomb, in a run of nine bombardments, and brought down an enemy machine the 11th of Aug., 1918.

*DINSMORE ELY

Lafayette Flying Corps; later Second Lieutenant, Volunteer Detached American Officer with French Escadrille S 120, Secteur Postal 102

Killed in airplane accident, April 21, 1918

Son of Dr. James Owen and Emma (Dinsmore) Ely; was born at Chicago, Ill., May 16, 1894. He attended the New Trier High School; the University and Chicago Latin Schools; and entered the Architectural School, M.I.T., in the fall of 1913. He was president of the Lambda Chi Alpha Fraternity, and vice-president of the Architectural Club. He completed his junior year in high standing and volunteered in May, 1917, for service in the Tech Unit of the American Ambulance Field Service, sailing for France on June 25, with the avowed purpose of getting into the Aviation Service as quickly as possible.

Arriving in Paris July 4, he secured his release the following day from the Ambulance Service, volunteered, and was accepted as a member of the Lafayette Flying Corps. He attended the French Aviation Schools of Avord, Pau, Tours, and Cazaux, and during his months of training had three thrilling escapes from death. On completion of his training, a qualified fighting pilot, he volunteered for active service under the French flag, and in Feb. arrived at the Toul sector as a member of the French Escadrille guarding the American lines. Here he remained in active service until March 29, 1918, when they were ordered to the great battle then centring around Amiens.

Passing through Paris, Ely was released from his French Squadron and commissioned 2d Lieut. in the U.S.A. But with the idea of more immediate service than seemed probable under the American forces still forming, he obtained permission to volunteer and return to his French corps as a detached officer, as his one desire was to be at the front.

In the last letter written by Lieut. Ely to his family on April 5, 1918, he said:

At present my one desire is to reach the defensive front. Right now it is hard for the French mind to grasp how much the Americans have wanted to help in this defensive during their first year of preparation. No matter how great the American organization is to be, if we suppose there are

300,000 Americans actually fighting in this offensive (no one knows numbers), we must keep things in scale by remembering that Germany alone has probably had more than a million and a half put out of action in this battle alone.

And I want to say in closing, if anything should happen to me, let's have no mourning in spirit or in dress. *Like a Liberty Bond, it is an investment, not a loss, when a man dies for his country.* It is an honor to a family, and is that the time for weeping? I would rather leave my family rich in pleasant memories of my life than numbed in sorrow at my death.

On April 21, 1918, Lieut. Ely was fatally injured in an airplane accident; he was taken to the hospital at Versailles with a fractured skull and passed away without regaining consciousness. He was buried with full military honors at Des Gonards' Cemetery, Versailles.

His last message — "Like a Liberty Bond, it is an investment, not a loss, when a man dies for his country" — has been used as a slogan throughout the country to help swell the Liberty Loans. Posters bearing these words went broadcast, and over a million full-page copies were printed in the newspapers of this country. Two weeks after Lieut. Ely's death $1,000,000 was subscribed as a memorial to him, on the last day of the Third Liberty Loan drive in Chicago, and in accordance with the request of Lieut. Ely, his $5000 life insurance was used to buy Liberty Bonds. A year after his death the wooden cross from his grave in France was presented to the Historical Society of Chicago, and lent inspiration at the conclusion of the Victory Loan drive. Of this cross the Librarian of the Historical Society wrote to the Chairman of the Victory Loan Committee:

The little white cross brought to my thought the thousands of those pale crosses that, like a thicket of Easter lilies, blanket the fields of France, and it seemed that there might be a message here that could be used to strengthen our morale at this moment.

And once more the young aviator's words helped swell the returns in his city and elsewhere.

For months Lieut. Ely's last message headed the casualty lists in the "Chicago Tribune," and cards with the printed paragraph upon them have brought comfort and inspiration to many bereaved hearts.

WILLIAM FITCH LOOMIS

LAFAYETTE ESCADRILLE, FIRST LIEUTENANT, A.S., U.S.A., ONE HUNDRED NINETY-THIRD, TWO HUNDRED THIRTEENTH AERO SQUADRONS

SON of Elihu G. and Marion H. (Fitch) Loomis; was born at Bedford, Mass., April 27, 1894. He was educated in the schools at Bedford; at Concord High School; Lawrence Academy; Groton; and Phillips Academy, Andover; and graduated from Amherst College in 1917, with the degree of A.B.

He sailed for France as member of the American Ambulance Service, May 19, 1917; he enlisted in the French Aviation Service and went through the French training schools, obtaining his license as a pilot; he served on the French front, flying with French companions for about six months, beginning in Nov., 1917. In 1918 he transferred into the U.S. Army with the rank of 1st Lieut. in Aviation, and was engaged in aerial service at Château-Thierry, St.-Mihiel salient, Verdun, and elsewhere, serving as Flight Commander and as a member of the "Hat in the Ring" Squadron. He received the Croix de Guerre from the French Government for faithful and efficient service. At the close of the war he returned to America and was honorably discharged.

Brothers in Service —

Ralph Lane Loomis, Ensign, Naval Aviation.
Hubert H. Loomis, 101st Regiment, F.A.
Samuel Loomis, 2d Lieut., 71st Coast Artillery.

RALPH LANE LOOMIS

LAFAYETTE FLYING CORPS, ENSIGN, NAVAL AVIATION SERVICE

SON of Elihu G. and Marion H. (Fitch) Loomis; was born at Bedford, Mass., April 13, 1887. He was educated in the public schools at Bedford; at Concord High School; Boston Latin School; and at Phillips Academy, Andover. He graduated with the degree of A.B. at Amherst, 1908; attended Harvard Law School, and was admitted to the Suffolk Bar, Boston, 1911; he practised law for a season and later engaged in business in Boston as one of the members of the firm of Loomis & Co., dealers in paper. On June 25, 1917, he sailed for France as a member of the American Ambulance Service, but upon reaching France he enlisted in the French Aviation Service and passed through the various aviation schools and obtained commission as a pilot; later, in 1918, he transferred into the U.S. Navy with the rank of Ensign; engaged in aviation work in connection with the officers of the English Navy, flying from Dunkirk and attacking enemy positions at Zeebrugge and Ostend; he was certified by his Commander to have been "a very good pilot and efficient officer in charge of men."

He is still in service, and stationed (May, 1919) at Pola, Istria.

Brothers in Service —

William Fitch Loomis, 1st Lieut., Lafayette Escadrille.

Hubert H. Loomis, Battery A, 101st F.A.; fought through the war with his regiment, being continually engaged at the front throughout the heavy fighting.

Samuel Loomis, 2d Lieut., 71st Coast Artillery.

ROBERT LOWELL MOORE

First Lieutenant, A.S., U.S.A., Escadrille Br. 29, G.B. 9

Son of James Lowell and Jane (Newell) Moore; was born in Cambridge, Mass., Jan. 12, 1896. He prepared for college at the high school, Wayland, Mass., and entered Harvard College, class of 1918. He left college at midyears in his sophomore year to join the Norton-Harjes Ambulance, and after six months' service returned in the fall of 1916 and finished his junior year.

He enlisted, May 17, 1917, and trained at the M.I.T. Ground School. He sailed for Europe, July 23, 1917, in the first group of aviators sent to France. He continued his training at Tours, Sept., 1917, Avord, Oct., 1917, and at Issoudun, where he remained from Nov., 1917, to Jan., 1918. He was commissioned 1st Lieut. on Nov. 20, 1917. Lieut. Moore was transferred to the Gunnery School at Cazaux, where he stayed from Feb. to April, 1918, as Pursuit Pilot. Subsequently, he spent some time in England at the Hythe Gunnery School. He returned to France, May, 1918, to act as Aerial Gunnery Instructor at the 7th Aviation Instruction Centre at Clermont-Ferrand.

He was sent to the front with Groupe de Bombardement 9, French Army, and was wounded, June 14, 1918, while engaged in a bombing expedition over Soissons. After his recovery two months later, he was put in charge of the Aero-Gunnery School at Clermont-Ferrand, Sept. to Dec., 1918.

In his report on the wounding of Lieut. Moore, Lieut. Mongin, a superior officer, wrote:

> On the 14th of June, on the return trip from a bombardment attack on Soissons, a formation of Bréguet aeroplanes, among which was Lieut. Moore, American aviator, was attacked by an enemy formation of pursuit planes at a height of 4800 metres over the German lines. At the first opening of fire, Lieut. Moore's observer, Lieut. Giquel, was killed; his body falling on certain controls, wedged them. Lieut. Moore, having lost control of his machine, fell, pursued by the two enemy planes which poured an incessant fire into his machine. Little by little he succeeded in regaining control of his plane, and continued to descend in regular spirals. The enemy planes steadfastly pursued him to an altitude of 1000 metres, pouring in their shot incessantly, and wounding him three times on the arm and right side.
>
> Thanks to his calmness, presence of mind, and skilfulness, Lieut. Moore succeeded in landing his machine, riddled with bullets and damaged in its

most essential parts, within our lines. Lieut. Moore was seriously wounded, and was at once despatched in an ambulance to the hospital at Guilly and evacuated immediately to Paris.

Citation

1st Lieut. MOORE, Pilot, Escadrille, Br. 29

A pilot of great bravery, possessing equally splendid enthusiasm and remarkable presence of mind. On the 14th of June, 1918, in the course of a combat above the enemy lines, his observer was killed, and he was forced to descend from an altitude of 5000 metres, pursued almost to the ground by two enemy planes, firing at him incessantly. Although he was wounded by three bullets and had his machine seriously damaged, he succeeded, thanks to his dexterity and courage, in reaching the ground.

(*Signed*) PÉTAIN

Lieut. Moore was honorably discharged from the Service at Garden City, N.Y., Feb. 10, 1919.

JENKIN R. HOCKERT

First Lieutenant, A.S.P.C., No. 2, Romorantin, France

Son of Bruno E. and Esther (Rylander) Hockert, of Hartford, Conn.; was born at Chicago, Ill., Sept. 10, 1894. He was educated in the public schools of Hartford, Conn.; graduated from Valparaiso University, B.S. 1912; and from Columbia University Law School, LL.B. 1917. He attended the R.O.T.C. at Plattsburg in 1917, and enlisted at Cambridge, Mass., Aug. 15, 1917. He attended the Ground School at M.I.T. from Aug. 3 to Oct. 6, and sailed for Italy on Oct. 17, 1917. He was trained at Campo Oveste Flying School, from Feb., 1918, to July, 1918; was commissioned 1st Lieut. May 13, 1918; and on June 14, 1918, received the Royal Italian Brevet as a pilot.

He was then ordered to France, where he was further trained: at Tours, from July 4 to July 19, 1918; and at Issoudun, from July 19 to Nov. 3, 1918. He acted as Ferry Pilot at Romorantin, France, on DH 4. He returned to the U.S. Jan. 31, 1919, and was honorably discharged on Feb. 10, 1919, at Garden City, N.Y. He now holds a commission in the Reserve Corps.

Brother in Service —

Frederick Hockert, 2d Lieut., U.S.A., 32d Infantry.

*WILLIAM HENRY MEEKER

Corporal, Lafayette Flying Corps, Escadrille 124

Killed in airplane accident, Sept. 11, 1917

Son of Henry E. and Jenny (Royce) Meeker; was born at New York City on Jan. 5, 1894. He was educated at Pomfret School, Conn., graduating in 1913; and at Harvard College, graduating in 1917. He had a very promising literary gift, and his articles and letters written overseas have been published in the press.

He drilled with the Harvard Regiment as Private, Corporal, and Sergeant. In the summer of 1916 he trained at the Thomas-Morse School at Ithaca, N.Y. Later, in the Harvard R.O.T.C., he was brevetted Corporal, Lieut., and Capt. On April 23, 1917, he enlisted in the Signal Officers' Reserve Corps, Aviation Section, at Cambridge. He sailed overseas, and received additional training at the French School at Avord, through June, July, and Aug., 1917. On July 29 he was brevetted Corporal at Avord. He reached Pau for training at the French School for Aviation Acrobacy on Sept. 10, 1917. He was killed on his trial flight at Pau, on Sept. 11, 1917, and was buried at Pau, France, on the same day.

That Corporal Meeker was one of the most promising young pilots, who needed but time to win distinction in his chosen Service, is shown by the citation issued on July 29, 1917, from the Commandant of the French School of Aviation at Avord, to Corp. Meeker, and to Samuel Skinner (Harvard, 1915), of which a translation follows:

> The Captain-Commandant of the School extends congratulations to the American pilots, Meeker and Skinner, for the skill and good-will of which they have given proof in the course of their instruction, which they have succeeded in completing in a remarkably short time, accomplishing their brevet of B.M. in less than three days. The Captain-Commandant presents these pilots, serving voluntarily in the French Army, as an example to all the pupils of the School, for the devotion and the excellent military spirit with which they are animated.

SHERBURNE EATON

Pilot, Lafayette Flying Corps, First Group

Son of Charles Edward and E. (Sherburne) Eaton, of Cambridge, Mass.; was born at Woburn, Mass., June 28, 1897. He was educated at Cambridge Latin School, 1915, and Harvard College, class of 1919. He was on the Harvard freshman and 'Varsity football squads.

He enlisted in the Foreign Legion at Paris, on March 2, 1917, and was soon transferred to Aviation, being sent to Avord for training on March 23. He was injured in a smash while training in July; and on Aug. 18, 1917, was brevetted Pilot, and made a member of the Aero Club of France. Again he was injured in a smash at Dijon in Sept., 1917. After finishing his training at Avord and Longwy, he was attached to the Lafayette Flying Corps for eight months, as a pilot. He was detached on special service to the U.S. Army, and attached to the 1st Aero Squadron as interpreter and instructor.

Eaton returned to the United States to lecture on the second and third Liberty Loans, and on the Red Cross drive with "Men from the Front" Section, U.S. Committee on Public Information, doing valuable service in four States. He acted as inspector of aeroplanes, and on the "Safety Committee." He spent three months, Aug. 23 to Nov. 28, 1918, at Louisville, Ky., in conjunction with the U.S. Field Artillery. On Nov. 28, 1918, he was honorably discharged.

Brother in Service —

Putnam Eaton, Chief Yeoman, U.S.N., Historical Staff, Intelligence Dept., London Headquarters.

ARTHUR RAYMOND KNIGHT

Second Lieutenant, A.S., U.S.A.

Son of Franklin P. and Annie J. Knight; was born at Newburyport, Mass., on Jan. 11, 1896. He attended the public schools of Newburyport and the Mass. Institute of Technology, where he played on the baseball team as catcher.

He enlisted on July 23, 1917, at Boston, and trained at the M.I.T. School of Aeronautics, where he was one of five highest honor graduates of Squadron 17. He was ordered to Egypt for advanced training; sailed for Liverpool on Nov. 11, 1917, to await transportation to the Mediterranean, but as no transports were available, he was transferred to France. He trained at Avord, Pau, and at Cazaux. He was sent from there to Gondrecourt, at the front, but as no machines were procurable, volunteered for observer in night bombing, and was sent back to Cazaux for further instruction in aerial gunnery; and from the latter place to Clermont-Ferrand Day Bombing School. From Clermont-Ferrand he went to Foggia, Italy, where he completed his training; thence to Modain, Italy, where he served with the Italian Air Forces, making day raids across the Adriatic Sea into Austria. He was sent to Chartres, France, and assigned to a French Bombardment Squadron and flew in day bombing. From this time on he followed the lines. Was three and one half months on day, and five months on night bombing.

At Plessis-Belleville most dangerous low-altitude day bombing was carried on. On one bombing raid at this latter place Lieut. Knight was nearly killed, his machine being riddled with bullets, necessitating its being discarded after his return to the aerodrome. He received a citation for this expedition. He continued flying over the lines at Gourgançon, Vinet, Arcis-sur-Aube, and La Perthe. He started night bombing at this latter place on single-motor Voisin machine. He moved forward to Mairy-sur-Marne; stayed there on bombing until transferred to Caproni machine at Villeneuve in Champagne. From Champagne he went to Épiez, remaining two and one half months, and flew from there over the Vosges Mountains to the Rhine. He flew here with Capt. Paul de Lesseps, the son of the French engineer who built the Suez Canal. Then he went westward to Alsace-Lorraine and continued bombing operations. He made, in all, 104 bombardments into enemy territory,

U.S.

and was decorated by General Pétain with the Croix de Guerre, with two citations. He was at Épiez when ordered, with three other lieutenants, to the United States to start a school of instruction in night bombing at Ellington Field, Houston, Tex. He sailed from Liverpool two days before the signing of the Armistice, and arrived in New York Nov. 16, 1918. He was instructor at Ellington Field for the two following months, and was honorably discharged July 1, 1919.

Brothers in Service —

David C. Knight, Private, U.S. Infantry.

Elliot P. Knight, Flying Quartermaster, Naval Aviation.

WILLIAM B. O'BRIEN

First Lieutenant, A.S.A., U.S.A.

Son of Cornelius and Anne (Early) O'Brien; was born in Wallingford, Conn., Jan. 5, 1891. He was a graduate of Yale College, 1911, and made records in swimming and wrestling. He enlisted Aug. 10, 1917, at New Haven, Conn., as Private, 1st Class, A.S.E.R.C., U.S.A. He attended the M.I.T. Ground School, graduating with the class of Oct. 6, 1917.

Oct. 18, 1917, he sailed overseas, and trained at Issoudun, France, attached to the 5th Foreign Detachment. Later he was sent to the École Militaire d'Aviation, at Châteauroux, Indre, for preliminary flying instruction. He was commissioned 1st Lieut. May 13, 1918; brevetted in Caudron, and made a member of the Fédération Aéronautiques Internationale, May 21, 1918. He was assigned to the American School of Perfectionnement for complete training as Pursuit Pilot, and graduated July 31, 1918, when he was ordered to the 1st Aircraft Acceptance Park at Orly, Seine, for duty as Transfer Pilot, while awaiting assignment to a Pursuit Squadron. He performed this duty until Dec. 17, 1918, when he was ordered to the U.S. and honorably discharged at Garden City, N.Y., Jan. 10, 1919.

WILLIAM AUGUSTUS WELLMAN

FIRST LIEUTENANT, U.S.A.S.; LAFAYETTE FLYING CORPS
FOREIGN LEGION; ESCADRILLE N 87

SON of Arthur G. and Celia Wellman; was born in Brookline, Mass., Feb. 29, 1896. He graduated from the Newton High School, where he proved himself an all-round athlete. At the time of enlistment he was in the wool business in Boston. He desired to enter the U.S. Aviation Service, but he was rejected, as the Service was full at that time. He therefore enlisted in the Norton-Harjes Ambulance Corps, of New York, in April, 1917, and sailed for France on May 22.

Soon after his arrival in France, he transferred from the Ambulance Corps, and enlisted in the Foreign Legion, June 27, 1917, becoming a member of the Lafayette Flying Corps. He trained at Avord, and received his pilot's license on Sept. 29, 1917, becoming a Corporal in the French Army, and refusing to accept a 2d Lieutenant's commission in the U.S.A. He was trained as a chasse pilot and as a bombing pilot; then went to Pau and Plessis-Belleville for training in acrobatics. Finishing his courses on Dec. 1, he was assigned to Escadrille N 87, in the Lorraine sector, near Nancy, at Lunéville, where he reported on Dec. 3, and made his first flight over the German lines on the following day.

On Jan. 19, 1918, Lieut. Wellman brought down his first Boche, in company with Thomas Hitchcock in another plane. The German Rumpeler, which had destroyed a French plane, was brought to the ground and the occupants killed. For this achievement both Hitchcock and Wellman received the Croix de Guerre. The latter's citation reads, translated, as follows:

> Corporal WELLMAN, WILLIAM AUGUSTUS, . . . of the Foreign Legion, pilot attached to Escadrille N 87. An American enlisted in the Foreign Legion, is distinguished as a remarkable chasse pilote by his enthusiasm and courage. On Jan. 19 he brought down an enemy aviator, who crashed to the ground near Bois Maut de la Croix.

In the next two months Lieut. Wellman had three more official and three unofficial victories to his credit. He was made Maréchal de Logis (Quartermaster, corresponding to Sergeant in rank). With Lieut. Hitchcock he went on special duty over the German lines to distribute President Wilson's Message to Congress.

On the second day of their flight they had a narrow escape, when flying only 100 yards above the Boches, who constantly shelled them. Lieut. Wellman's machine was destroyed, after he had succeeded in escaping just over the first-line French trenches.

On March 9, the day the Rainbow Division made its first and successful attack on the enemy, Lieut. Wellman was detailed to fly over them with the French patrol — the only American airman at that time and place. He flew as leader of the lowest patrol, at a height of 1000 metres, with eight machines following him. He first destroyed a biplane Rumpeler, sending it to the ground in flames at 4.20 P.M. and a few minutes later, at 4.45 P.M., brought down a one-man Albatross. For this achievement he received a second gold palm-leaf on his Croix de Guerre, and the following citation, which included recognition of two previous victories:

> The American pilot, Maréchal de Logis WELLMAN, WILLIAM AUGUSTUS, pursuit pilot, showing the finest qualities of bravery and enthusiasm for attack. On Jan. 20, having gone in pursuit of an enemy biplane, above Nancy, he chased him to his terrain for more than 25 kilometres within the lines, shooting the hangars at short range and killing the pilot.
>
> On Feb. 10 he shelled at low altitude an enemy aviation ground.
>
> On March 9 he brought down an enemy biplane de réglage in the region of P——, and almost immediately after brought down an escorting enemy monoplane.

On March 21 he was shot down by anti-aircraft guns, at the height of nearly three miles. His shelled machine went into a spinning nose dive that changed as by a miracle into a sweeping spiral, over the forest of Parroy. The machine struck the trees and splintered into fragments; he clung to the top of a big fir tree, and clambered down, badly injured but alive. On March 29 he was honorably discharged from the French Army, as unfit for further Aviation Service, and returned to America.

After treatment and recuperation he enlisted in the U.S. Aviation Service, receiving a 1st Lieutenant's commission, on Sept. 16, 1918. He became Advisory Instructor of Combat Flying at Rockwell Field, San Diego, Cal. He has written a most readable and interesting book, "Go Get 'Em!"

Brother in Service —

Arthur Ogden Wellman, 2d Lieut., A.S., U.S.A.

ARTHUR OGDEN WELLMAN

Second Lieutenant, A.S., U.S.A.

Son of Arthur G. and Celia Wellman; was born in Brookline, Mass., Oct. 31, 1894. He was educated at the Newton High School, where he was a member of the football, baseball, and hockey teams throughout his course.

Lieut. Wellman enlisted at Princeton, N.J., in Jan., 1918, and trained at the Ground School at Princeton, West Point, Miss., and at Dayton, O. He was commissioned 2d Lieut., A.S.A., in Aug., 1918; but did not, like his brother, see service on the other side, as the Armistice intervened.

He was honorably discharged at West Point, Miss., on Jan. 1, 1919.

Brother in Service —

William A. Wellman, 1st Lieut., Lafayette Flying Corps.

EDWARD DAVID JUDD

LIEUTENANT (*j.g.*), U.S.N.R.F.; LAFAYETTE FLYING CORPS, ESCADRILLE SPAD 3 (*Les Cigognes*); BRITISH NAVAL DAY BOMBING SQUADRON; NORTHERN BOMBING GROUP

SON of Dr. David H. and Lillian M. (Hanna) Judd; was born in Boston, Mass., Aug. 31, 1894. He graduated from the Roxbury Latin School, 1912, and from Harvard College, A.B. 1916. On Jan. 6, 1917, he enlisted in the American Ambulance Field Service, and was attached to S.S.U. 4 of that Service until June 28, 1917, working in the Argonne and Champagne sectors.

On July 6 Lieut. Judd joined the Foreign Legion of the French Army for Aviation Service, and became a member of the Lafayette Flying Corps. He was brevetted "Pilote Aviateur" on Oct. 1, 1917, at Avord, France. He went through the acrobatic school at Pau, and the finishing school at Plessis-Belleville, then joined Escadrille Spad 3, at Dunkirk, France, on Dec. 1, 1917. This escadrille moved to Soissons and later to Beauzée, just behind Verdun.

While at Beauzée Lieut. Judd was released from the French Service to join U.S. Naval Aviation. He was commissioned Ensign on Jan. 19, 1918, and sent to the Naval Air Station at Dunkirk, to fly scout seaplanes on anti-submarine patrols in the North Sea, off the Belgian coast, at that time held by Germany. On May 28, 1918, he was transferred back to land flying on day bombing machines. After a month at the Army Day Bombing School at Clermont-Ferrand, he was sent to join English Squadron 218, at Calais, for training in actual day bombing, later to become a Flight Commander in a Naval Day Bombing Squadron. While with this English Squadron Lieut. Judd made raids over Zeebrugge, Bruges, and Ostend.

The day bombing work of the Navy having been taken over by the Marines, he was transferred to the staff of Capt. D. C. Hanrahan at Paris, Commander of the Northern Bombing Group. After a month there, on Sept. 6, 1918, Lieut. Judd was returned to the United States to instruct in day bombing. He arrived in America on Sept. 1, 1918, and was sent to Miami, Fla., to instruct in the Marine Flying Field there. He remained in Miami until Feb. 28, 1919, when he was put on inactive status of the U.S.N.R.F., as a Lieut. (j.g.), dating from Oct. 1, 1918.

CHARLES DABNEY HORTON

SERGENT-PILOTE, ESCADRILLE, SPA 75, G.C. 14

SON of Charles Dabney and Charlotte L. (Ogston) Horton; was born in St. Louis, Mo., June 3, 1891. He was educated at St. John's School, Ossining, N.Y.; at Blair Academy, Blairstown, N.J.; and at Dartmouth College, A.B. 1915. He was noted for his swimming at Blair Academy, and at Dartmouth belonged to the Dartmouth Outing Club in 1914, took 1st Prize for the 100-Yard Ski Dash, and 2d prize for the Cross-Country Ski Race.

He enlisted in the French Army Aviation Service in Paris on Aug. 20, 1916. He was trained at the French flying schools at Buc, Juvisy, and Avord, and was made "Sergent-Pilote" on Sept. 14, 1917. He was attached to Escadrille C 17, Sop. 255, Spa 69, and Spa 75. He took part in engagements in Flanders in 1917; at Fismes, Chemin des Dames, and St.-Quentin in 1918. As a recognition of his excellent work at St.-Quentin he was awarded the Croix de Guerre. He was discharged from the service of the French Army on Jan. 20, 1919, in Paris, France.

Married, Jan. 10, 1917, Miss Helen Wheelock Hubbard.

TALBOT OTIS FREEMAN

FIRST LIEUTENANT, A.S.A., U.S.A.. QUARTA SQUADRILLA UNDICESSIMO GRUPPO, ZONA DI GUERRA, ITALIA
ONE HUNDRED FORTIETH U.S. AERO SQUADRON

SON of Daniel Allen and Lucy T. S. Freeman; was born in Longwood, Mass., Nov. 9, 1890. He graduated from the Noble and Greenough School, and from Harvard College, S.B. 1914; member of the Institute of 1770, D.K.E., Hasty Pudding, and "Fox" Clubs (Digamma). He made the Harvard-Yale freshman record, 120 yards, high hurdles, and belonged to the 'Varsity track team from 1911 to 1914. For a year he trained with Battery A, M.V.M.

He enlisted in the Air Service in Boston on June 20, 1917, and was assigned to the M.I.T. Ground School from June 20 to Aug. 25. On Sept. 11, 1917, he joined the 4th Squadron of the "First Foreign Detachment" at Fort Wood, Bedloes Island, N.Y. He sailed overseas on Sept. 25, 1917, arriving in Paris on Oct. 16. He was then ordered to the 8th Aviation Instruction Centre at Foggia, Italy, where he was trained from Oct. 28. He passed his first "brevet" on Jan. 13, 1918; his second "brevet" and R.M.A. tests on Feb. 14; and was commissioned 1st Lieut., A.S.A., U.S.A., on March 2, 1918. On May 28 he qualified as night and day Caproni bombing pilot. Lieut. Freeman finished his final training at Campo Scuola Cascina Malpensa, Galleratte, Milano, on July 1, 1918. He was subsequently ordered to Verona, where he joined the 4th Squadron, 11th Group, on July 16. He remained on active duty on the Italian front until late in Aug., taking part in the raids over Pola, the Austrian naval base. During this time he was piloting the Caproni planes, and was recommended for the Italian Croce di Guerra on Aug. 20. On Aug. 25 he was detached from the Italian Squadron, and assigned to the Chief of the Air Service at Tours, France, from Aug. 28 to Oct. 1. On Oct. 7 he was ordered to Handley-Page Night-Bombing Aerodrome in England, where he qualified as B.E. – 2 E. Pilot on Oct. 10 and as Liberty D.H. 4 Pilot on Nov. 5. On Dec. 1, 1918, he sailed for New York. He was honorably discharged at Camp Mills, Garden City, N.Y., on Dec. 30, 1918.

Brother in Service —

Daniel Allen Freeman, Jr., 2 years Lieut. (j.g.), in U.S. Navy.

*BRIGGS KILBURN ADAMS

Second Lieutenant, Eighteenth Aero Squadron
Bombing Group, R.F.C.

Killed in action, March 14, 1918

Son of Major Washington Irving Lincoln and Grace (Wilson) Adams; was born in Montclair, N.J., May 6, 1893. He was educated in the Montclair public schools, and at Harvard College, class of 1917. He was leader of the 'Varsity Musical Clubs at Harvard, and a member of D.K.E.

He drove a motor ambulance in France during the summer of 1916, and before returning to America to complete his college course he enrolled for service the following year in the Lafayette Escadrille.

In May, 1917, he volunteered for active war service in the Royal Flying Corps, and had his preliminary training at Camp Borden, Can., and Fort Worth, Tex. In Nov., 1917, he received his commission as 2d Lieut., R.F.C., and sailed for England in Dec. He graduated first, in a class of twenty, with an average of 94, the highest grade which had been achieved up to that time. After completing his training at various camps in England and Scotland, he volunteered for active service in France before he was required to "go out," and crossed the Channel with a single companion in Feb., 1918.

He was assigned to the Bombing Group of the 18th Squadron, R.F.C., at Aire, France, and at once began his flying on the battle front. He chose the bombing group, because, as he wrote, in destroying the enemy's munitions, fortifications, and equipment, he was "making war on war." To quote from a letter to his mother:

> I feel no bitterness against the Huns as individuals. It is war that I hate, and war that I am willing to give all to end as permanently as possible; for it is n't the men that war kills, it is the mother's heart which it destroys, that makes it hateful to me.

In another letter he wrote:

> Even if I don't come back, it is all right, Mother, for you know we can't hope to gain such wonderful ends without paying big prices, and it is not right to shirk payment.

On March 4, 1918, while in active service on the western front, he fell and was buried with military honors in the military cemetery

RFC

near St.-Omer, France. "Death is the greatest event in life," he wrote in one of his eloquent letters to his mother, "and it is seldom that anything is made of it. What a privilege, then, to be able to meet it in a manner suitable to its greatness."

A few of his letters were first printed in the "Harvard Alumni Bulletin"; subsequently a larger collection appeared in the "Atlantic Monthly" for Oct., 1918. They caused a widespread expression of deep interest, and thoughtful readers assigned to them a high place in the spiritual literature of the war. Of them Professor Francis G. Peabody of Harvard says:

> They are not only gallant and beautiful in their feeling, but singularly elevated in their style, as though his new experience had lifted him into new levels of expression and given to his language something of the clearness and freshness of the upper air.

And Arthur Stanwood Pier, who collected the letters in a volume called "The American Spirit," wrote to Major Adams:

> He never wrote anything for me which could compare with these letters, and nothing else that has been written about the war that I have read, can compare with them. They are the most beautiful bits of writing that have come out of the war — beautiful in style, color, and motion. . . . No one else has taken me up in the air, and shown me what it must be to fly; no one else has presented so vivid a figure of War as it should be portrayed.

In a letter to his mother, he wrote:

> I go about, as it were, *hands with palms out*, all about my heart, holding things outside of it. I am conscious of things I don't like, discomforts, sometimes . . . but I won't let them get into the inside where they hurt. If I can change them, I can do it just as well keeping them outside, and if I can't change them — well, what does it matter? — they are outside.

Lieut. Adams, through his father, Major Adams, was a lineal descendant of Henry Adams, of Braintree, Mass., the common ancestor of Samuel Adams, the Patriot, and John Adams, the second President. On his mother's side, Lieut. Adams was descended from the Wilson family of Virginia, of which one member was killed in action at Monmouth in the Revolutionary War, and another fell in the War of 1812. His father, Major Adams, was in active service with the Q.M.C. for over a year. Lieut. Adams also had a brother in the Service, Wilson I. Adams, 2d Lieut., F.A., in active service about five months.

WALTER ROGER AVERY

First Lieutenant, A.S., U.S.A., One Hundred Forty-Eighth U.S. Aero Squadron

Attached to the Thirteenth Wing, Royal Air Force

Son of Nicholas F. and Mary Henderson (Taylor) Avery; was born at Charlestown, Mass., Feb. 6, 1894. He attended the public schools in Boston and Pepperell, Mass., and graduated from Tufts College in 1914.

He entered the employ of Sloane, Huddle, Feustel & Freeman, consulting engineers, and was carrying on his work in Chicago at the time of his enlistment, May 13, 1917.

He attended the first Officers' Training Camp at Fort Sheridan, Ill. (Co. I, Ill. Engineers). He was one of eight men to be chosen for the Air Service, and was transferred to the Aviation Section June 18, 1917; he graduated from the School of Military Aeronautics, Champaign, Ill., Aug. 1, 1917, and went overseas Aug. 18, 1917, with the first detachment of aviators to go across. He trained in England at Oxford University Ground School, receiving flying training at Stamford, Joyce Green, London Colney, Hounslow, and Marke; during this time he was injured in a "crash," in which his companion was killed, and spent three months in English hospitals.

He was commissioned 1st Lieut. May 29, 1917, and was assigned to the 148th U.S. Aero Squadron (Pursuit), attached to the 13th Wing, R.A.F., Sept. 6, 1918. In the following weeks he took active part in patrols, bombing, and observation expeditions, and participated in a fight in which between 80 and 90 machines were engaged; although outnumbered about two to one, his group suffered no casualties and brought down enough enemy machines to win a congratulatory letter from the General in command.

He was cited for extraordinary heroism in action on July 25, 1918, and was awarded the Distinguished Service Cross.

On Oct. 1, while flying at a low altitude, some distance over the lines, his engine was put out of action by an enemy machine gun and he was forced to land a few kilometres southeast of Cambrai, behind the German lines, where he was captured. He was confined in the prison camps at Caudry, Solesmes, and Le Quesnoi, until Oct. 10, when he entrained for Germany; some hours later he escaped from his guards and jumped from the train, moving at the rate of

25 miles an hour, near Valenciennes; for the next two days he travelled by compass without food or water, hiding in ditches during the daylight and crawling through the middle of a German transport camp. Forced to take shelter in a shell-hole by the Allied bombardment, he was recaptured by the enemy, and while being marched through the streets narrowly escaped death from bombs dropped by his own Squadron.

He was imprisoned from Oct. 18 to 31 at Siognies, under the poorest conditions, suffering from insults, hunger, and filthy surroundings; on Nov. 2 he was transferred to Maransart, where, on Nov. 6, he escaped with a British officer, by a rope suspended from a barn, between guards stationed outside.

Aided by friendly Belgians he remained in hiding during the following week, travelling back by degrees to Siognies, where he was located on Nov. 11, and witnessed the evacuation of the town the next day by the enemy. On Nov. 14 Lieut. Avery was returned by airplane to his Squadron at Toul, which had given him up for lost. He was for some time confined in the hospital as a result of his ill-treatment by the Germans.

He was honorably discharged at Garden City, N.Y., Feb. 5, 1919.

ROYAL WINTER WETHERALD

ENSIGN, U.S.N.R.F., U.S.N., A.S.

SON of James I. and Eliza (Phelps) Wetherald, of Boston, Mass.; was born in Newton, Mass., Dec. 29, 1893. He was educated at the Noble and Greenough School, Boston; St. Andrew's School, Concord, Mass.; and Mass. Institute of Technology. He played on the football and track teams. Previous to enlistment he completed the prescribed Infantry and Cavalry Course of the U.S. Military Training Camp, Fort Oglethorpe, Ga., on May 30, 1916.

He entered the Curtiss School of Flying at Newport News, Va., on March 5, 1917. He received a certificate as pilot after 600 minutes' instruction in Curtiss F Boat type and land tractor J.N. 4. He enlisted in Naval Air Service on April 19, 1917. On Nov. 5 he passed the Naval Aviator's tests and examinations at Naval Base, Hampton Roads, Va.; and on Dec. 19, 1917, was commissioned Ensign, U.S.N.R.F.

After receiving his commission Ensign Wetherald was detailed to instruct students in flying, until ordered to Fort Worth, Tex., to take a course of instruction at the Aerial Gunnery School of the Royal Flying Corps. After graduating from this school he returned to Washington and received foreign orders; but before sailing was ordered back to Hampton Roads as Ordnance Officer and Instructor in Charge of the Officers' School of Gunnery. He organized the Ordnance Department at that station and fitted with ordnance the first seaplanes that were ever used in active patrol work off the Virginia Capes. During this time he instructed many of the officers in flying and aerial gunnery who were afterwards sent abroad.

During the German submarine activities off the U.S. coast, while still acting as Ordnance Officer, Lieut. Wetherald patrolled the coast of Virginia. On Nov. 18, 1918, he was honorably discharged, at Hampton Roads, Va.

Married, May 11, 1918, Rosemonde Wyman.

*ARNOLD WHITTIER HILL

LIEUTENANT, ROYAL AIR FORCE

Killed in airplane accident, July 13, 1918

SON of Arthur W. and Josephine B. Hill; was born in Malden, Mass., June 6, 1897. He was educated at the Malden Grammar and High Schools, 1915. From earliest boyhood Lieut. Hill showed the keenest interest in flying and in flying machines. While in high school he won a silver cup for special flying at a meet of the Waltham Model Aeroplane Club. He made a double somersault and spiralled to the ground, a feat unusual for an amateur in those days.

On Jan. 1, 1918, Lieut. Hill volunteered in the Royal Air Force at Toronto, Can. He trained at Camp Mohawk, Can., and had technical training at the University of Toronto. He learned to fly at Fort Worth, Tex., and was recommended for Instructor in the School of Special Flying at Toronto. He was commissioned Lieut. in June, 1918.

On July 13, 1918, Lieut. Hill was killed in an accident while flying at Armour Heights, Toronto, Can. He was buried at Mt. Auburn, Mass.

A letter from the Chaplain to Lieut. Hill's family said in part:

> In speaking with Captain Leach, the Commanding Officer of the School of Special Flying, he said it was a pure accident which caused the death of Lieutenant A. W. Hill; he was a promising flyer, a good officer, and personally a very fine fellow. His death cast a deep gloom over the airdrome. Speaking personally, I know he was very popular among his fellow officers and all who knew him in the airdrome. There is no doubt that he took his duties very seriously and showed wonderful ability. There is every evidence that he was a fine, clean-living, manly fellow, who commanded the respect and confidence of all who knew him. He will not be forgotten. Be assured that his passing was due to no mistake or neglect on his own part or the part of any one, but just one of those unaccountable accidents that have taken from us so many of our fine, heroic boys.

GARDINER GREENE HUBBARD

CAPTAIN, SQUADRON 254, ROYAL AIR FORCE, ENGLAND

SON of Charles Eustis and Caroline Dennie (Tracy) Hubbard; was born in Boston, April 19, 1878. He fitted for college at the Browne and Nichols and the Noble and Greenough Schools, and graduated from Harvard College in 1900. He was prominent in athletics (running, jumping, hurdling, pole-vaulting, and golf), playing on the 'Varsity, team in his senior year. After graduation he made a trip round the world, and then spent over three years in Paris, at the Beaux-Arts, studying architecture. On his return he went into an office in New York. Some years later he visited Prof. Bell at Cape Breton, who was at that time experimenting on flying machines, and Hubbard became interested in the subject. This resulted in his spending the winter there and designing and building an aeroplane in the Baddeck shop. He then went to Pau and took lessons in aviation and received his certificate. Later he built another machine at Ipswich, Mass., and did some flying in New York State. He was a member of Squadron A, N.Y. State Cavalry, when the war broke out.

In Nov., 1914, he went to Belgium, with Francis Colby and ten other young men to form an ambulance corps, attached to the Belgian Cavalry. He remained there until the summer of 1915, when the ambulance corps disbanded. Hubbard was urged to join the Lafayette Escadrille, but decided to go to England and enter the Royal Flying Corps. He received his commission in the fall, and went to the front on active duty and remained there until spring.

He was then sent back to England to serve as an instructor. Later he was detailed at Coventry, to fly new aeroplanes to Farnborough, Aviation Headquarters. From there he went to Norwich to test out new machines. He then went to the Military School at Christ Church, Oxford, as Instructor in the Mechanism of Aeroplanes. He remained there for about a year, receiving his Captaincy there. He then went to assist in establishing an aerodrome at Denham, near London, where he was brevetted Major. In the summer of 1918 he was sent to Prawle's Point, South Devon, to establish a Coast Patrol.

Father in Service: Charles Eustis Hubbard, Company A, 45th Mass. Volunteers Civil War.

MELVIN STORY DICKINSON

Second Lieutenant, Royal Air Force

Son of David Taggart and Carrie N. (Story) Dickinson; was born at Cambridge, Mass., Nov. 11, 1895. He was educated at the Cambridge Latin School, and at Harvard College, class of 1918. At college he won his numerals in his freshman year in the high jump.

He went to Toronto, Can., in Sept., 1917, to join the Royal Air Force; attended training camps at Long Branch, Camp Borden, and the School of Aeronautics at Burwash. In Jan., 1918, his training in flying began at Fort Worth, Tex., Camp Taliaferro, and Benbrook. In March, 1918, he sailed overseas with the Royal Air Force, and finished his training at Scampton Aerodrome, Lincoln, and Shrewsbury. He was commissioned 2d Lieut. in July, 1918. At Scampton he was recommended for a Bristol fighter. On account of his excess height (he is 6 feet, 7 inches tall), he was sent to Shrewsbury for Bristol bombing-machine training. He was then assigned as pilot in a battleplane, and was preparing to go overseas when his knee was badly injured in an airplane crash, while he was a passenger. He became instructor at Shrewsbury and Thelford. In Dec., 1918, he began a course in wireless telephony at the R.A.F. Winter Aerodrome, Bournemouth. Later he was to have been officer in charge of this school; but he was incapacitated on account of his injured knee, and was honorably discharged by the Medical Board, as permanently unfit for further air service with the R.A.F.

*VICTOR RALEIGH CRAIGIE

SECOND LIEUTENANT, ROYAL AIR FORCE

Killed in accident, April 7, 1918

SON of Capt. Horace Walpole Craigie (of the British Army), of London; was born in New Brunswick, Can., May 22, 1892. At an early age he was adopted by Mr. and Mrs. James Brown and subsequently made his home in Boston. He received his education at the Mt. Hermon Preparatory School, the Boston Y.M.C.A., and the Harvard Graduate School of Business Administration.

At the time of the outbreak of the war in Europe, Craigie, then in business with the Berkshire Life Insurance Co., desired to enlist, and made several applications in Canada, but failed to obtain his mother's consent. He was a member of Troop A, 1st Squadron of Cavalry, M.V.M., and trained one year at the M.V.M. Training School.

When the U.S. entered the war he made application to attend the 1st Plattsburg Camp, but was not eligible because of failure to receive his final papers for Americanization. He then enlisted in the Royal Flying Corps, in Canada, where he began his training in June, 1917, at Toronto University, Camp Mohawk, and at Camp Borden; he continued training at Taliaferro Field, Tex., where he proved himself the best shot with machine gun in the division. He was commissioned 2d Lieut. in Toronto, in Nov., 1917, and sailed overseas Dec. 14, 1917, continuing his training in Stockbridge and Langmere near Chichester, Eng. There he had about completed his course and was eagerly awaiting orders to be sent to France, when he was killed in a collision on April 7, 1918.

Before going overseas, Lieut. Craigie wrote to his mother:

> I thank God that I have been accepted to take part in this damnable slaughter for the freedom of future generations and the race. Had I held back I should feel myself a traitor to the whole civilized world.

Later he wrote:

> Certainly I forgive you for not allowing me to get into the fray sooner, although it has grieved me much not to have been one of the first to put the harness on in the great cause for freedom and right. However, may God permit me to reach the German lines.

He was buried with full military honors at St. Andrew's Church, Oving, Sussex, Eng.

*HENRY BRADLEY FROST

FIRST LIEUTENANT, SEVENTEENTH AERO SQUADRON

Killed in action, Aug. 26, 1918

SON of Frank Clifton and Mattie (Bradley) Frost; was born at Arlington, Mass., Aug. 8, 1892. He prepared for college at the Arlington High School, graduated from Dartmouth in 1914, and from the Thayer School of Civil Engineering in 1915. While in college he played on the Dartmouth hockey team.

In July, 1916, he joined the National Guard, in Iowa, and the following year enlisted in the Aviation Service. He attended the Ground School, M.I.T., during the summer of 1917, and was sent overseas to continue his training in England, at Oxford, Grantham, Lincoln, Tadcaster, and Turnberry; also at Ayr, Scotland.

This course extended from Sept., 1917, to March, 1918, and on April 2, 1918, he was ordered to France where he was attached to the 17th Aero Squadron, and sent to the front. He was on active duty until Aug. 3, when he had two weeks' furlough which he spent in England. On returning to France he was made Flight Commander and was leading his patrol in a battle with enemy planes on Aug. 26, when he was seen to fall behind the German lines, near Bapaume. He was at first reported missing, and later his family were informed that he was alive and a prisoner in Germany. It was not until more than six months after he was reported missing that the War Department announced that Lieut. Frost had died on the day he was shot down, at the main dressing-station at Boursiers, France. He was buried in the military cemetery on the Cambrai-Bapaume road at Boursiers.

*JAMES GRANTLEY HALL

First Lieutenant, Sixtieth Squadron, Royal Air Force

Reported killed in action, Aug. 8, 1918

Son of Charles Edwin and Edith J. Hall, of Malden, Mass.; was born in West Dennis, Mass., Jan. 8, 1896. He was educated in the Medford and Malden High Schools, and at Burdett Business College. He left college to enlist. He won several medals and ribbons for running-races. In Jan., 1913, he was awarded a silver medal by the Humane Society for bravery in trying to save the life of a chum in a skating accident.

He enlisted in the Royal Flying Corps, at Boston, in July, 1917, after having been several times refused by the U.S. because he lacked half an inch of the required height. He went to Toronto and trained at different camps in Canada and later in Texas. He was commissioned 2d Lieut. Nov., 1917, in Toronto, and sailed overseas on Dec. 22, 1917. He landed in England and was sent to the front, in France. He was in active service, flying a scout plane, and had three Hun planes to his official credit. He was commissioned 1st Lieut., in May, 1918. He was doing admirable work, when he was shot down in combat on the Picardy front and reported killed, on Aug. 8, 1918; though the report has not been officially confirmed by the Air Ministry.

Lieut. Hall's Major wrote his parents that he was a most promising officer and had done wonderful work in his Squadron. From his letters it is assumed that he was on the Picardy front, and it was on the day before the British began their smash there that he engaged the Germans, and failed to return. The battle was at several thousand feet, and as long as Lieut. Hall was in sight he appeared to be under control and heading for the British advanced lines. Unless shot down by anti-aircraft gun-fire it seemed that he might land safely.

He is said to be buried one and a half kilometres south of Maricourt, France.

SIDNEY SPALDING BATCHELDER

FIRST LIEUTENANT, A.S., U.S.A., SIXTY-FOURTH SQUADRON, R.A.F.
TWENTY-FIFTH AERO SQUADRON, FIFTH PURSUIT GROUP

SON of Dr. Henry Flanders and Caroline E. (Taft) Batchelder, of Dedham, Mass.; was born in Danvers, Mass., Nov. 10, 1895. He attended the Dedham High School, and graduated from the Mass. Institute of Technology in 1917.

He enlisted at Plattsburg, N.Y., on May 12, 1917, and was one of the first ten to be sent from the Plattsburg Training Camp to the Ground School at M.I.T. on June 18. There he was one of three chosen for a ground course at Oxford University, England, and sailed overseas on Aug. 18, 1917. He remained at Oxford from Sept. 4 to Oct. 22, 1917, and was attached to the Royal Flying Corps in Sept. He was then transferred to Stamford, Eng., to Harling Road and Marske-by-the-Sea for training as a scout pilot.

He was commissioned 1st Lieut. in the Signal Reserve Corps, on May 13, 1918, and was attached to the 64th Squadron, Royal Air Force, serving in France from July to Sept., 1918. He was withdrawn to the American Air Service in Sept., and assigned to the 25th Aero Squadron for patrol duty on the Rhine through Nov. and Dec., 1918.

Lieut. Batchelder was honorably discharged from the service at Garden City, N.Y., on Feb. 4, 1919.

Brother in Service —

Hollis G. Batchelder, Lieut., Medical Corps., on duty with A.E.F., 76th Division, 301st Field Hospital; Surgeon-in-Chief, Camp Hospital 26.

*THOMAS CUSHMAN NATHAN

First Lieutenant, A.S.A., U.S.A.
Attached to Royal Air Service

Killed in airplane accident, March 20, 1918

Son of Frank N. and Elizabeth (Kimball) Nathan, of Newton Centre, Mass.; was born at Dorchester, Mass., Jan. 21, 1897. He graduated from Newton High School, class of 1915; attended Dartmouth College one year; then transferred to M.I.T., class of 1920, leaving there to enlist at the end of his freshman year. He played four years on the Newton High School football team; was captain of the freshman football team at M.I.T. For three years he was on the school track team, winning many cups and medals.

On March 17, 1917, he enlisted, at the age of 20, in the U.S. Aviation Service. He trained at Miami, Fla., and at the Ground School, Berkeley, Cal. In Aug. he was made Commander of his Squadron, and a few weeks later was put in charge of the eight highest honor men, picked to finish their training in England. These were among the first 50 aviators ready for service abroad. He went to Oxford, Eng., on Aug. 12, 1917; and having trained there was sent to Stamford, Eng., for scout-patrol work on the coast. Later he was sent to the Flying School at Ayr, Scotland, to test planes. On March 3, 1918, he was commissioned 1st Lieut., and was ordered across the Channel. Lieut. Nathan was to have sailed for France on March 22, but two days before that date he was killed at Ayr, Scotland, while testing a Spad plane, a wing of which collapsed, so that it fell. He was given a funeral with full military honors, both British and American.

A letter to his father from the English Lieutenant in command of the School at Ayr says:

> Your son's death was a very severe loss to all those who knew him in England. He was not only extremely popular and well liked, but an excellent soldier, and I have heard from many sources that he was considered the best American pilot that had ever been to the Flying School at Ayr.

GEORGE E. SPRAGUE

C.Q.M. (A.), U.S.N., Two Hundred Seventeenth Squadron
Royal Air Force
Seventh Squadron, Northern Bombing Group, U.S.N.

Son of Mr. and Mrs. Walter Sprague, of Saugus, Mass.; was born in Boston, Mass., on Nov. 16, 1896. He was educated at the Saugus High School, where he played football and basket-ball for four years, and at Boston University.

He enlisted in Naval Aviation early in April, 1917, in Boston, and after a few weeks' training at the Ground School in Pensacola, Fla., sailed for France on May 25, 1917, as a member of the First Aeronautical Detachment, U.S.N., which was the first official unit of U.S. forces to land in France, disembarking at St.-Nazaire, June 7, 1917.

Sprague was designated as an observer and assigned to the Centre d'Aviation Maritime, at St.-Raphael, on the Mediterranean coast. Here he took the French seaplane observers' course. He was then ordered to the Aerial Gunnery School at Cazaux, where he received his brevet as a military observer. For a number of months he acted as a Gunnery Instructor in the U.S. Naval School of Aerial Gunnery at Montchic-Lacanau, Gironde. After an additional course at the U.S. Army School of Bombing at Clermont-Ferrand, Puy-de-Dome, he went to the front with the first squadron of daylight bombers which the Navy had on land work. He had several months of active service over the lines with Squadron 217 of the Royal Air Force, with Squadron 7 of the First Marine Corps Aviation Force, and with the Northern Bombing Group, U.S.N. Soon after the Armistice was signed, he was sent to England for training as a pilot. He was ordered home in Dec., 1918, after having completed eighteen months of foreign service. He was honorably discharged from the service at the U.S. Naval Station, Pelham, N.Y., on March 15, 1919.

JOHN LAVALLE, JR.

FIRST LIEUTENANT, A.S.A., U.S.A.
ATTACHED TO THIRTY-THIRD WING, R.A.F.

SON of John and Alice C. (Johnson) Lavalle, of Boston, Mass.; was born in Nahant, Mass., on June 24, 1896. He was educated at the Noble and Greenough School, at St. Paul's School, and at Harvard College. He belonged to the Harvard R.O.T.C. from April to June, 1916; attended the Officers' Training Camp in Plattsburg in July, 1916; and had intensive training with the Harvard R.O.T.C. from April to July, 1917. He passed the examination for the Aviation Service in April, 1917, but because his record was lost in Washington for three months, did not formally enlist until July 2, 1917, in Cambridge. He was assigned to the Ground School at M.I.T., where he remained from July 2 to Sept. 1, 1917.

He left the U.S. on Sept. 18, 1917, with the "Italian Detachment," which never reached Italy, but was sent to Oxford and Grantham, Eng., and then split into several groups for flying instruction. He trained at the Ground School, Oxford, from Oct. 5 to Nov. 2, and at the School of Machine Gunnery, Harrowby Camp, Grantham, from Nov. 3 to Dec. 3. He was then transferred to Rockford, where he stayed till Jan. 27, 1918, when he was ordered to Southend, and later to Amesbury, Jan. 28 to April 1. He was in the hospital in London from April 1 to Aug. 8, leaving to return to Amesbury. Lieut. Lavalle was attached to the 33d Wing, R.A.F., and was sent to 58 T.S., Cramwell, Eng., where he expected to join a night-bombing Handley-Page Squadron, which, however, was disorganized. On his return to Amesbury, he was made Instructor. He was posted to No. 1 School of Fighting and Aerial Gunnery, Turnberry, Scotland, on the day of the Armistice; returned to Liverpool, and sailed for the U.S., arriving in New York on Dec. 4,1918.

He was commissioned 1st Lieut. on March 20, 1918, and honorably discharged from the Service at Camp Mills, Mineola, N.Y., on Dec. 26, 1918.

Married: Oct. 3, 1919, Ellen Tufts.

*ELLIOT ADAMS CHAPIN

First Lieutenant, Royal Air Force, Ninety-Ninth Squadron, B Flight

Killed in action, June 27, 1918

Son of Cyrus S. and Alice (Bigelow) Chapin, of Newton Centre, Mass.; was born May 10, 1895, at Somerville, Mass. He was educated at the Newton High School, class of 1913; and at Phillips Andover Academy, graduating with the class of 1914. He entered Harvard College in the class of 1918. In his freshman year he played on the Gore Hall football team, and in 1915 captained the Gore Hall baseball team.

At the close of his junior year, in April, 1917, he enlisted in the U.S.N.R.F. Coast Patrol, after having been refused by the U.S. Aviation Service, because of a minor defect in one eye. Being eager to serve in Aviation, however, he applied for and obtained an honorable discharge from the U.S.N.R.F., effective upon his enlisting in the British Royal Flying Corps, which he did on Aug. 26, 1917. He reported at Toronto, Can., on Sept. 6, and received ground and flying training at Deseronto and Long Branch; he continued his training at Camp Hicks, Fort Worth, Tex., where, in Dec., 1917, he was commissioned 2d Lieut. On Dec. 31, 1917, he sailed from Halifax on the *Tunisan*, as part of the convoy with the ill-fated *Tuscania* when she was torpedoed off the Irish coast. Lieut. Chapin volunteered, when the Captain called for "extra submarine watch," and afterward wrote his family that "it was the most exciting three hours he had ever spent."

After further intensive training at Old Sarum, Salisbury, Eng., he was commissioned 1st Lieut. in April, 1918, only seven months after beginning training. Early in May, 1918, he was ordered to France, and with his observer flew his plane, a large de Haviland bomber, over the Channel and across France to the aerodrome of the 99th Squadron, R.A.F., 6 miles south of Nancy. His Squadron was a bombing squadron, whose duties were to harass the enemy lines of communication, railways, ammunition dumps, and aerodromes.

On June 27, 1918, Lieut. Chapin was sent with others to bomb the railway at Thionville, north of Metz. After successfully dropping their bombs, the formation was attacked by a large number of Fokker scouts. In a desperate fight a shot passed through the

petrol tank of Lieut. Chapin's plane, causing an explosion which sent the machine down in flames from 1300 feet. Lieut. Chapin fell at Thionville, 25 miles within the enemy lines, and was killed. As the machine went down he was seen to turn to his observer and shake hands with him. His grave is as yet unidentified.

In a letter informing Lieut. Chapin's family of his death, Major Pattison, Commanding Squadron 99, R.A.F., writes:

> Your son is a great loss to this Squadron, as he was one of our best pilots, and also most popular amongst the other officers. He had been in a number of successful duties over the lines, and was a fine, stout-hearted officer.

One of his brother officers also writes:

> His loss is very keenly felt amongst us all, as he was one of the best. He always had a smile, and a kind word for every one.

And later, this officer wrote:

> There have been many tales of bravery, but I think it must be nice for you to know that your son died a hero's death, and faced it without fear. He was a son for any parent to be proud of, and we all loved him. In fact he was the finest type of Christian manhood that could possibly be found.

Lieut. Chapin's maternal grandfather, George E. Bigelow, was killed in the Civil War at the battle of Fredericksburg. His great-grandfather, Capt. John Bigelow, fought in the Revolutionary War, and was delegate to the Convention to ratify the Constitution.

*WILLARD FREDERICK SWAN

Sergeant, One Hundred Eighty-Second Aero Squadron

Killed in airplane accident, Feb. 6, 1918

Son of Frederick A. and Emma Ida (McDaniels) Swan; was born at Saugus, Mass., July 6, 1898. He was educated in the public schools of Saugus, at the Hawley School of Electrical Engineering, and Boston Y.M.C.A. (Automobile Course). He worked for a year as apprentice with the Burgess Aeroplane Company, of Marblehead, Mass., while it was under Government control; and was advanced to the position of foreman of the Flying Squad in July, 1917. He left this company to enter the U.S. Aviation Branch of the Army on Oct. 29, 1917. He trained at the Kelly Field, Everman Field, and Hicks Field, Tex., receiving high marks; and was recommended by his Captain, on Jan. 3, 1918, for a commission.

In a letter of Jan. 29, 1918 he said:

I had a wonderful flight yesterday with a boy from Boston. We were up for an hour and ten minutes. Believe me, at 6000 feet I got a good look at Texas.

Jan. 28:

Our Captain's plane collapsed 3000 feet up to-day. It happened before my very eyes and I shall never forget it. It was the worst thing that could have happened to the Squadron, because Captain Payne was a worker and was pushing this Squadron ahead very fast.

The death of his beloved Captain greatly affected him. On Feb. 4 he wrote:

Was in the air to-day two hours and ten minutes, and during that time we did about everything that was ever done in a flying machine. I had the controls 45 minutes.

Feb. 7:

I had two beautiful flights to-day with Lieut. Marquand. This morning we did not go very far, but this afternoon went to Dallas, about 44 miles from here. To-morrow I expect to make a trip to Denton, about the same distance, only in the opposite direction.

He never made that trip; for on Feb. 8 he was instantly killed in an airplane crash, at Hicks Field. His Lieut., Joseph Lersch, with whom he was making the flight, was nearly killed by the same fall.

Lieut. Lersch wrote of the accident a year later:

> I wish I could tell you in detail the happenings of that February morning. What I remember is that we started up about 9.45. In my recollections of Willard, I think of him as always making the most careful examination of the plane before a flight. His cautiousness was an outstanding characteristic as a "mechanic," and while, as I say, happenings just preceding are not clear, I can picture him, as was his habit, making the usual tests before going up. I know that while aloft we discovered some engine trouble and landed; after attempting to remedy it we went up again. I should say we had been flying about ten minutes when the crash came. I can remember falling; I think, too, I realized striking the ground, but there was no pain. . . . It seems certain that Willard must also have escaped conscious suffering. The cause of the crash was, in my opinion, a "frozen control.' Willard was my 52d student. It seems a hopeless thing to try and convey sympathy for his family in writing. I know that resignation to the sacrifice of such a boy — one so full of promise and who had the admiration and affection of every last man in the Squadron — is a heroic thing. . . .

Sergeant Swan is buried at Camden, Me.

Willard Swan's last words to his parents on leaving home were to the effect that he was not going to fight for selfish gain, for any honor or praise which he might win in the Service; not for the good of his country only; but Service in the highest sense.

US

*LE ROY GATES WOODWARD

FIRST LIEUTENANT, A.S.A., U.S.A.

Killed in airplane accident, Aug. 16, 1918

SON of Charles Herbert and Nellie R. (Oatman) Woodward; was born at Watertown, Conn., Dec. 28, 1893. He attended the public schools of Watertown, was president of his class in the High School (1912), and graduated from the Pratt Institute, Brooklyn, in 1916. He was captain of class baseball team (Pratt Applied Electricity), and played on 'Varsity basket-ball, tennis, and football teams.

He enlisted June 21, 1917, and attended the Ground School, M.I.T., receiving further training at Scott Field, Belleville, Ill. He was commissioned 1st Lieut. at Washington, D.C., Dec. 24, 1917, and sailed overseas Feb. 25, 1918, continuing his training as chasse pilote at 3d Aviation Instruction Centre, Issoudun. He took the gunnery course at Cazaux, and returned to Issoudun for three days' combat work before going to the front.

On Aug. 16, the second day of this combat flying, he was killed in an airplane accident, two days before he was to have gone to the front. He was buried in the Military Cemetery 32, at Issoudun.

Lieut. Woodward was very ill during the first of his stay in France.

After his recovery he wrote to his mother:

> I'm back on the OK list again, and am feeling like a two-year-old. I started to fly again about a week ago and went through the rouleurs, the 23 doubles and singles, and 18 metres all in about a week, and am now over on the 15-metre machine, which is the smallest machine we have. I probably will be here a couple of weeks or so, perhaps not as long as that; then I have to have a gunnery course — that will take about another week, and then yours truly will be ready for that longed-for crack at the Hun. . . .
>
> As we progress from one field to the next, planes get smaller and better, and I'm really in love with the "li'l' babies." I know I will make good because I love the work and have so much confidence in myself. I feel at home quite as much when I'm upside down in the air, at an altitude of a couple of miles, as I do when I am flying level at a few feet off the ground. But never have a fear, 'cause above all things I'm careful, 'cause I'm always thinking of you.

Brother in Service: Russell Johnson Woodward, 2d Lieut., 25th Engineers, A.E.F.

Grandfather in Service: John Andrew Woodward, 22d Connecticut Volunteers, Civil War.

*JOHN LESTER HUBBARD

First Lieutenant, A.S., U.S.A., Tenth Aero Squadron

Killed in airplane accident, Aug. 18, 1918

Son of Henry F. and Julia (Calligan) Hubbard, of Providence, R.I.; was born in New Rochelle, N.Y., Nov. 9, 1895. He was educated at the Moses Brown School, Providence, R.I., and at Harvard College, class of 1918. At the Moses Brown School he was one of the editors of the school paper, president of his class in junior and senior years, and at graduation won the Harvard Prize. At school he was captain and catcher for two years of the baseball team, and captain of the football team in his junior and senior years. At Harvard he won his "H" for playing on the 'Varsity lacrosse team.

He joined the R.O.T.C. at Harvard, and was sent to the 1st Training Camp at Plattsburg. He was one of the first to answer the call from Washington for volunteers for the Aviation Corps, enlisting in April, 1917. He was sent to the M.I.T. Ground School for training, and graduated as an honor man. He sailed overseas from Halifax on Oct. 29, 1917, for final training, which he received at Avord, Tours, Cazaux, and Issoudun. He was commissioned 1st Lieut. on May 13, 1918, and was attached to the 10th Aero Squadron, Aviation Corps, U.S.A.

He was killed on Aug. 18, 1918, as a result of the fall of his airplane, during the final phase of his training, at Issoudun, France, and was buried with full military honors in the Government Cemetery connected with the 3d Aviation Instruction Centre, A.P.O. 724, Issoudun.

A quotation follows from a letter sent to the parents of Lieut. Hubbard by the Aero Club of America:

> Although the sacrifice is great, it is a consolation to feel that your son's patriotic and faithful service to our Country, for which he gave his life, and the indomitable spirit which he has shown, will serve as a noble example and be an added incentive to young men, especially to his nearest and dearest friends and companions, to fight for the cause of Liberty and Freedom. We believe the Air Service, in which your son was engaged, is the most important of all forms of combat. . . . His name will be inscribed upon the records of this Club among those who gallantly answered their Country's call, and who nobly gave their lives in her defence.

*WALTER FRANCIS BUCK

Second Lieutenant, A.S., U.S.A.

Killed in airplane accident, Sept. 7, 1918

Son of Rev. and Mrs. Walter P. Buck, of New London, Conn.; was born in Provincetown, Mass., July 18, 1896. He graduated from the High School, Brockton, Mass., and attended Wesleyan University, 1913–14; Mass. Institute of Technology, 1915–16. He was proficient in tennis, rowing, riding, and motoring. He enlisted at Fort Slocum in April, 1917, and was sent from there to Kelly Field No. 2, San Antonio, Tex. He went to Princeton, N.J., for theoretical training; then back to Kelly Field, where he was commissioned 2d Lieut. in the spring of 1918. Lieut. Buck soon became Pioneer Instructor at Kelly Field, and trained 44 cadets in solo flying without an accident. He was then appointed Instructor of Instructors, teaching them "stunts" and military tactics. He longed for active service, but was kept at the less interesting work of training other flyers.

He had passed his final examinations and was awaiting further promotion at the time of his death.

On Sept. 7 Lieut. Buck had been flying in battle formation all the morning at Kelly Field. On coming down, a mechanic asked him to go up with him to test a certain airship. When 4000 feet high, both wings fell from the plane, and were found later a city block apart. The Government stopped at once the use of all ships of that make. It is supposed that the steel pins were removed and wooden ones substituted by some one sympathizing with the enemy.

Lieut. Buck was buried at Cedar Grove Cemetery, New London, Conn. The Government showed every possible honor on the occasion. Five airships, driven by officers whom Lieut. Buck had instructed, flew above the train for 30 miles out of San Antonio, dropping flowers on the coach. A full military funeral was held at New London, by order of the Kelly Field Commander. An airship hovered over the cortège, and dropped flowers into the grave of the aviator.

Married, April 26, 1918, Mab Casey, of San Antonio, Texas.

Brother in Service —

Willis L. Buck, entered Hydroplane Service as soon as possible after his brother's death. Assigned to M.I.T. for training.

*GORDON STEWART

Cadet, A.S., U.S.A., Second Aviation Instruction Centre Tours, France

Died in Service, Jan. 9, 1918

Son of Edward J. and Helena (Felt) Stewart, of Brookline, Mass.; born in Millis, Mass., March 15, 1896. He was educated at the Brookline High School, Chauncy Hall School, Boston, and at the Mass. Institute of Technology. He was an all-round athlete; coxswain of the high school crew for two years, and captain in 1915, when the crew won the interscholastic cup; a member of the swimming team for three years; member of the gymnasium team, winning two medals from the Harvard Interscholastic Gymnasium Association. He was prominent in various branches of sport at Chauncy Hall, and held the Greater Boston interscholastic diving championship for two years. He was a member of Sigma Alpha Epsilon Fraternity at Tech.

Immediately after the declaration of war, Stewart left the M.I.T. to enlist, with his brother Theodore, in the American Ambulance Field Service, reaching France aboard the first ship to dock after the declaration. He served from April to Oct., 1917, except for two and a half months spent in the hospital with a bad fracture of the arm. In Aug., 1917, his ambulance section was cited for exceptional bravery at Verdun. On Oct. 15, 1917, he enlisted in the Aviation Corps at Paris. He trained at Tours, and was about to graduate from the Aviation School there, when he fell ill with spinal meningitis and died within ten days, on Jan. 9, 1918, at Tours, France. He is buried in the American Cemetery, Indre-et-Loire, at Tours, France. His French instructor, when he heard of his death, wept, not wholly for Gordon, but, as he said, "for the loss to the Allies." He was accounted the most promising pupil that had passed through the school at Tours.

Brother in Service —

Theodore F. Stewart, ambulance driver; wagoner, Co. D, 2d Corps Artillery Park, France.

*CHARLES EDWARD JONES

CADET, A.S., SIGNAL CORPS, A.E.F., FOURTH AVIATION INSTRUCTION CENTRE, FRANCE

Killed in airplane accident, Feb. 15, 1918

ONLY son of Edward Archie and Isabel (Abbe) Jones; was born at Pittsfield, Mass., on Jan. 7. 1894. He attended the public schools of Pittsfield, and prepared for college at the Hill Preparatory School at Pottstown, Pa.; he graduated from the Yale-Sheffield Scientific School (Mechanical Engineering), with high honors, in 1915; the year following he took a special course in chemistry at the M.I.T. in order to fit himself for his father's business, the manufacture of paper-mill machinery.

In the summer of 1916, and again in 1917, he attended the Officers' Training Camp at Plattsburg, enlisting from there in the aviation section of the Army, June, 1917. In Aug. he was transferred to the Ground School, M.I.T., at which time he entered the 13th Squadron, graduating from there in Oct. He was assigned to Mineola, N.Y., for training, and from there was sent abroad Oct. 27, 1917, and trained at Tours, France, until Dec. 26, 1917, when he was transferred to a French flying school at Avord. There he was killed in an airplane accident on Feb. 15, 1918, two weeks before the time when he was to have been commissioned 1st Lieutenant. He was buried in the Protestant Cemetery, at Avord, on Feb. 18, and on March 25 memorial services were held for him in Pittsfield, at the First Congregational Church.

In paying tribute to his memory the Rev. Mr. Gregg said:

"This young soldier, whom we are commemorating, did not pretend to greatness. His last thought would have been to esteem himself above his fellows. Yet it is remarkable that wherever he went, other people and especially his contemporaries and comrades, admired him, respected him, and loved him. One of these, a cadet, who was with him both at the aviation school in Cambridge and in France, wrote: "I have never known anybody who was a better example of the highest type of an American. Of all the men in our detachment there was no one who was a better citizen, actually and potentially, none whom the nation could so ill afford to spare. By his straightforward living under conditions not the most favorable he was a constant inspiration to all of us."

Cadet Jones was descended from two Captains of Revolutionary fame, on his mother's side from Capt. Thomas Abbe, of Enfield, Conn., and on his father's, from Capt. Samuel Pelton, of Pittsfield.

*WILLIAM HALSALL CHENEY

First Lieutenant, A.S., S.O.R.C.

Killed in airplane accident, at Foggia, Italy, Jan. 20, 1918

Son of Charles P. Cheney and Mary C. Cheney (Schofield), of Peterboro, N.H.; was born at Colorado Springs, Colo., Jan. 15, 1897. He was educated at St. Mark's School, and at Harvard College, class of 1920. He was captain of St. Mark's School football team in 1915–16; and member of the Harvard freshman football team in 1916. During his vacations in 1915 and 1916 he took preliminary training in Aviation at Newport News, Va.

He left college in his freshman year to enlist in U.S. Aviation Service. March 31, 1917, he entered the School of Military Aeronautics at Urbana, Ill., and graduated as Honor Student on July 25, 1917. He sailed overseas and took advanced training in flying in Italy, and was the first American to win the Italian Military Flying Brevet, on Oct. 18, 1917. He was commissioned 1st Lieut. A.S., S.O.R.C. on Nov. 23, 1917.

On Jan. 20, 1918, Lieut. Cheney was accidentally killed at Foggia, Italy, in an airplane collision which resulted in the death of two other aviators.

The accident is described in the following letter from Headquarters of Major Ryan, commanding the U.S.S.C., Foggia, under date of Jan. 20, 1918.

With the profoundest feeling of sympathy for you and sorrow for your loss, I wish to inform you of the death of your son, 1st Lieutenant William H. Cheney, Aviation Section, Signal Officers Reserve Corps, a member of this command, on January 20, 1918.

Your son served under my command since leaving the United States, and by his delightful personality, keenness for work, and devotion to duty proved himself a man, a soldier, and a gentleman in every respect and one worthy of the greatest respect and admiration by all with whom he came in contact.

His death, which was instantaneous, was one of those almost impossible and wholly unavoidable accidents. He was piloting a machine with Lieut. Oliver B. Sherwood as observer and flying over the training field. At the same time another machine, piloted by Aviation Cadet George A. Beach, was also in the air. A very low cloud of fog blew over the training field and closed around your son's machine. He immediately turned to get out of the fog, and as the machine emerged, it struck the machine of Cadet Beach who was also endeavoring to avoid the fog. Both machines fell to the ground, a distance of about one hundred and fifty feet.

The funeral was held from the Italian Military Hospital in Foggia, at two o'clock in the afternoon of the twenty-first, and was attended by troops and officers of the American, Italian, French, and English Armies. All three men were buried with full military honors.

This noble sacrifice, although very hard to bear, is one every soldier is ready to make at any time for his country, and it was a comfort to know that he died as he desired, a soldier, a flier, honorably, in the defense of his country, of liberty and democracy for the world.

(*Signed*) WM. ORD RYAN
Major, J.M.A., Signal Corps

From Special Order, issued by Headquarters, Foggia, Italy, Jan. 22, 1918:

1st Lieut. W. H. Cheney, A.S., S.O.R.C., 1st Lieut. O. S. Sherwood, A.S., S.O.R.C., and Aviation Cadet George A. Beach, S.E.R.C., were men who on every occasion and in every way showed their bravery, desire, and eagerness in serving their country in all things and in all ways.

1st Lieut. W. H. Cheney answered the call of his country by enlisting in the S.E.R.C. on March 31, 1917; entered School of Military Aeronautics at Urbana, Ill., graduating therefrom as an honor student on the 25th day of July, 1917. After completion of the course at the S.M.A., he was sent abroad as a member of the A.E.F. He was the first member of this command to complete his Italian Military Flying Brevet, this on October 18, 1917, was commissioned as 1st Lieutenant, A.S., S.O.R.C., on November 23, 1917, and thereafter, as well as before, showed his abilities as a soldier and endeared himself to all men of his command. . . .

The great sacrifice of these brave young soldiers is not only an inspiration to this entire command and to the American Air Service at large, but also America's first offering of life in Italy to the great cause of the Allied Nations.

The command mourns at their loss and desires to express its deepest sympathy to their bereaved families.

(*Signed*) WM. ORD RYAN
Major, J.M.A. Signal Corps, Commanding

PETER K. CONSTAN

SECOND LIEUTENANT, A.S.A., U.S.A., BOMBER

SON of Constantine P. and Amalia J. Perentesis Konstantarogiannis, of Greece; was born in Sparta, Greece, Jan. 30, 1888. He is now a citizen of Boston. He was educated at Olivet College, A.B., and at Harvard University (post-graduate). Immediately after the declaration of war, he made application for the Officers' Training Camp at Plattsburg, but was rejected as being a fraction of an inch below the minimum height. Constan applied for the 2d Plattsburg Camp, and was this time rejected for being three pounds underweight. Just then the age for Aviators was raised, and he enlisted in U.S. Air Service at Cambridge, on Sept. 14, 1917.

He attended successively the M.I.T. Ground School, Nov. 3, 1917, to Jan. 6, 1918, and the School of Military Aeronautics, Princeton, N.J., Jan. 6 to graduation, Jan. 19, 1918. From Jan. 25 until April 20 he was trained as a pilot at Kelly Field, San Antonio, Tex. He then transferred to aerial bombing, and was ordered to the Concentration Camp at Camp Dick, Dallas, Tex. On June 28, 1918, he was ordered to Ellington Field, Tex., to train as a *bombier*. He finished his training and was recommended for a commission on Sept. 13. A week later he was ordered to the Aerial Gunnery School for Bombers at San Leon, Tex., a branch of Ellington Field. He was commissioned 2d Lieut. on Oct. 25, 1918. He graduated from this school on Nov. 2, and returned to Ellington Field to await orders for overseas.

Lieut. Constan has taken up a course for piloting and will remain at Ellington Field until it is finished.

In an interesting letter, Lieut. Constan shows his appreciation of American citizenship and of the New England tradition:

> I am a native of Greece. But I am an American none the less. Without a hyphen. I am very proud of the fact that I was an American citizen when I first set foot upon this continent, almost fourteen years ago, my father having been naturalized some years before my arrival. I am also a New Englander, more specifically a Bostonian. At least, I consider myself one, inasmuch as I have made Boston, or one of its suburbs, my home for the last seven years. It will be a matter of infinite pride to me to be included among the New England Aviators.
>
> New England's past records are among the highest. Let us hope that this one will not fall short of the mark; that the Past will welcome it as a worthy companion; that the Future will look up to it with pride.

*ROBERT SWIFT GILLETT

FIRST LIEUTENANT, A.S., U.S.A., CHIEF OBSERVER, ONE HUNDRED NINETIETH AERO SQUADRON, SECOND PROVISIONAL WING

Killed in airplane accident, Sept. 17, 1918

SON of Arthur Lincoln and Mary Bradford (Swift) Gillett; was born at Hartford, Conn., March 5, 1895. He was educated at Westminster School, Simsbury, Conn., graduating in 1912; and at Amherst College, class of 1916. He attended the Harvard Law School, but left in the spring of 1917 to go to Plattsburg.

He attended Plattsburg Camp in 1916, and Plattsburg Officers' Training Camp in the summer of 1917. He enlisted May, 1917. He was commissioned 2d Lieut., F.A., and was ordered to Camp Devens, where he was attached first to Battery 1, 302d F.A.; then to Headquarters Co., 302d F.A. He was commissioned 1st Lieut., F.A., early in the winter of 1918. He was ordered to take examination as Aerial Observer, and was sent for training successively to Post Field, Fort Sill, Okla.; Camp Dick, Dallas, Tex.; Selfridge Field, Mt. Clemens, Mich.; and Park Place, Houston, Tex. He was with the 191st Squadron, 2d Wing, Air Service. At Park Place he was made Chief Observer of the 2d Wing, consisting of the 190th and 191st Squadrons.

He was killed in an airplane accident near Kingsville, Tex., on Sept. 17, 1918. He was interred in Hartford, Conn., Sept. 21, 1918.

Married, Oct. 13, 1917, Marjorie Stafford Root; one child, Mary; born July 22, 1918.

*RALPH SANGER

Captain, U.S.N., A.S., C.O. Ferry Pilots, Orly Field, France

Killed in airplane accident, Aug. 29, 1918

Son of William Thompson and Ellen (Horswell) Sanger, of New York City; was born at Cambridge, Mass., May 31, 1882. He was educated at St. Mark's School, Southboro, Mass., and at Harvard College, A.B. 1904. He rowed on the Harvard freshman crew and on the Harvard four-oared crew.

He attended the Officers' Training Camp at Plattsburg in Aug., 1917, graduating with a commission as Capt. of Infantry, about Nov. 27, 1917. He transferred to the Aviation Service and went first to Fort Sill, Okla., then to Austin, Tex., for eight weeks' training in machine-gunnery and wireless telegraphy. He continued his instruction in flying at Hazlehurst Field, Mineola, N.Y., beginning in April, 1918. He passed all tests and received his wings in July, when he received overseas orders, and sailed for France. He was given command of 250 officers, known as ferry pilots, at Orly Field, France, on Aug. 20. He was killed in an aerial accident on Aug. 29, 1918, and was buried at Suresnes, France.

The officer in charge of the Transfer Section, who had been in very close touch with Capt. Sanger from the time he came to take charge of the Transfer Pilots, wrote of him:

> I enjoyed my work with him, and for him, so much. To work under him was excellent training. He insisted that everything should be exactly right, and his attitude towards us was always such that no one wanted to fall short of the standard. . . . I thought perhaps I might tell you how much I miss him and how much the other pilots feel his loss.

Married, Nov. 16, 1904, Virginia Osborn.

*ARTHUR MAXWELL PARSONS

SECOND LIEUTENANT, A.S.A., U.S.A.

Killed in airplane accident, July 3, 1918

SON of Charles M. and Alice M. (Call) Parsons; was born at Gloucester, Mass., Dec. 11, 1895. He was educated in the public schools of Gloucester and at the Mass. Institute of Technology. He was a member of Theta Chi Fraternity at M.I.T. He played baseball and football at Gloucester High, and won his letters. At M.I.T. he won his numerals in wrestling, and was on the football team. He was Captain of the High School Cadets in his senior year, and 1st Lieut. in the M.I.T. Regiment. After graduation, and before the war, he practised civil engineering, and had experience in planning and building roads with the Mass. Highway Commission. In 1917 he worked five months for the West Virginia Railroad, laying tracks in the coal mountains.

He enlisted at Boston, on Nov. 10, 1917, and trained six weeks at M.I.T. and two weeks at Cornell University. From there he went to Dallas, Tex., and was among 50 men chosen to train with the Royal Flying Corps. In April, 1918, he was commissioned 2d Lieut., and was transferred to Hicks, Tex., where he served as Instructor in the Gunnery School. On July 2, 1918, he met with an accident while going for help for a fellow aviator, which resulted in his death on the following day. He was buried in Gloucester.

Lieut. Parsons had a narrow escape from accident on his altitude test, when his motor stopped and he came down 8000 feet, but he escaped without injury. He never had an accident with the cadets he was called to instruct. He had 150 hours of solo flying to his credit.

*RAYMOND B. MESSER

First Lieutenant, A.S.A., U.S.A.

Killed in airplane accident, Feb. 20, 1919

Son of Bradley A. and Hattie (Boden) Messer, of Lowell, Mass.; was born in Lowell, Sept. 12, 1894. He graduated from the Lowell High School, where he made a record as long-distance runner, and was manager of the baseball team in 1913. He attended the Lowell Textile School for three years.

He enlisted as mounted orderly in the 6th Mass. Regiment, on March 30, 1917, at Lowell, and was chosen to attend the Officers' Training Camp at Plattsburg. There he volunteered for Aviation Service, and was sent to the Ground School, M.I.T. When he had completed a six weeks' course, he was transferred to Mineola, N.Y. He was commissioned 1st Lieut. in Sept. 1917.

He went overseas, Nov. 13, 1917, and trained at Issoudun, France, graduating there in Feb., 1918. He was subsequently ordered to several other training-fields as an instructor. On July 13, 1918, he was sent into the zone of advance. He hoped to get to the front, but was stationed at Châtillon-sur-Seine as instructor and tester of planes. He was killed in an airplane collision there on Feb. 20, 1919, and was buried at Châtillon-sur-Seine on Feb. 22, 1919.

Lieut. Messer's superior officer wrote concerning his death:

> Raymond joined us as a pilot shortly after the Second Corps Aeronautical School was organized at Châtillon-sur-Seine. I was in charge of the flying at that school from its organization. It did not take many days to find what a really valuable man your son was, and he was at once put to work as an instructor in Sopwith and Bréguet planes, in addition to his duties as a staff pilot. He was a skilful pilot; his judgment was good; and his attitude toward his equals and superiors was one of unvaried courtesy. He was extremely popular, and to quote one of the old officers, "No accident ever hit the fellows quite so hard as Messer's death." Like the rest of us, he found it a source of great regret, not being able to get to the front. But the training of observers was so important that he could not be spared. If ever a man served his country well, it was Messer.

*EUGENE DORR MORSE

SECOND LIEUTENANT, A.S.A., U.S.A.

Killed in airplane accident, Nov. 6, 1918

SON of Fitz Albert and Helen D. (Cotting) Morse; was born in Brookline, Mass., Dec. 7, 1895. He was educated at the Country Day School, Boston; and at Harvard College, class of 1919. At school he played baseball and football, and was captain of the football team in 1914. At college he was assistant manager of his freshman baseball team, and 2d assistant manager of the Harvard, 1917, hockey team.

He left college in his sophomore year to enlist, on Oct. 23, 1917, at Boston. He received his ground training at M.I.T. and Cornell University, graduating on Jan. 26, 1918, and was assigned to Ellington Field, Houston, Tex., for flying instruction. He passed his reserve military aviator test on May 2, and was commissioned 2d Lieut. in the Air Service on that date. He was then assigned for advanced training in reconnaissance successively to Camp Dick, Dallas, Tex.; Post Field, Fort Sill, Okla.; and Taliaferro Field, Hicks, Tex. On Aug. 13, 1918, he embarked for duty overseas, arriving in France on Sept. 7, 1918. There was a great demand for bombers; and Lieut. Morse was assigned to the 7th Aviation Instruction Centre, near Clermont-Ferrand, for instruction in that branch. On completing the course in bombing he was detailed as instructor in flying, and was on such active duty when he was killed in an airplane accident, Nov. 6, 1918, at Clermont-Ferrand. He was buried in the U.S. Military Cemetery of that town.

According to proceedings of the Board of Officers convened to investigate the accident which caused Lieut. Morse's death, he was flying with an observer doing aerial gunnery practice at about 500 feet altitude, when the machine became in some way disabled and fell to the ground. Lieut. Morse was killed and the observer was slightly injured. In the findings of the investigation Lieut. Morse was not only exonerated from all blame, but was highly commended by his superior officer, who spoke of him as a good pilot and a man of ability and good judgment.

*HARRY HUBBARD METCALF

SECOND LIEUTENANT, A.S.A., U.S.A.

Died of pneumonia, Oct. 13, 1918

SON of Walter C. and Jessie F. (Willson) Metcalf; was born at Southboro, Mass., July 4, 1894. He prepared for college at Exeter, and William Nolen's, Cambridge, and was a member of the class of 1917, at Harvard College. In the spring of 1915, he entered the American Ambulance Service in France, and was one of the first to volunteer to drive at the front; his section was twice mentioned in the orders of the day at Pont-à-Mousson. He was a member of the Harvard Gun Club and one of the best intercollegiate shots. When the Harvard Flying Corps was organized by Frazier Curtis, in 1916, he was made temporary Flight Captain. He was one of the first ten men sent to the Harvard Flying School at Buffalo, in 1916, and the first to qualify there for his pilot's license, which he received from the Aero Club of America, Aug. 30, 1916.

On Nov. 19, 1916, he offered his services to his country, having previously been a member of Battery A, M.V.M., and was sent to Miami, Fla., in March, 1917. He was ordered to the School of Military Aeronautics, M.I.T., Cambridge, Nov. 2, 1917 (graduating Jan., 1918), and to Princeton University, Jan. 7, 1918, being transferred to Park Field, Memphis, Tenn., Jan. 14, 1918.

He was commissioned 2d Lieut. March 17, 1918, and was kept at Park Field as officer in charge of formation flying. He was twice recommended for promotion, by Major Jernegan and Col. Mc.Chord.

On Oct. 13, 1918, he succumbed to pneumonia at Park Field, Memphis, and was buried from his home at Westboro, Mass., with military honors. The long-wished-for overseas orders came to him after he was taken ill.

In a letter to Lieut. Metcalf's family, Frazier Curtis wrote:

> What he did for army flying can only be realized by the few of us who know that in March, 1916, we had only 24 army flyers qualified for the Western Front, and that the Harvard Flying Corps was the first successful attempt to get college men interested in the flying game.

Married, Jan. 1, 1918, Helen T. B. Williams, of Pasadena, Cal.

Brother in Service —

Walter W. Metcalf, Lieut.-Col., 305th Infantry, A.E.F.

*ROLAND JOHN WINTERTON

Second Lieutenant, A.S.A., U.S.A., Second Provisional Training Squadron

Killed in airplane accident, April 16, 1918

Son of Roland B. and Catherine M. (O'Brien) Winterton; was born in South Boston, Mass., May 7, 1889. He attended the South Boston High School, where he was prominent in athletics. He was devoted to yachting, and was librarian and an active member of the South Boston Yacht Club. He left his business as civil engineer and surveyor to enlist at the 1st Plattsburg Camp, May 7, 1917. Having been assigned to the Air Service, he was sent to the U.S.A. Aeronautical School, M.I.T., in Oct., 1917. On Dec. 19 he was transferred to Ellington Field, Houston, Tex., attached to the 1st Prov. Training Squadron, and later to the 2d Squadron. On March 25 he was commissioned 2d Lieut., A.S.

On April 16, 1918, while acting as pilot of an airplane in which he and Cadet Jones of Worcester had been doing camera work near Webster, Tex., both aviators were killed at Ellington Field in an unexplained tail-spin, falling about 2000 feet to the ground. Lieut. Winterton was instantly killed; Cadet Jones lived about an hour. It is believed that the accident was due to a faulty engine.

The following extract is from a letter from his friends and brother officers to the mother of Lieut. Winterton:

> Those who have known Roland and lived with him during his period of training wish to express their deepest sympathies to his mother in her sorrow. We knew him to be a gentleman and a soldier, as well as a stanch and patriotic citizen of our country, the United States of America. His name will long remain in our hearts, acting as an incentive, and giving us strength to help us through this conflict. We feel that there is no more beautiful passage from this earth than in the service of our country, for the cause of democracy. These words can but slightly express the feeling of loss we hold in our hearts.

A Resolution offered by the South Boston Yacht Club reads:

> He answered the nation's call and with characteristic courage chose the Aviation Service. A thorough yachtsman, he was always willing and ready to lend a hand; and the remaining men of the Club bear testimony to his sterling worth as a sailor and as a man.

US

*FORREST DEAN JONES

Cadet, Fifth Aero Squadron

Killed in airplane accident, April 16, 1918

Son of William H. and Gertrude E. (Dudley) Jones, of Worcester, Mass.; was born in Nashua, N.H., Sept. 23, 1895. He was educated in the public schools of Worcester, Mass., and at Amherst Agricultural College. He was a member of the South High School crew, which won a number of races at Lake Quinsigamond. Before enlisting he did war garden work, farming alone a large garden in Millbury.

He enlisted at Boston, in Oct., 1918, and was sent first to M.I.T. Ground School for a few weeks, then to Cornell University, from Jan. 1 to March 2, 1918. He was then ordered to Ellington Field, Houston, Tex., attached to the 5th Cadet Aero Squadron.

On April 16, 1918, he was killed in an aeroplane accident at Ellington Field, and was buried in Lebanon, N.H. He was to have received his commission after this last flight, in which he and Lieut. Roland Winterton met their death. The two New Englanders, Cadet Jones and his pilot, Lieut. Winterton of South Boston, had just finished their daily lesson or "stunt," and were preparing to come down, when it was noticed that they were in a tail-spin; whether intentionally or not will never be known. They were unable to recover, and dashed about 2000 feet to the ground. Winterton was instantly killed, and Jones lived about an hour. There were several other accidents at the Field the same day, all of which were believed to have been due to faulty engines. Lieut. Jones had always been deeply interested in Aviation, and had hoped to engage in the Aerial Mail Service after the war.

Brother in Service —

Leon D. Jones, Corporal, Co. C, 104th Infantry.

Brother-in-law in Service —

Leroy W. Gardiner, Corporal, Co. C. 104th Infantry. Died from wounds received in action, July 7, 1918.

*ROBERT JAMES BARRON

CADET, A.S., U.S.A.

Died in Service, trying to rescue drowning comrades

SON of James T. and Elizabeth (Nixon) Barron; was born in Portland, Ore., March 22, 1896. He was educated in the Portland public schools, Volkmann's School, Boston, and the Boston University College of Business Administration. At the time of his enlistment, he was by occupation a salmon-packer, vice-president of the Thlinket Packing Co., and Nooksack Packing Co., of Portland, Ore. He was a trained athlete, and when examined for the Aviation Service, at Portland Ore., he was pronounced the finest specimen of physical manhood ever seen by the examiner.

He enlisted at Boston, June 3, 1917, as cadet in the Aviation Service. He entered at once the Ground School, M.I.T., and finishing his course there was transferred to the Aviation Field at Essington, Pa.

On Aug. 22, 1917, Cadet Barron met his death by drowning, in an attempt to rescue two cadets of his class precipitated into the Delaware River by an accident to their hydroplane. He swam to their assistance, but his strength proved unequal to battle with the strong current and rough waters and he was drowned before reaching them. By order of the War Department he was accorded a military funeral of an officer of rank; and also by order of the War Department the Aviation Field at Fort Worth, Tex., formerly known as "Everman Field," was renamed "Barron Field," in his honor. The highest peak on Mansfield Peninsula, off southeastern Alaska, 4000 feet high, has also been named Mount Robert Barron by our Government to commemorate the Aviator who gave his life for his friends. Personal letters were received by the family of Cadet Barron, from President Wilson, Secretary Baker, Senator Chamberlain, and others, praising his heroic act. He was buried at Mount Calvary Cemetery, Portland, Ore.

Letter from President Wilson:

THE WHITE HOUSE
WASHINGTON

12 *December*, 1917

MY DEAR FRIENDS:

May I not send you a word of very heartfelt sympathy? The death of your son in an heroic effort to save two of his comrades from drowning has

excited my sympathy not only, but my very profound admiration. I hope that your grief will be tempered in some degree at least by a knowledge of the peculiar distinction with which your son died.

Cordially and sincerely yours

(*Sgd*) WOODROW WILSON

Cadet Barron's grandfather, Robert Nixon, served in the Civil War, and met his death also by drowning, on a transport *en route* from the South to New York.

*HOWARD B. HULL

SECOND LIEUTENANT, A.S., U.S.A., GUNNERY OFFICER
ELLINGTON FIELD

Killed in airplane accident, Sept. 8, 1918

SON of Mr. and Mrs. Charles N. Hull, of Bridgeport, Conn.; was born Jan. 4, 1895. He was educated in the Boston public schools; at the Roxbury High School, 1912; and at Harvard College, A.B. 1916. He attended the 1st Plattsburg Training Camp, from May to Aug., 1917, and was commissioned 2d Lieut. Aug. 14, 1917. From Aug. 27 to Sept. 1, 1917, he was stationed at Camp Devens, Mass. He was attached to the Royal Flying Corps for special duty at Camp Borden, Ontario, Canada, from Sept. 1 to Oct., 1917. He was made Gunnery Officer of the 17th U.S. Aero Squadron, and stationed at Fort Worth, Tex., from Oct. 12 to Nov. 12, 1917.

Upon completion of the course at Ellington Field, Tex., he was appointed Gunnery Officer in that Aviation School, where he remained until Aug. 28, 1918, when he was transferred to Selfridge Field, Mt. Clemens, Mich., for a three weeks' specialization in gunnery, as a fighting observer in a pursuit plane, the final phase of that important work.

On Sept. 8, 1918, Lieut. Hull met his death as the result of a collision at 8.50 A.M. between two planes in mid-air, at the height of 2000 feet, in "combat practice."

*FREDERIC PERCIVAL CLEMENT, Jr.

First Lieutenant, A.S.A., U.S.A.

Killed in airplane accident, July 4, 1918

Son of Frederic P. and Maud (Morrison) Clement; was born at Elizabeth, N.J., March 20, 1895. He attended the Watertown, N.Y., public schools, and graduated from the Morristown School, N.J., where he won the highest scholarship prize each year; he obtained more scholarship prizes than any other boy in the school (Greek, Latin, French, History, and English) and played on the football and track teams.

He graduated from Harvard College in 1916; while there he was assistant manager of the Freshman track team, manager of the 'Varsity track team, and a member of the executive committee I.C.A.A.A.A.; he belonged to the Institute of 1770, the Hasty Pudding Club, the Delphic Club, and the Signet Society.

He spent one year at the Harvard Law School, leaving in May, 1917, to enlist in the U.S. Service. He attended the 1st Officers' Training Camp at Plattsburg, and volunteered on the first call for aviators, and on June 19, 1917, entered the M.I.T. Ground School. From there he went to Mineola, N.Y., and was made a Reserve Military Aviator Sept. 1, 1917. On Sept. 18 he was transferred to Kelly Field, San Antonio, Tex., and on Oct. 5 commissioned 1st Lieut. in the Aviation Section of the Signal Reserve Corps; he went to Fort Sill, Okla., in Oct. as instructor in training observers, and in Nov. was ordered into the 4th Aero Squadron, scheduled for overseas duty; these orders were changed and he was stationed at Fort Dick, Dallas, Tex., where he was instrumental in getting a flying section started, and where he was the head of the court-martial department; he made out a series of lectures covering 150 cases. In April, 1918, he was sent to Taliaferro Field, Hicks, Tex., where he was considered the best flyer.

On July 4, 1918, Lieut. Clement was in charge of the exhibition flying at the Fair Grounds, Camp Dick; he had been thrilling his audience of 20,000 persons with daring aerial manœuvres, when his plane suddenly went into a tail-spin and crashed to the earth. Lieut. Clement was hurried to the Camp Dick Hospital, but died before reaching there; his companion, Cadet Arnold Hald, was not seriously injured.

Shortly before his death Lieut. Clement established a new altitude record for Dallas, when he attained a height of 16,700 feet.

At the time of his death he was flying in a model J.N. 4–H Curtiss plane decorated with the Iron Cross to represent a German scout plane. With several other planes he appeared in battle formation dropping imaginary bombs. Lieut. Clement was playing the part of the German scout plane attempting an escape, when the accident occurred.

He was buried with military honors from Trinity Church, Rutland, Vt., and interred in the family lot there, at Evergreen Cemetery.

Lieut. Henri Le Maître, the famous French Ace, was present at the exhibition of flying when Lieut. Clement met his death. He expressed himself as amazed at the work of the Camp Dick flyers. Never, he said, in all his experience, both at the front and in America, had he seen such flying. He spoke especially of the daring and skilful work of Lieut. Clement.

Brother in Service —

Roger C. Clement, Harvard Regiment 1916–17, commissioned 1st Lieut. Nov. 27, 1917, promoted to Capt. Aug., 1918, at Camp Devens.

GEORGE H. TRIDER, Jr.

Second Lieutenant, A.S.A., U.S.A.

Son of George H. and Hannah A. (Ziegler) Trider; was born in Waltham, Mass., Sept. 13, 1890. He was educated in the Waltham public schools and at Massachusetts Agricultural College.

He enlisted Sept. 27, 1917, at Cambridge, Mass., and trained first at M.I.T. Ground School, from Dec. 1, 1917, to Jan. 6, 1918; then he was transferred to Princeton University, U.S.S.M.A., where he graduated on Feb. 2, 1918. He was attached to the Cadet Detachment, 13th Squadron, at Camp Dick, Dallas, Tex., from March 2 to March 13, and had flying training at Taliaferro Field, Fort Worth, Tex., from March 13 to June 28, 1918. He was commissioned 2d Lieut. June 21, 1918, with brevet grade, R.M.A. He was ordered to Flying Officers' Detachment, Camp Dick, from June 28 to July 25; and acted as machine-gun instructor, at Wilbur Wright Field, Fairfield, O., from July 27 to Aug. 24, 1918.

Receiving overseas orders, Lieut. Trider sailed from Hoboken on Aug. 30, 1918, landing in Brest on Sept. 12. He trained as a pursuit pilot at the 3d Aviation Instruction Centre, Issoudun, from Sept. 22 to Oct. 12, when he was attached to the American Aviation Acceptance Park at Orly, until Jan. 20, 1919, ferrying airplanes to the front and to other points.

Lieut. Trider had various narrow escapes from death, even though he saw no actual combat. On Oct. 8, 1918, he wrecked a Nieuport and was injured. During a bombing-raid at Nancy the auto in which Lieut. Trider and thirteen other aviators were riding was struck and rolled down an embankment in the dark. Only one aviator, Lieut. Richard Banks, was killed, the others having a marvellous escape.

Lieut. Trider was honorably discharged at Camp Dix, N.J., on Feb. 23, 1919.

WILLIAM BARTLETT BACON

First Lieutenant, A.S., U.S.A., Instructor, Aerial Gunnery School, Second A.I.C., Tours, France

Son of William and Karolen (Bartlett) Bacon of Brookline, Mass.; was born in Brookline, March 26, 1897. He was educated at the Country Day School, Newton, Mass., and entered Harvard College with the class of 1919. He graduated from the Curtiss Aviation School, Buffalo, N.Y., in 1916.

He enlisted in the Air Service in Boston on May 18, 1917, and was a member of the first class graduated from the Ground School, M.I.T. On July 15, 1917, before completing the course, Bacon received overseas orders and sailed for France on July 23, 1917. He had his preliminary training on Caudrons at the French Aviation School at Tours, where he remained from Aug. 16 to Sept. 28, 1917. He then received instruction on Nieuport 23-metre and 18-metre machines, at the French School, Avord, from Sept. 29 to Oct. 21, 1917. From Oct. 22, 1917, to Jan. 8, 1918, he was at the 3d Aviation Instruction Centre at Issoudun, where he was trained in formation flying, acrobatics, and cross-country flying, on 15-metre Nieuports. He was then transferred to the French School at Cazaux for work in aerial gunnery (Lewis gun), where he remained until the end of Jan. He was subsequently ordered to Hythe, Kent, Eng., where he spent from Feb. 9 to Feb. 23 at the R.F.C. School in a course in aerial gunnery (Vickers gun). After graduating from another course in aerial gunnery (Vickers gun), this time at the R.F.C. School, Turnberry, Ayrshire, Scotland (March 1–12, 1918), he was assigned as Instructor to the Aerial Gunnery School, 2d Aviation Instruction Centre, at Tours, in charge of range and aerial practice, from March 25 to Sept. 15, 1918; and from Sept. 15 to Nov. 11, 1918, was Staff Chasse Pilote on camera-gun practice.

He was commissioned 1st Lieut. on Nov. 20, 1917. He returned to the U.S. on March 25, 1919, and was honorably discharged from the Service on May 14, 1919.

JOHN WHITIN LASELL

Second Lieutenant, A.S.A., U.S.A., Three Hundred Fifty-Fourth Aero Squadron, Sixth Observation Group

Son of Josiah M. and Mary F. (Krum) Lasell, was born in Whitinsville, Mass., Nov. 30, 1897. He was educated at the Hotchkiss School, Conn., and at Williams College. At Hotchkiss he played on the football team, and at Williams played on the freshman football team. In the summer of 1916 he attended the Officers' Training Camp at Plattsburg.

He enlisted at Minneola, Fla., on Aug. 22, 1917. He trained at M.I.T. Ground School, Sept. 29, 1917, to Nov. 24, 1917; and at Love Field, Dallas, Tex., from Nov. 28, 1917, to Feb. 23, 1918. He was commissioned 2d Lieut. Feb. 16, 1918, and trained at Camp Dick, Dallas, Tex., Feb. 23 to March 18; Post Field, Fort Sill, Okla., March 18 to April 15, 1918; Camp Dick, April 15 to June 29; Taliaferro Field, Fort Worth, Tex., June 29 to July 31.

Lieut. Lasell sailed overseas on Aug. 9, 1918, and was stationed at St.-Maixent, France, from Aug. 22 to Sept. 25, 1918; at Issoudun, 3d Aviation Instruction Centre, Sept. 27 to Oct. 16; with the 354th Squadron, Oct. 20 to Nov. 26, at Antreville. He was then ordered to Saizerais, in the Marbache sector. He was stationed at Tours, 2d A.I.C. from Nov. 28 to Dec. 21; and at Bordeaux, Dec. 21 to 25. He sailed for home on Dec. 26, 1918, arriving in the U.S. on Jan. 7. He was honorably discharged at the U.S. Army General Hospital No. 10, Boston, Mass., on Feb. 20, 1919.

Brother in Service —

Josiah Lasell, 2d, Captain, C. O. 302d Hq. Co., 16th Division.

*FREDERICK ARTHUR KEEP

Second Lieutenant, A.S.A., U.S.A., Twenty-Eighth Aero Squadron; Seventy-Eighth Aero Squadron

Killed in airplane accident, May 6, 1918

Son of Frederick Heber and Alice (Leavitt) Keep, of Milton, Mass.; was born at Wollaston, Mass., Nov. 23, 1892. He was educated at Milton public schools, Milton Academy, and Harvard College, class of 1915.

He was a cadet in the Harvard R.O.T.C., 1916 and 1917. He attended Plattsburg Training Camp from May 13, 1917; was commissioned 2d Lieut., I.O.R.C., Aug. 15, 1917, and ordered to active duty at Camp Devens on Aug. 28, 1917. From here in a few days he was ordered to the Royal Flying Corps, Camp Borden, Ont., then to the University of Toronto for courses in military aeronautics. Leaving there for Fort Worth, Tex., on Nov. 8, 1917, he became attached to the 28th Aero Squadron, Taliaferro Field, Fort Hicks, Tex. He was injured in an airplane accident, Nov. 22, 1917, when his leg was fractured; and did not report for duty until about March 20, 1918. He was then attached to the 78th Aero Squadron. He was again injured in an airplane accident, at Fort Worth, Tex., on May 3, 1918, when his machine got into a tail-spin and crashed. He died on May 6, as a result of his fall, at Fort Worth, Tex. He was buried at Milton, Mass.

BRADFORD BROOKS LOCKE

First Lieutenant, A.S.A., U.S.A., Third Aviation Instruction Centre, Issoudun, France

Son of Warren A. and Madeline (Weedman) Locke, of Cambridge, Mass.; was born in Cambridge on Oct. 14, 1891. He attended the Cambridge Latin School, and graduated from Harvard College in 1913. At Harvard he played on the freshman hockey team in 1910, and on the 'Varsity soccer team in 1911, 1912, and 1913.

Prior to the declaration of war he was 2d Lieut. in the 1st Armored Motor Battery, in the National Guard of New York. He enlisted in the Air Service at Mineola, N.Y., July 19, 1917, and was assigned to the Cornell Ground School, Ithaca, N.Y., where he remained from Aug. 20 to Oct. 13. On Oct. 25 he sailed overseas as Aviation Cadet.

He was trained at the 3d Aviation Instruction Centre, Issoudun, France, from Nov. 17 to March 21. He was commissioned 1st Lieut. on May 18, 1918, and was on the staff at Issoudun.

Lieut. Locke was honorably discharged from the Service at Mitchel Field, Garden City, N.Y., on April 20, 1919.

Brother in Service —

Arthur W. Locke, A.R.C., Camp Devens, Ayer, Mass.

*JOHN WATLING BRADLEY

SECOND LIEUTENANT, INSTRUCTOR, A.S., U.S.A.

Killed in airplane accident, July 4, 1918

SON of John and Selina A. (Watling) Bradley, of Groton, Mass.; was born at Quincy, Mass., Dec. 13, 1890. He was educated at the Groton High School and at the Mass. Agricultural College, Amherst, graduating in 1914, with the degree of B.S. He received a Government appointment and became attached to the Bureau of Entomology at Washington, working at the laboratory at Melrose Highlands until his enlistment.

He enlisted Nov. 27, 1917, and went to the Ground School, M.I.T., for training; was transferred to Princeton, N.J., in Dec., and from there was sent to Camp Dick, Dallas, Tex. He was again transferred to Wilbur Wright Field, Dayton, O., and was there commissioned 2d Lieut. on June 17, 1918. He was killed in a fall on July 4, 1918, while instructing cadets at Wilbur Wright Field.

Lieut. Bradley's Commander wrote to his mother that Bradley was one of the most promising aviators at the Field, and that they had expected a brilliant career for him.

Brother in Service —

William G. Bradley, 2d Lieut., A.S., U.S.A.

US

WILLIAM GEORGE BRADLEY

SECOND LIEUTENANT, A.S., U.S.A.

SON of John and Selina A. (Watling) Bradley; was born at Quincy, Mass., Aug. 11, 1892. He was educated at the Groton High School and Mass. Agricultural College, Amherst.

He enlisted at the Ground School, M.I.T., in Sept., 1917, and was trained there, at Princeton, N.J., Camp Dick, Dallas, Tex., at the Flying School, Kelly Field, San Antonio, Tex., and at Brooks Field, San Antonio, Tex. Soon after reaching Kelly Field, Bradley was flying with his instructor who was driving the ship, when it fell, killing the instructor and injuring Bradley. In Nov., 1918, he was commissioned 2d Lieut., receiving Instructor's rating on Jan. 6, 1919. At the closing of Brooks Field he was honorably discharged, Jan. 7, 1919.

Brother in Service —

Lieut. John Watling Bradley, Instructor in Aviation; killed in accident on July 4, 1918.

JOHN WINTHROP EDWARDS

FIRST LIEUTENANT, A.S.A., U.S.A.

SON of John Couper and Elizabeth (Morrill) Edwards, of Marion, Mass.; was born in Brookline, Mass., Nov. 18, 1896. He was educated at the Noble and Greenough School; Milton Academy, 1914; and at Harvard College, 1918.

He enlisted in June, 1917, at Boston, and trained at the M.I.T. Ground School, and at Mineola, N.Y. He sailed for France in Oct., after receiving his commission as 1st Lieut., A.S., U.S.A., and continued his training at the French and U.S. Aviation Schools in France, notably at Issoudun. Lieut. Edwards spent the winter of 1917–18 on the Brittany coast. In the summer of 1918 he trained student officers from the U.S. at Issoudun, in the use of de Haviland machines.

After the Armistice, Lieut. Edwards was chosen special courier for Gen. Patrick, Chief of the U.S. Air Service. His official duty was to take by airplane from Tours to Paris the completed MS. of the history of the American Air Service in France. He received a special recommendation for this courier work from Col. Hiram Bingham, his Commanding Officer; special commendation also for his work in training student officers. He was honorably discharged on Feb. 20, 1919, at Paris.

Married, Nov. 30, 1918, Marcelle Moch, of France.

Brother in Service —

B. Allison Edwards, Capt. U.S.A., 302 F.A., A.E.F.

Grandfather in Service —

Lewis Allison Edwards, M.D., Col., U.S.A.

JOE GARNER ESTILL, Jr.

First Lieutenant, A.S.A., U.S.A.

Son of Joe Garner and Mary (North) Estill; was born in Lakeville, Conn., May 6, 1894. He attended the New Haven public schools, graduated from Hotchkiss School, and Yale Scientific School. He holds the record of Hotchkiss School for half-mile, 2′5″.

He enlisted in Boston on May 21, 1917, and trained at M.I.T. Ground School; had flying training at Mineola, N.Y., and was stationed at Kelly Field, San Antonio, Tex., for a short time. On Oct. 3, 1917, he was commissioned 1st Lieut. in Aviation Section, Signal Service.

Lieut. Estill returned to Mineola, and was ordered overseas on Oct. 30, 1917. He reported at Issoudun, at the 3d Aviation Instruction Centre; and was sent later to Châteauroux to fly with the French; thence to Coëtquidan, for pilot, at the American Artillery Observation School for some months. He then went back to Issoudun and finished his training in all forms of flying — scout flying, aerial gunnery, acrobacy, bombing.

He was made assistant tester of planes at Issoudun, after finishing training at Cazaux. Two weeks later he was made tester of planes at St.-Jean de Monts, Vendée. After a few weeks there he had the misfortune to slip in alighting from his plane, and the propeller almost completely severed his left arm above the elbow. He was rushed to Base Hospital 34, Nantes, and his arm was saved.

Brothers in Service —

Wallace Estill, 2d Lieut. F.A.C.O. T.S., Camp Zachary Taylor.
Gordon North Estill, member S.A.T.C., at Yale.

STERLING RUSSELL CHATFIELD

First Lieutenant, A.S.A., U.S.A., Two Hundred Second Squadron (Italian)

Son of Minotte Estes and Stella Stowe (Russell) Chatfield; was born in New Haven, Conn., Sept. 14, 1891. He attended the Taft and Cheshire Schools, and graduated from the Sheffield Scientific School, Yale, in 1915. He was on the football and hockey teams at Taft and Cheshire Schools, and holds the half-mile track record at Taft.

On Dec. 15, 1915, he enlisted in Co. F (New Haven Grays), 2d Regiment, Conn. Infantry. He was on duty at the Mexican Border from June 20 to Nov. 8, 1916, and was appointed Corporal, Feb. 8, 1917. He was sent as one of 25 non-commissioned officers to the 1st R.O.T.C. at Plattsburg, May 20, 1917. He was honorably discharged as a Corporal from U.S. Army on Aug. 16, 1917, by reason of enlistment in S.E.R.C., Aug. 10, 1917. About July 20, Chatfield was sent as Acting Sergeant in charge of 15 men, to U.S. Ground School, M.I.T., and during the school term he was Acting Sergeant of the class, graduating as a cadet on Sept. 29, 1917. He was honorably discharged as Corporal from Nat. Guard of U.S. on Aug. 5, 1917, when the regiment entered Federal Service.

He sailed for France on Oct. 17, 1917, and trained at Issoudun until Feb. 8, 1918, when he was transferred to Campo Avest, Aviation Camp, at Foggia, Italy. Having finished his preliminary training at Foggia, he received his *brevetto* on June 8, 1918, and was made a member of the Aero Club d' Italia. He was transferred to Campo Sud, Foggia, on June 9.

On June 25, 1918, he was commissioned 1st Lieut. Air Service (Aeronautics), of the National Army, and started instruction on Caproni machines. Lieut. Chatfield was later sent to Foggia Renantico, near the Italian front, as pilot bomber of a 600 h.p. Caproni biplane. He left for St.-Maixent, France, on Nov. 10, 1918.

On Dec. 16 he sailed from Bordeaux for America. He reported at Garden City, N.Y., and was honorably discharged on Jan. 8, 1919.

H. POTTER TRAINER

FIRST LIEUTENANT, A.S.A., U.S.A., EIGHTH AERO SQUADRON

SON of Harry Reeves and Celia E. (Potter) Trainer, of Brookline, Mass.; was born in Boston Dec. 8, 1891. He was educated in the Brookline public schools, the Stone School, Boston, and Harvard College, A.B. 1915. He was a member of the freshman hockey team; captain of the second hockey team in 1914 and 1915; a member of the Institute of 1770, D.K.E. Fraternity, Hasty Pudding Club, and Owl Club. He attended the Officers' Training Camp at Plattsburg, from July 12 to Aug. 8, 1916.

On April 16, 1917, he enlisted for four years, at Boston; reported at Mineola, N.Y., on April 23, and completed his R.M.A. tests on July 3. He was commissioned 1st Lieut. Aviation Section, S.O.R.C. July 18, 1917. On July 25, he was sent to Mt. Clemens, Mich., for further instruction. He was on active duty with flying status orders from Aug. 11, 1917. On Oct. 25, he was ordered overseas as Supply Officer attached to the 8th Aero Squadron. He sailed on Nov. 22, arriving in England on Dec. 8. He was immediately detached from the Squadron and attached to the Royal Flying Corps. The greater part of the next seven months he spent in three different hospitals with pleuro-pneumonia and mastoiditis. In Oct., 1918, being discharged as physically fit he resumed flying duties. At London Colney, Herts, Eng., he learned to fly SE 5. (combat) machines, and was on duty at that station as a scout pilot when the Armistice was signed. Lieut. Trainer was honorably discharged on Dec. 28, 1918, at Garden City, N.Y.

CHARLES LAKEMAN WARD

SECOND LIEUTENANT, A.S., U.S.A., STUDENT OFFICER
LOVE FIELD, DALLAS, TEXAS

SON of Charles W. and Mabel (Brace) Ward; was born in Brookline, Mass., Dec. 3, 1895. He was educated at the Browne and Nichols School, Cambridge, at Brookline High School, and at Harvard College, B.S. 1917. He was on his class football and soccer teams; and played on the Love Field football team, while in Service.

He attended the Officers' Training Camp at Plattsburg in 1916, and trained with Harvard R.O.T.C. in 1917. He enlisted at Boston in April, 1917, and attended the 1st Officers' Training Camp at Plattsburg from May to Aug., 1917. He was appointed to the 301st Mass. Infantry with the commission of 2d Lieut. on Aug. 15, 1917; and trained at Camp Devens, Mass., until March, 1918. He was stationed at Aviation Ground School, Austin, Tex., from March to May, 1918, detached from Service for instruction as a pilot. He attended Princeton Ground School in June, 1917; and Chanute Flying Field, Rantoul, Ill., from July to Oct., 1918. He was appointed Reserve Military Aviator in Oct., 1918, and transferred to Love Field, Dallas, Tex., where he spent Nov. and Dec., 1918.

Lieut. Ward was honorably discharged from the Army on Dec. 13, 1918, at Love Field, Dallas, Tex.

Grandfather in Service —
Captain Andrew Abbot Ward, U.S.N., Civil War.
Grandfather in Service —
Sergeant David Elwell Saunders, U.S.A., Civil War.

MARSHALL HEADLE

First Lieutenant, A.S.A., U.S.A., Second Aviation Instruction Centre

Son of Rev. Edwin Charles and Clarendo (Yeomans) Headle, of Bolton, Mass.; was born in Winthrop, Mass., March 21, 1893. He was educated at the Winthrop High School, and the Mass. Agricultural College, Amherst. He was one of the first in rank at college, though having to work his way through. He played baseball, and was the best shot in the rifle team.

He enlisted in Aviation at the beginning of the war, at Springfield, Mass., and was trained at M.I.T. Ground School. He sailed overseas and landed in France Sept. 17, 1917. He started flying under French instructors at Tours, and was trained with the Caudron plane, receiving his Reserve Military Aviation grade, in Feb., 1918, and the French brevet at the same time. For the next two months he took advanced flying on Nieuports, at Issoudun, in the 3d Aviation Instruction Centre, returning to Tours in March, 1918, when he began instruction in flying, and acted as staff pilot in the 2d Aviation Instruction Centre. From Aug., 1918, to March, 1919, he was Chef de Piste in the Observation Training Camp at Tours. He was then appointed instructor in the A.E.F. University, Beaune, France.

Brother in Service —

Herbert Wallace Headle, Corp., Co. E, 23d Engineers.

ROBERT WALKER HARWOOD

SECOND LIEUTENANT, A.S.A., U.S.A

SON of Herbert J. and Emilie Augusta (Green) Harwood; was born at Littleton, Mass., July 16, 1897. He was educated at Concord (Mass.) High School, and at Harvard College, class of 1920. At college he became a member of Delta Kappa Epsilon, Institute of 1770, Delta Upsilon, and was on the board of the *Harvard Crimson.* He was the holder of the Harvard interscholastic pole vault record, 12′ ⅝″, and was a member of the Harvard freshman and 'Varsity track teams. He attended the Plattsburg Camp in 1916, and trained with the Harvard R.O.T.C. in 1917.

He enlisted at Boston on Dec. 24, 1917. He attended the U.S. School of Military Aeronautics, Princeton, from Feb. 16 to April 13, 1918; was stationed in turn at Camp Dick, Dallas, Tex., April 22 to May 13, 1918; Scott Field, Belleville, Ill., May 15 to Sept. 26, 1918, and was commissioned 2d Lieut. A.S.A., on July 27, 1918. He was stationed at Park Field, Memphis, Tenn., Sept. 27, 1918, to Jan. 25, 1919. At Park Field, Lieut. Harwood was Officer in Charge of Formation Flying. He was honorably discharged on Jan. 25, 1919, at Park Field, to finish his course at Harvard College.

Brothers in Service —

Herbert E. Harwood, 1st Lieut., A.S. (M.A.)

Jonathan H. Harwood, Capt. 303d F. A. Eight months' service in France as Battalion Commander; commanded Officers' Artillery School at Camp Devens, Mass.

LOYAL R. SAFFORD

SECOND LIEUTENANT, A.S.A., U.S.A., THIRD AVIATION INSTRUCTION CENTRE, ISSOUDUN, FRANCE

SON of Charles R. and Drusilla A. (Robinson) Safford of Wollaston, Mass.; was born in Atlantic, Mass., on Oct. 4, 1897. He was educated at the Quincy (Mass.) High School; at Boston University, and at the Mass. Institute of Technology. In school and college he played baseball and basket-ball.

He enlisted in Boston on Aug. 29, 1917, and was assigned to the Ground School, M.I.T., on Nov. 17, 1917. He was later transferred to the Ground School at Princeton University, from which he graduated on Feb. 9, 1918. He continued his training at Camp Dick, Dallas, Tex., Feb. 12 to April 3, 1918, and at Kelly Field, San Antonio, Tex., April 4 to April 23. He was then sent to Hazelhurst Field, N.Y., attached to the 1st U.S. Coast Patrol. He received his commission as 2d Lieut. on June 4, 1918, and was ordered to Camp Dick, Dallas, Tex., on June 15, and from there to Wilbur Wright Field, Dayton, O. He was then transferred to Hoboken, N.J., for overseas service, and sailed Sept. 8, 1918.

On arriving at Brest, Sept. 20, Lieut. Safford was assigned to the 3d Aviation Instruction Centre at Issoudun, France, at which he remained until Jan. 8, 1919. He was ordered to Angers on Jan. 8, and to Brest on Feb. 3. He sailed for America on Feb. 8, arriving at Philadelphia on Feb. 21, 1919. Lieut. Safford was honorably discharged at Camp Dix, N.J., on Feb. 23, 1919.

Brother in Service —

Henry W. Safford, Corp. 301st Infantry, A.E.F.

RALPH MAURICE PHELPS

FIRST LIEUTENANT, A.S.A., U.S.A.

SON of Robert Wiley and Martha Gibson (Palmer) Phelps, of Gloucester, Mass.; was born in Clinton, Mass., April 11, 1892. He was educated in the public schools of Gloucester and at Dartmouth College, A.B. 1914. At college he was a member of the Mandolin and Glee Club, the Outing Club, and Kappa Sigma Fraternity. He later engaged in the automobile business.

On June 20, 1917, he enlisted in the Aviation Service, and was ordered to the M.I.T. Ground School, where he remained until Aug. 20, when he was sent to Flying School at Scott Field, Belleville, Ill. He left Belleville Nov. 20, 1917; was commissioned 1st Lieut. Dec., 1917, and reported to Mineola, N.Y., about Dec. 20. He received instruction there until Aug. 20, 1918, when he sailed overseas and was stationed at Sussex, Eng., at the Handley-Page Acceptance Park No. 1. There he acted in many capacities as Assistant Flying Adjutant, until the signing of the Armistice, when he assumed the duties of Adjutant, until the camp was dismantled. About Nov. 20 he went to London as liaison officer, and worked in conjunction with the British Flying Forces, until English Aviation affairs were settled, receiving permission from the Royal Air Force to wear the insignia of the Eagle and Crown, for services rendered. Lieut. Phelps was ordered to Paris about Jan. 20, 1919, as a liaison officer.

Married, Aug. 3, 1917, Harriet Hazeltine Gage, of Haverhill, Mass.; a son, Ralph M., Jr., born May 31, 1918.

*WILLIAM ST. AGNAN STEARNS

First Lieutenant, A.S.A., U.S.A., Seventh Aviation Instruction Centre, France

Killed in airplane accident, May 25, 1918

Son of Richard Sprague and Carrie (Gill) Stearns, of Jamaica Plain, Mass.; was born in Eastbourne, Eng., Sept. 8, 1895. He fitted for college at the Noble and Greenough School, and graduated from Harvard College in 1917, with a high record for scholarship. He was a member of the Institute, D.K.E., and Hasty Pudding Club; and was for two years captain of the Harvard rifle team. He attended the Plattsburg Camp in 1915.

He enlisted in May, 1917, from M.I.T., where he was in the first squadron of 25 to receive ground instruction. He was transferred to Mineola, N.Y., about July 10, 1917, passed his Reserve Military air test Aug. 11, 1917, and was sent to San Antonio, Tex., for a month of training. He sailed for France on Nov. 1, and continued his training at Issoudun. From there he went to the bombing school at Clermont-Ferrand. In Jan., 1918, he was commissioned 1st Lieut., and was made instructor at the 7th Aviation Instruction Centre, Clermont-Ferrand. He was acting as chief pilot and testing a machine, on May 25, 1918, when he fell, and was killed in the execution of his duty. With him was George M. Martin, who was also killed. He is buried at Clermont-Ferrand.

Capt. Walker M. Ellis, Officer in Charge of Training at Clermont-Ferrand, after stating that on account of the skill, judgment, and ability of Lieut. Stearns, he had retained him as instructor, wrote:

> Though he did n't like it, he accepted his assignment cheerfully and did splendidly as an instructor. . . . We soon grew to have absolute confidence in him. He was above all things reliable. He never did any spectacular flying, but every movement in the air was perfect, and he knew what he was doing every instant of the time. . . .
>
> There were two or three Fiats, which were ready for testing. . . . It seems that he had taken up one. . . . The immediate cause of the trouble was a vertical bank at about 2000 feet, during which the nose of the machine fell, which resulted in a tail-spin. . . . He was instantly killed. . . . No other accident ever did, or will, affect me as that one did. He was such a dear boy; and he represented the very best in young American manhood.

Brother in Service —

George Gill Stearns, 1st Canadian Reserve Battalion.

VOLNEY DALTON HURD

Second Lieutenant, A.S., U.S.A., Six Hundred Forty-Fourth Aero Squadron

Son of George W. and Jessie (Dalton) Hurd; was born in Boston, May 2, 1898. He was educated at the English High School, Boston, and had one year at Northeastern College.

He enlisted on Oct. 26, 1917, at Boston, and was trained at M.I.T. Ground School and Cornell University, later going to Gerstner Field, Lake Charles, La. He was commissioned 2d Lieut. on May 9, 1918, as pursuit pilot, and sailed overseas Sept. 17, 1918. He was attached to the 644th Squadron at Issoudun, France. On May 8, 1918, he fell 800 feet with his machine, completely wrecking it, but escaping with a few minor cuts and bruises. He was appointed one of the eight instructors in France of aerial fighting and tactics. When his school closed he became interested in furthering entertainments for those in Service and was attached to the Show Detail, taking a company of 25 enlisted men organized as a minstrel show, to all the camps and stations in France; he and two other officers comprising the orchestra. He had just reached the front when the Armistice was signed.

Citations

1. In accordance with instructions from Commanding Officer the following is submitted: 2d Lieut. Volney D. Hurd, A.S. On Nov. 11, 1918, Lieut. Hurd was detailed as Combat Instructor at Field No. 8. Despite his lack of previous experience as an instructor, his alertness and ability to fly soon made his work noticeable in its thoroughness. He displayed a willingness to work and a precision in his efforts that marked him as an exponent of the efficiency of the field. His careful analysis and correction of the faults of his pupils made them pilots of high standard.

(*Signed*) H. L. Wingate
Captain, A.S.

You would not have been selected to be a member of the teaching force of the largest and most important flying school in France if it had not been that you showed unusual ability as a pilot and reliability and trustworthiness as an officer. Your self-sacrifice and loyalty in training others to achieve brilliant victories merits the highest commendation.

(*Signed*) Hiram Bingham
Lt.-Col., A.S., Commanding

FREDERIC WYLLIS CALDWELL

SECOND LIEUTENANT, A.S.A., U.S.A., FORTY-EIGHTH AERO SQUADRON, FIRST PROVISIONAL WING

SON of Frederic Atherton and Sylvia (Woodin) Caldwell, of Kingston, R.I.; was born at Toledo, O., Sept. 22, 1892. He was educated at the Woonsocket (R.I.) public schools, and at Rhode Island State College, where he was on the basket-ball and track teams.

He enlisted in the Aviation Service at Cambridge, Mass., July 15, 1917. He graduated from the M.I.T. Ground School Nov. 17, and was ordered to Garden City, N.Y., for overseas training. He was transferred to the Flying School, Love Field, Dallas, Tex., Dec. 25, 1917, where he completed his course and was commissioned 2d Lieut. April 20, 1918. He was sent successively to Camp Dick, to Langley Field, Hampton, Va., and to Taliaferro Field, Fort Worth, Tex., where he was retained as instructor until Oct. 2, 1918, when he was again transferred to Garden City for overseas service. He was attached to the 48th Squadron, 1st Provisional Wing, at Mitchel Field, Garden City. Later he was transferred to Hazelhurst Field, Mineola, N.Y. He is a member of the Aero Club of America.

On Feb. 15, 1919, Lieut. Caldwell was sent to Ancon, Panama, for special flying work. He is still in Service.

Brother in Service —
Seth Atherton Caldwell, Ensign, U.S.N.

Grandfather in Service —
Charles Henry Bromedge, Line officer, U.S.N., in Civil War. Commanded gunboat *Itaska* at capture of New Orleans. Commodore in blockade squadron.

Great-grandfather in Service —
Charles Henry Caldwell, officer, U.S.N.; died at sea from wound received in Mexican War.

Great-great-grandfather in Service —
Charles Caldwell, Marine officer, U.S.N.

WALTER FREDERIC THOMAS

SECOND LIEUTENANT, A.S.A., U.S.A., STAFF PILOT
SECOND CORPS

SON of Mr. and Mrs. Frederic William Thomas; was born at Melrose, Mass., Dec. 28, 1888. He was educated at the Melrose High School, the Allen School, Newton, Mass., and at Dartmouth College, where he was a member of Theta Delta Chi Fraternity. Before the war he served in Co. L, 8th Regiment, M.V.M.

He joined the National Guard, U.S.A., on June 28, 1916, and served as Regiment Supply Sergeant of the 8th Regulars at Camp Cotton, Tex., on the Mexican Border; being honorably discharged in May, 1917. He enlisted in Aviation Service on May 14, 1917, at the 1st Plattsburg Officers' Training Camp, and attended first the M.I.T. Ground School, graduating Dec. 8, 1917. He received flying training at Park Field, Memphis, Tenn., and was there commissioned 2d Lieut. on March 22, 1918. He sailed for France on May 19, 1918; received Nieuport training at the 3d Aviation Instruction Centre, Issoudun, France; qualified as an observation pilot at the 2d Aviation Instruction Centre, Tours, France; and studied aerial gunnery at St.-Jean-des-Monts, Vendée, France. On Oct. 20, 1918, he was ordered to the Zone of Advance, and was assigned to 2d Corps Aeronautical School as staff pilot, at Châtillon-sur-Seine. At the time of the Armistice he was training observers in photographic missions, infantry liaison and artillery *réglage.* His was the last school in France to close after the Armistice; and Lieut. Thomas was still continuing his work there in Feb., 1919.

SEYMOUR SOULE

Flying Cadet, A.S., U.S.A.

Son of Allen P. and Harriet L. (Seymour) Soule, of Hingham, Mass.; was born in Malden, Mass., April 5, 1891. He was educated in the public schools of Hingham, and at Colby College, where he played on the 'Varsity football team. Previous to enlisting he served three years in Co. H, 2d Regiment, Maine Nat. Guard; two years in Battery A, 1st Regt. Mass. F.A., seeing Service on the Mexican Border in 1916.

He enlisted in Aviation on Oct. 23, 1917, at Boston, and was assigned to Princeton Ground School, Nov. 24, 1917. He graduated Feb. 2, 1918, and served as Squadron Commander for five weeks, when he was transferred to Camp Dick, Dallas, Tex., on Feb. 5, 1918. From there he was sent to Ellington Field, Houston, Tex., on March 8, 1918. On April 1, 1918, Cadet Soule received an injury from a collision in the air, while training at Ellington Field, which resulted in his physical disqualification for the Air Service. He was recommended for a commission on June 25, 1918; but was discharged on July 8, 1918.

Quoting from the Findings and Recommendation of the Headquarters Board, at Ellington Field, dated June 25, 1918:

> The Board is of the opinion that on account of the physical disqualifications of this cadet, he should be removed from flying status and discontinue his training as pilot. He is an excellent type of man, his record is absolutely clean at this School, and his services as a cadet in training for a commission have been satisfactory in every respect except physically, and inasmuch as he had had some 45 hours' training and is particularly acquainted with the Air Service, the Board recommends that he be considered as a candidate for a commission as Adjutant, or as a Supply Officer, and if this be not approved, it is recommended that he be discharged from the service of the United States.

Mr. Soule was assigned to duty as Inspector and Tester of Airplanes at Detroit Acceptance Park, by the Bureau of Aircraft Production, on Sept. 9, 1918. He resigned from this duty on Dec. 10, 1918.

Married, June 23, 1917, Eleanor Patterson.

HOWARD C. HOYT

SECOND LIEUTENANT, A.S., U.S.A

SON of George O. and Mary Etta (Cook) Hoyt; was born at Haverhill, Mass., Dec. 29, 1891. He was educated in the Haverhill Schools, at Deering High School, Portland, Me., and at Dartmouth College.

He enlisted at Boston on April 15, 1917, and attended the 1st Plattsburg Camp that spring and summer; and the S.M.A., M.I.T., Cambridge, from Oct. 10 to Dec. 1, 1917. He was successively trained at Rich Field, Waco, Tex., Dec. 7, 1917, to April 11, 1918; Camp Dick, Dallas, Tex., April 16 to May 10; Hoboken, N.J., May 16 to June 1; Camp Dick, Dallas, Tex., June 12 to June 29; Post Field, Fort Sill, Okla., June 29 to Aug. 3, 1918. He was commissioned 2d Lieut. on March 30, 1918. After finishing his course at Fort Sill, he was chosen temporary instructor, but was released at his own request. At Taliaferro Field, Fort Worth, Tex., where he was ordered from Aug. 8 to Sept. 4, 1918, on finishing his course he was again appointed instructor. But after making a special plea, Lieut. Hoyt was again released and obtained overseas orders. He was put in command of a casual company and stationed at Hoboken, N.J., and Camp Merritt, from Sept. 16 to Oct. 13, 1918. This delay prevented him from seeing active service. He sailed overseas, however, in Oct., and was stationed in France from Oct. 26, 1918, to Jan. 26, 1919, when he was ordered back to America, and honorably discharged at Garden City, N.Y., on Feb. 14. 1919.

Brother in Service —

George S. Hoyt, Serg't, 1st Class, Q.M. Corps.

FRED DON POLLARD, Jr.

Second Lieutenant, A.S.A., U.S.A.

Son of Fred Don and Lois (Bryant) Pollard of Proctorsville, Vt.; was born in Proctorsville, Jan. 13, 1892. He attended the Black River Academy, Ludlow, Vt., and graduated from Dartmouth College in 1911.

He enlisted at Camp Devens, Ayer, Mass., on Sept. 17, 1917, and served as Corporal in the 301st Infantry until Jan. 5, 1918, when he was transferred to the Air Service. He attended the Ground School at Cornell University from Jan. 5 to March 5, 1918, and was then ordered to Camp Dick, Dallas, Tex., where he remained until April 23. He was sent to Park Field, Tenn., where he stayed from April 23 to Aug. 28, and where he was commissioned 2d Lieut., A.S.A., on July 16, 1918. Subsequently he received further training at Post Field, Fort Sill, Okla., from Aug. 28 to Oct. 28; and at Taliaferro Field, Tex., from Oct. 28 to Nov. 13, 1918. He was ordered to the Air Service Dépôt, Garden City, N.Y., where he was held from Nov. 13, to the date of his honorable discharge from the Service on Dec. 19, 1918.

Married, Dec. 16, 1918, France Ganguet.

Brothers in Service —

Rowland P. Pollard, Corp., Co. C, 310th Infantry.
Bryant F. Pollard, 3d Serg't., 58th F.A.
Roy G. Pollard, Private, Dartmouth S.A.T.C.

Sister in Service —

Mary V. Pollard, Dietitian, Ellis Island Hospital.

CHARLES KINGMAN PERKINS

FIRST LIEUTENANT, A.S.A., U.S.A., SECOND AVIATION INSTRUCTION CENTRE

SON of Rev. Sidney Kingman and Jennie H. (Shattuck) Perkins, of Manchester, Vt.; was born in Haverhill, N.H., Oct. 21, 1891. He was educated at the York (Me.) High School, and at Amherst College, A.B. 1912. For two years after graduation he was Assistant Register and Assistant to the Dean of Amherst. He then entered business with the Sears Manuf. Co., of Walpole, Mass. Just prior to his enlistment he was treasurer of a company which was to furnish the Government with surgical dressings.

He enlisted at New York City on July 17, 1917. From Aug. 20 to Oct. 13 he studied at Cornell University Ground School. On Oct. 27, 1917, he sailed for France with the 10th Detachment of Flying Cadets. From Nov. 17 to Feb. 10, he trained in flying at Issoudun, 3d Aviation Instruction Centre. From Feb. 10 to May 16, he was first student, then instructor, in aerial gunnery at Cazaux. From May 16 to Aug. 16 he had pilot's training at 2d and 3d A.I.C. From Aug. 16 to Nov. 27 he was staff pilot attached to 2d A.I.C. He was commissioned 1st Lieut. on May 18, 1918. He was honorably discharged at Garden City, N.Y., on March 18, 1919.

Brother in Service —

Roger Conant Perkins, Chief Quartermaster, U.S.N.R.F.; killed in seaplane accident, March 14, 1918.

*ROGER CONANT PERKINS

CHIEF QUARTERMASTER, U.S. NAVAL RESERVE FLYING CORPS

Killed in the fall of a seaplane, March 14, 1918

SON of Rev. Sidney Kingman and Jennie H. (Shattuck) Perkins, of Manchester, Vt.; was born at West Springfield, Mass., Nov. 6, 1895. He was educated in the schools of York, Me., and Manchester, Vt., and at Amherst College, class of 1917. He was a member of the Amherst football team, and was manager of the 'Varsity baseball team at the time of his enlistment. He was also a member of the Sphinx Club and the Scarab at college.

He enlisted at New York City on April 9, 1917. He trained at the M.I.T. Ground School, where he stood second in his class, with the honorary rank of brevet Ensign. On Feb. 12, 1918, he was sent to Key West, Fla., for training in flying. He had been up 16 times alone, and was making his 50th flight, when his seaplane fell, on March 14, 1918, and he was killed. He is buried in Manchester, Vt.

A former teacher said of him: "Roger was a leader of boys and promised to become a leader of men."

Brother in Service —
Charles Kingman Perkins, 1st Lieut., U.S.A.S.

ARTHUR L. RICHMOND

CAPTAIN, A.S.A., U.S.A.

SON of Arthur Jones and Rosita (Lavalle) Richmond, of Boston, Mass.; was born in Boston, Aug. 31, 1896. He was educated at St. Mark's School, and at Harvard College. He was trained by the Harvard Undergraduate Aero Training Fund at the Thomas Aviation School, Ithaca, N.Y., from July to Oct., 1916, and flew at Marblehead in the winter of 1916–17.

He enlisted in the Air Service at Boston, Mass., on March 1, 1917, and was ordered to complete his training at the Curtiss Aviation School, Miami, Fla., where he remained as Sergeant, S.E.R.C., from March to June, 1917. He was subsequently ordered to Kelly Field, San Antonio, Tex., for advanced flying, for the month of July. He was commissioned 1st Lieut., Sig. R.C.A.S., on June 25, 1917, and was put in command of the 22d Aero Squadron, U.S.A., attached to R.F.C., at Leaside, Toronto, Can., from Aug. to Oct., 1917. He was then made Assistant Officer in Charge of Flying at Scott Field, Belleville, Ill., from Oct. to Dec., 1917. He was then assigned to Park Field, Memphis, Tenn., from Dec., 1917, to Oct., 1918, first as Assistant Officer in Charge of Flying, and later as Officer in Charge of Flying. He was commissioned Capt., S.C., Regular Army, on Feb. 19, 1918. He was ordered to the port of embarkation, Hoboken, N.J., on Oct. 15, 1918, sailed Nov. 11, and was turned back. Capt. Richmond was honorably discharged at Hoboken, N.J., on Dec. 9, 1918, to enter the reserve forces.

He flew almost 12,000 miles cross-country for the Third Liberty Loan, covering territory from Pensacola, Fla., to Chicago, Ill., Kansas City, Mo., and Dayton, O.

RICHARD W. SEARLE

Second Lieutenant, A.S.A., U.S.A., One Hundred Sixty-Eighth Aero Squadron, First Army Observation

Son of Mr. and Mrs. Charles Putnam Searle; was born in Boston, Mass., July 7, 1891. He graduated from the Stone School and from Harvard College, S.B. 1914. At college he played on his class football teams, and was a member of his class crew. At one time he was a member of Battery A, 1st Mass. F.A., N.G.

He enlisted in Sept., 1917, at Cornell University, and trained there in the School of Aeronautics, graduating on Jan. 26, 1918. He then trained successively at Ellington Field, Houston, Tex.; Camp Dick, Dallas, Tex.; Langley Field, Hampton, Va.; and Taliaferro Field, Hicks, Tex. He was commissioned 2d Lieut. on May 2, 1918, and ordered overseas.

Lieut. Searle sailed from Hoboken, N.J.; on Sept. 15, 1918, landed at Brest, France, and trained at St.-Maixent, Deux Sœurs, France; Issoudun, and Colombey-les-Belles; being assigned to the 168th Aero Squadron, 1st Army Observation, at Mannonville.

He was honorably discharged at St.-Aignan, Loire-et-Cher, France, on April 5, 1919.

*LAURENCE HILL CATE

ENSIGN, U.S. NAVAL RESERVE FLYING CORPS

Died of pneumonia, Oct. 9, 1918

SON of Frederick and Joanna (Lane) Cate, of Weymouth, Mass.; was born in Weymouth, April 19, 1896. He graduated from Thayer Academy, Braintree, Mass., in 1916, and was there captain of the baseball team. He entered Bowdoin College with the class of 1920. At Bowdoin he played baseball, and was a member of Zeta Psi Fraternity. He trained with the Harvard R.O.T.C. for three months and enlisted in Boston in July, 1917, in the Naval Aviation Service. After a ground course at M.I.T., he was sent to Hampton Roads, Va., and thence to Pensacola, Fla. He was commissioned Ensign in the Naval Reserve Flying Corps on March 11, 1918, and had been recommended for Junior Lieutenant at the time of his death. He died of pneumonia following influenza on Oct. 9, 1918, at Pensacola.

His Squadron Commander wrote of him:

> A good aviator, conservative flyer with a cool head. Rather young in appearance but above the average in brains, industry and reliability. He has a very pleasant personality. He is a conscientious worker.

In the official report it was stated:

> For some time he was a flight instructor in an N 9 Squadron, teaching elementary flying. He was taken from this duty to be made an Assistant Division Commander in a division of flying boats, and soon became a Division Commander in the F boat squadron. From this duty he was promoted to be Assistant Patrol Officer, and later to the position of Patrol Officer, which he held at the time of his death. As Patrol Officer he had full charge of all navigation training flights out into the Gulf, and of all rescue work in connection with these flights. He was also in charge of all ground instruction in Navigation. His status was commensurate with that of a Senior Squadron Commander. His classification as to type of pilot was "HS Pilot." I have in official files of the School . . a confidential report to me from the Commander of the Squadron V. The comment made was "fine officer," and was signed by Squadron Commander, Lieut. V. F. Valdes.
>
> I feel that I knew Laurence well, personally, and can say without hesitation or reservation that he was one of the most liked and admired officers of the Seaplane School.

Brother in Service —

Melville F. Cate, Ensign, U.S.N.R.F.

*ROBERT FITZGERALD CLARK

Ensign, U.S. Naval Reserve Flying Corps

Killed in airplane accident, Aug. 21, 1918

Son of Robert Jones and Harriet (FitzGerald) Clark; was born at Dedham, Mass., on Sept. 13, 1898. He was educated at the Noble and Greenough School, Boston, and at Harvard College, class of 1920.

He attended the Officers' Training Camp at Plattsburg in 1916, and the Harvard R.O.T.C. in 1917. In April, 1917, he enlisted in the Naval Reserve Flying Corps; enrolled May 9, Quartermaster, 1st class (Aviation). On June 27 he was sent to Pensacola, Fla., where he was in training for six months; there he was commissioned Ensign, U.S.N.R.F.C., Class 5, on Dec. 17, 1917.

He sailed overseas Jan. 13, 1918, and on arrival in England was assigned to duty with the Royal Naval Air Service, and for six months served at different stations on the English coast, among them, Westgate, Portland, and Felixstowe. On July 17, 1918, he was detached and ordered to Paris, where he was assigned to the U.S.N. Air Station at Brest, France; here he won the respect and confidence of his commanding officers, and he was acting as Chief Pilot of the station when he was killed, while flying in the performance of his duty, on Aug. 21, 1918. He was buried at Kerfautras Cemetery, Brest, France.

*WINTHROP FLOYD SMITH

ENSIGN, U.S.N.R.F.

Died of pneumonia, Oct. 10, 1918

SON of Henry Floyd and Jennie (Saville) Smith; was born in Ashmont, Mass., July 28, 1893. He attended the Henry L. Pierce School, Dorchester, Mass.; Phillips Exeter Academy, and spent one year at Williams College. He graduated from Mass. Institute of Technology. He was an all-round athlete. At Phillips Exeter he was a member of Alpha Nu Fraternity, and managing editor of the *Exonian* in his senior year. He was a member of D.K.E. at Williams. In 1915 and 1916 he attended the Officers' Training Camps at Plattsburg.

On May 8, 1917, he left the business in which he was engaged to enlist in the Naval Reserve Corps at Newport, R.I. He trained at the M.I.T. Ground School, and after passing all tests was sent to Key West, Fla., for a twelve weeks' course in flying. He was there commissioned Ensign, the first week in April, 1918. He was then sent to Bay Shore, N.Y., as Instructor in Aviation. He was a very successful navigating aviator, and trained several hundred students from April 22 to Oct. 10. He also acted as patrol pilot for submarines. He had a narrow escape in June, 1918, when a defective engine caused him to fall into the sea while hunting submarines. He remained clinging to a wing of his plane for 24 hours without help, as passing ships suspected him to be a German decoy. When finally rescued, he was so exhausted that he could not have held on an hour longer. In Sept. Ensign Smith was stricken with influenza, but recovered in two weeks and returned to his duties as instructor. At this time he made a flight with Major Shaw, a British aviator, and performed many difficult manœuvres. Less than three weeks later he was stricken with double pneumonia, and died after a few days' illness at Bay Shore, N.Y., on Oct. 10, 1918. He was buried at Woodlawn Cemetery, Malden, Mass.

Paternal grandfather in Service: served in the Civil War.

Great-grandfather in Service: Dr. John Sprague of Malden, surgeon in Revolutionary War.

Great-great-grandfather in Service: Jonathan Webb of Quincy, Captain in Revolutionary War.

*ARTHUR HOUSTOUN WRIGHT

FIRST LIEUTENANT, NINTH SQUADRON, FIRST MARINE AVIATION FORCE

Died of broncho-pneumonia, Oct. 31, 1918

SON of Rev. Arthur Henry and Claude Houstoun (Hopkins) Wright; was born Jan. 27, 1895, at Warehouse Point, Conn. He was educated in the public schools of Newburyport, and at St. Paul's School, Garden City, N.Y.; entered Trinity College, class of 1918, where he spent two years; he was a member of the Delta Kappa Epsilon Fraternity.

On April 7, 1917, he enlisted in the U.S. Naval Reserve, and was for two months attached to the Mosquito Fleet. In June he was transferred to the U.S. Naval Aviation Force and sent in July to Canada to train with the Royal Flying Corps, at Camp Borden, Toronto, and other flying fields. He was commissioned Ensign in Nov., 1917, and, after two weeks' training at Norfolk with the seaplanes, was sent as instructor to Miami, Fla., where he was in charge of the gunnery school; in May, 1918, he was commissioned 2d Lieut. and transferred to the Marine Aviation Corps, instructing in the bombing school. He was commissioned 1st Lieut. in July, 1918, and sailed for overseas July 18, with the 1st Marine Aviation Force.

On Aug. 9 Lieut. Wright was sent to Squadron 218, Royal Air Force, B.E.F., where he reported for duty, with 2d Lieut. Charles A. Needham detailed as his observer. At 5 A.M. next morning he was ready to fly over the lines on a bombing-attack against the submarine docks and harbor at Ostend, which was situated at that time fifteen miles behind the Hun lines.

On Aug. 10 his record shows him to have dropped 8 25-pound bombs on the mole at Zeebrugge. He was also credited with two raids against the submarine base at Bruges, where he was under fire from one of the most powerful Hun anti-air craft batteries. On one of these raids the Squadron was attacked by Fokker scouts, whom he helped materially in beating off. He was ordered to return to the American Escadrille, on Aug. 22, to act as instructor.

In Sept. he was sent to the U.S. Naval Aircraft Base at Eastleigh, Eng., to supervise the assembling of airplanes arriving from America, and later he flew a plane across the English Channel, to

the U.S. aerodrome at the front. On Oct. 7 he piloted Capt. D. C. Hanrahan, U.S.N., across the Channel to Dover, Eng., in order that Hanrahan might attend an important conference with the British authorities, and returned flying over the Channel in a heavy fog, in order that he might be back in time to participate in the first raid that Squadron 9 made against the Hun.

On Oct. 14, with the late Gunnery Serg't David F. Price, as observer, he flew one of 7 American-built airplanes, equipped with Liberty motors and American guns, in a bombing-raid against the railway junction at Thielt, Belgium. This raid destroyed the very important railway yards and seriously hindered the Hun retreat at this strategic point. In the course of this raid 12 Boche fighting-scouts attacked the 7 American planes and 3 Germans were shot down. All the American airplanes returned safely, although two were so badly disabled that they were never flown again, and one observer was seriously wounded. This was the first time that a flight of fully American-built and armored airplanes, with American-trained pilots and observers, had flown over the Flanders front.

On Oct. 17, after flying 25 miles to the rear of the German lines, he dropped 4 112-pound bombs on the important railway yards at Steenbrugge. In the afternoon of the same date a flight, led by the late Major Douglas B. Roben, again bombed Steenbrugge and, owing to better visibility, the flight was able to report direct hits.

On Oct. 18 Lieut. Wright led a raid against the retreating German troop-trains at Eecloo, Belgium, in order to destroy certain important trains in the vicinity. This was successfully accomplished as the flight reported 8 direct hits, without any loss to themselves, although Wright's machine was perforated in wings and fuselage, by machine-gun bullets from ground batteries.

On Oct. 23 Lieut. Wright was stricken with influenza and died at the British General Hospital 30, Calais, France, on Oct. 31, 1918. On Nov. 4, 1918, he was buried with full military honors in the British Military Cemetery, Les Baracques, Calais, France.

Lieut. Wright was one of the founders of the Pursuit School of Aerial Bombing at Miami, and at the time of his death was on the eve of promotion to a captaincy.

Married, July 1, 1918, Susan March Lowell.

*RALPH TALBOT

LIEUTENANT (*j.g.*), NORTHERN BOMBING SQUADRON, U.S. NAVAL AVIATION SERVICE

Killed in airplane accident, Oct. 25, 1918

SON of Richard J. and Mary (O'Connell) Talbot; was born at South Weymouth, Mass., Jan. 6, 1897. He prepared for college at the Weymouth High and the Mercersburg preparatory schools, and entered Yale in the class of 1920. In college he played on the football, baseball, and cross-country teams in his freshman year. From June 1 to Sept. 15, 1917, he attended the DuPont Flying School, and on Oct. 15, 1917, enlisted in the U.S. Navy.

He was sent to the M.I.T. and received further training at Key West, and at Miami, Fla. He was commissioned Ensign, about April 5, 1918. In July, 1918, he went overseas attached to the Northern Bombing Squadron.

Lieut. Talbot proved a daring and efficient flyer and was the only member of his squadron who succeeded in bringing down an enemy plane. On Oct. 25, 1918, he went up to test a motor, which proved to be bad, and he crashed into a high embankment and was instantly killed, at La Fresne, France. He was buried on Oct. 31, in the British Military Cemetery at Les Baracques, Calais, France.

The following extracts are from a letter written by a fellow aviator who was Talbot's tentmate:

Our pilots were sent to a British school for a bit of practice after so long an absence from flying. Dick (Talbot) was the first from our squadron to go, leaving Sept. 15. His flying attracted so much attention there that he was allowed to take a Camel scout out, a privilege not given to the rest of our pilots. Dick finished there about the 22d, and was given our only De Haviland 4, with Liberty motor, to operate with the British. About this time they were engaged in dropping bully beef to a detachment of French troops cut off from their supply base, and he got some of that work. It was quite dangerous as the tins were dropped from under 500 feet, and the ships were exposed to a terrific machine-gun and rifle fire. It took stamina of the highest sort to stand the gruelling, but Dick enjoyed it. He used to laugh about his aerial grocery work. Then he went on high bombing with the British, bombing Ostend and Bruges from 12,000 feet. As his machine was so fast he was given the very hard task of protecting the rear of the squadron. He could dive and circle about without being out-distanced. On his first, or almost first raid, the squadron engaged in a running-fight with a superior number of Huns, and Dick with his gunner,

Corporal Robinson, shot down one Boche plane, for which he was given official credit by the British, and commended by a letter from the commanding officer of the First Marine Aviation Force. After a few more raids, he was recalled to stand by until our squadron was ready.

On its first raid, Dick had motor trouble and hung about 500 feet below the squadron. After two hours the ships straggled in one by one, but Dick and Capt. Lytle were missing. Several hours later Dick came in with his plane shot very badly and his gunner missing. It developed that eleven Huns had dived on him, firing. Robinson shot one down, and his gun jammed. At that instant he received a stream of bullets through his left arm rendering it useless. While he was working with the gun Dick turned on the planes with his forward gun, but after three or four shots they jammed. Then Robinson recovering shot down a second. The third dived and shot him through the chest and stomach. Dick turned on the third with all guns useless, one of the most daring magnificent bluffs of the war. Then Robinson having fainted and fallen on the control Dick dived to within a hundred feet of the ground and started back across miles of hostile territory, with the third Hun on his tail, firing constantly. Dick's account to me was most graphic. Twisting, turning, zooming trees, he fled with every ounce of power, while above the roar of the motor he could feel the zip of the bullets as every part of the plane was struck. At every house a Boche would snipe at him with rifles, and he passed under a barrage the Huns were laying on the trenches with heavy artillery. Finally he passed over the zigzag line of trenches, saw familiar uniforms and the scout left him. Again he showed his coolness by landing at a Belgian airdrome and rushing the unconscious Robinson to a hospital, undoubtedly saving his life. The Belgian Major was very enthusiastic over his conduct, and it is understood was going to recommend both Dick and Robinson for medals for heroic conduct. Whether this will go through, I don't know.

The fatal accident happened about 1.15 the afternoon of Oct. 25. Just after lunch he went out to make a short motor test. The motor was bad, and he crashed into an earth embankment. His passenger was thrown thirty feet and the machine instantly burst into flames. But Dick did not know because death was instantaneous and painless. So passed a gallant officer, a daring flyer and a most Christian gentleman.

*FRANK W. RILEY

Ensign, U.S.N.R.F., Instructor in Aviation, Naval Air Station, Miami, Florida

Died of pneumonia, Oct. 12, 1918

Son of Frank J. and Ellen M. (Hart) Riley of Dorchester, Mass.; was born in Boston, on Aug. 13, 1894. He was educated at the English High School in Boston, and at the Roxbury Latin School.

When war was declared, he was in the employ of the Schumaker-Santry Co. of Boston. He enlisted on July 25, 1917, at the Charlestown Navy Yard, and was assigned to the Ground School at M.I.T. He was sent from there, Jan. 19, 1918, to Key West, Fla., where he was commissioned Ensign on March 25, 1918. He was subsequently detailed to the Naval Air Station at Miami, Fla., as Instructor in Aviation.

From Miami, he and Electrician Walter P. Clark set out on Friday, June 7, 1918, in a regular U.S.N. hydroplane, in search of the German submarine which was then terrorizing the Atlantic Coast. Before they had gone 25 miles from shore, engine trouble developed and they were forced to descend, landing in the Gulf Stream. That afternoon and by turns all night, they labored over the engine, but were unable to make it work. On the afternoon of June 8, when the heavy plane showed signs of sinking, they sighted a four-masted schooner. Mounting the wings of their plane, they signalled frantically, but the schooner, thinking their craft to be a camouflaged U-boat, sped away. At dawn, June 9, sharks began to hover about the submerging plane, but at about 8 o'clock that day a Norwegian freighter came into view, and its captain made out the figures of the two men signalling from the wings. They immediately made for the plane. When Ensign Riley and his companion were picked up, they had drifted 150 miles from land.

On Oct. 12, 1918, Ensign Riley died of pneumonia, at Miami, Fla., and was buried at Calvary Cemetery in Boston, Oct. 17, 1918.

*MARTIN LUTHER HOPE

Cadet, Marine Flying Corps

Killed in airplane accident, Miami, Fla., Oct. 22, 1918

Son of Rev. William Frederick and Martha (Festner) Hope, of Meredosia, Ill.; was born in Independence, Kan., on Oct. 27, 1897. He attended the elementary schools of Portland, Ore., and Pittsburgh, Pa. He graduated from the Central High School, Pittsburgh, with honors, after three years' work, and won the scholarship offered by the Harvard Club of Western Pennsylvania. He entered Harvard College with the class of 1919, but graduated in 1918, *summa cum laude.* In 1916 he was a member of the Freshman Debating Team against Yale; in 1917–18, a member of the 'Varsity Debating Team and the winner of the Interclass Debating Championship Cup. On graduation he was awarded the George B. Sohier Prize of $250 and the Bowdoin Prize of $100. He also received the John Harvard Scholarship and a Detur as a mark of high academic distinction. He was elected to Phi Beta Kappa, in Feb., 1919, four months after his death; this is believed to be the first instance of the conferring of the honor of Phi Beta Kappa posthumously.

He enlisted in the 1st Marine Aviation Corps in Boston, on June 5, 1918, and was assigned to the Ground School, M.I.T., for instruction. He was ordered to the Marine Flying Field in Miami, Fla., in Aug., 1918, where he was soon regarded as the best flyer at the field. On Oct. 22, 1918, he was killed. The accident occurred during target practice; the pilot, Paul Gering, lost control of the machine which crashed to earth, killing both men. At the time of his death, Cadet Hope was about to receive his wings as a full-fledged pilot, having been recommended for a commission as 1st Lieut. on Oct. 9, 1918. After his death he was awarded Golden Wings by custom. He was buried in Meredosia, Ill.

An extract from a letter from fellow cadet officers to Mr. Hope's father, dated Oct. 24, 1918, follows:

> In the midst of the great loss come to our camp in the loss of your son, we ask to join our grief with yours. . . . Months of constant comradeship have brought a deep respect and lasting admiration . . . for his sober judgment, unselfishness and fine qualities as a friend. We feel that death in an effort to win this war is the highest honor a man can attain. . . .

The Secretary of the Harvard Chapter of Phi Beta Kappa, in sending Mr. Hope's key to his father, wrote on March 12, 1919:

Martin's remarkable achievement in getting the *summa cum laude* in three years singled him out as one of the most brilliant men in the class; and after all that he had done, we felt that election to Phi Beta Kappa was the least we could do in recognition of his unusual success.

Prof. Chester Noyes Greenough, Acting Dean of Harvard College, wrote on June 2, 1919:

As you know, we give as prizes to our best scholars, books which we call "Deturs," and these books are treasured by men who receive them as one of the most valuable souvenirs of their college career. Your son, had he lived, would have received a detur, and I should have been very proud to hand it to him and to say to him that I felt confident that his future career would justify the promise of his work with us. Your son's death in the service of his country makes it impossible for me to do more than to send you the book which he has so richly earned and to try to say to you not only what I say to every recipient of a detur — that the College is proud of his scholarship — but also to tell you that the College feels not only pride in the success of its students, but grief and sympathy when they are cut off at the beginning of their careers.

The patriotic spirit of Martin Luther Hope is finely shown in a letter written Oct. 19, four days before his death:

I was recommended for my commission about two weeks ago; it will arrive shortly now. I was chosen as an instructor, but have gotten around the matter now. And so I am to leave with the next squadron.

Grandfather in Service —

Frederick C. Festner, Captain, 29th Wisconsin Regiment, fought in Civil War, and was wounded at Memphis, Tenn.

JOHN PERRIN

LIEUTENANT (*j.g.*), U.S. NAVAL RESERVE FLYING CORPS

SON of Arthur and Mary (Schlesinger) Perrin; was born in Brookline, Mass., April 23, 1895. He was educated at the Country Day School, Newton, Mass., the Volkmann School, and at the Stone School, Boston. He entered Harvard College in the class of 1920. He was on the Volkmann four-oared crew, and at the Stone School, rowed stroke on the winning eight-oared crew against Cascadilla, in 1916. At Harvard, during his freshman year, he was on the crew squad until the war stopped athletics. He attended the Officers' Training Camp at Plattsburg in 1916, and trained with the Harvard R.O.T.C., 1916–17.

He enlisted in the N.R.F.C. in Boston, in April, 1917. He was sent to Pensacola, Fla., for both ground work and flying instruction, and served there as Instructor and Beach-Master for a few weeks in 1917. He was commissioned Ensign on Dec. 17, 1917.

He sailed overseas on Jan. 13, 1918, and after a week in France was ordered to England, and attached as pilot to the Royal Naval Air Service at Great Yarmouth, under the command of Capt. Samson (later Col.), D.S.O., one of the few men on whose head a price was set by the Germans. The Great Yarmouth Station sent patrols daily to the German, Dutch, and Friesian coasts, and in one night accounted for 5 Zeppelins out of 7 that attempted a raid on London. He remained at the Great Yarmouth Station through Aug., acting as a pilot for "Shorts" and "Schneider Sea-Scouts." An account of one of Lieut. Perrin's experiences follows:

One morning a flight of five "boats" started for the other side after a Zeppelin which made its customary dawn patrol down the German coast. Each flying boat carried five men, eleven machine guns, wireless set, and gasoline for ten hours. Getting off the water in the pitch dark and forming in formation is quite a stunt; but by means of flashes of light we signalled to each other, and finally got into formation, and kept it in the dark all the way across the 200-odd miles to the German coast. We reached it at dawn off Borkum Island, about the place where Germany joins Holland; below us was the English light seas fleet with a destroyer which towed a Sopwith scout on a lighter. A lighter is a barge about sixty feet long, and a Sopwith scout (called a "camel" because of its hump) is a fast land plane that is good for getting Zeps. These camels have such a powerful engine and can climb so fast that they can get off a lighter and into the air before they have travelled the length of the lighter (60 feet). Flying a camel from a lighter had only been attempted once before, and unsuccessfully at that.

We skirted the German coast, keeping in close formation, at an altitude of 3000 feet. Suddenly I saw the Zeppelin at about 17,000 feet coming down the coast toward us, about three miles off the German coast. We signalled the find to the leading boat, dived in formation down to the water so as to be invisible from the "Zep," tore back to the destroyer and signalled it. At once the camel, with Flight Lieut. Culley as pilot, took off the lighter, and followed us back up the coast toward the "Zep" until we got in sight of it. Before the camel left us, we had to drive off a flight of German planes which were attacking it; the camel was helpless because it carried only explosive ammunition for the "Zep" instead of bullets. Although we successfully protected the camel and drove off the German planes, we knew that we did not have much time, for they were sure to be back in large numbers as soon as the vanquished machines spread the news. Suddenly we picked up a German S.O.S. from the "Zep," and then it burst into smoke and fell.

It was risky to stay around the German coast any longer, for we expected an overpowering number of enemy planes to come out after us at any second; but we stayed and were successful in finding the camel and conducting it back to the destroyer. The original orders were to turn for home as soon as the "Zep" had been shot down; the camel was to fly south, and the pilot to intern himself in Holland after destroying the machine. This would have meant that the Allies would have lost his services for the rest of the war. We met him on the way to Holland to carry out his orders, and took him to his destroyer. Then Flight Lieut. Culley made a stall landing with his land plane on the water alongside the English destroyer, which quickly got two small boats under the wings of the camel before it could sink, and the whole thing was hoisted aboard. We all got home safely, feeling satisfied at shooting down a "Zep" under the very noses of the Huns.

After eight months' work at Great Yarmouth, Ensign Perrin was transferred to Felixstowe, where he flew "boats." He was subsequently returned to the American command, and stationed at Lough Foyle, Ireland. He was commissioned Lieut. (j.g.) on Oct. 1, 1918.

Lieut. Perrin was placed on inactive service on Jan. 13, 1919, at the U.S. Naval Air Station, Bay Shore, New York.

Brother in Service —

Hugh Perrin (Harvard R.O.T.C.), seaman, U.S.N.R. (In training for Naval Aviation at M.I.T. in the Naval Unit, when the Armistice was signed.)

*DONALD CARY PERO

ENSIGN, U.S. NAVAL AVIATION SERVICE

Lost at sea, Aug. 24, 1918

SON of George Francis and Margaret (Cary) Pero, of Indian Orchard, Mass.; was born in Springfield, Mass., Jan. 14, 1896. He was educated at Springfield High School, and Mass. Institute of Technology, class of 1919. He received class honors during his four years at high school.

He left M.I.T. in his second year, to enlist in the Naval Reserve, May 7, 1917. He attended the 1st class of Naval Aviators at M.I.T.; then went to the Naval Air Station, Norfolk, Va.; and later to the Naval Air Station, Pensacola, Fla., where he completed his training and was commissioned Ensign, U.S.N.A.F., on Feb. 4, 1918. He was stationed at Rockaway Beach, N.Y., as instructor, and placed on patrol duty; and it was while he was engaged in this service that Ensign Pero met his death, on Aug. 24, 1918.

Two seaplanes were out on patrol duty in a heavy fog. One was commanded by Ensign Pero, the other by Ensign H. Stevens, each with two machinists. According to the pilot of the other plane, it was only Ensign Pero's superior handling of his machine that prevented the loss of both crews in the collision that ensued. As soon as the approaching plane broke through the fog in front of him, Ensign Pero attempted a dive. The front end of his plane cleared the approaching one, but the tail was ripped off and all control of the plane was lost. It was seen to go into a nose-spin and disappear, falling straight down. The other plane circled over the spot for nearly an hour, but found no trace of any of the crew, three in all. Mine-sweepers and patrol vessels searched the vicinity for the missing men, but to no avail. The second seaplane landed safely on the water and aided in the unsuccessful search.

The accident took place 12 miles southeast of Fire Island Lightship, at about seven in the evening, and at an altitude of about 3000 feet.

Brother in Service —

Joseph H. Pero, U.S.N.A.R.F., enlisted May, 1917; served in France as chief printer in the Photographic Section.

*DEAN EDMUND LOCHMAN, Jr.

Lieutenant (*j.g.*), U.S. Naval Aviation Service

Killed in seaplane accident, May 19, 1919

Son of Mr. and Mrs. Dean Edmund Lochman; was born in Salem, Mass., Nov. 10, 1897. He attended the Lincoln, Bowditch Grammar, and Salem High School, graduating from the latter in 1916. Early in 1916 he joined the Salem Cadets, who were then reorganizing into artillery.

On June 25, just before graduating from high school, he was sent with the artillery to the Mexican Border. He returned from Mexico in Nov., and entered business with the Salem Electric Lighting Co. When the U.S. entered the war, he was interested in Naval Aviation, and applied for a discharge from the Army in order to enter the Navy. He passed his physical examinations and started a three months' preliminary course at M.I.T. Ground School. In Oct., 1917, he was sent to Pensacola, Fla., to finish his work; and was commissioned Ensign in Dec., 1917. On Feb. 16 he was ordered overseas, and was stationed first in England, then at a U.S. Naval Base on the south coast of Ireland, where he remained until the signing of the Armistice. He returned home on Dec. 28, 1918.

Lochman was anxious to continue his Aviation work. On Jan. 26, 1919, he received orders to leave at once for New York, to prepare to go to Coco Solo, in the Panama Canal Zone. He was married that same evening to Miss Evelyn Bowker, of Salem, and together they went to New York. They sailed for Panama on Feb. 6, 1919. Upon arrival he was commissioned Lieut. (j.g.), which rank he should have received in the preceding Oct. while in England, but for some reason the commission was delayed.

On May 19, 1919, Lieut. Lochman was killed in a seaplane accident at Coco Solo, Panama. He is buried in Harmony Grove Cemetery, Salem, Mass.

ROGER WILSON CUTLER

Lieutenant, U.S. Naval Aviation Service

Son of George C. and Mary Franklin (Wilson) Cutler; was born in Brookline, Mass., Nov. 3, 1889. He was educated at Volkmann's School, Brookline, and at Harvard College, graduating in 1911. He engaged in all kinds of athletics — track, football, baseball, golf, and basket-ball. He was captain of the 'Varsity crew in 1911. In 1914 he was stroke of the Union Boat Club crew at Henley, Eng.

He acted as a radio operator in a naval cruise (P.S. No. 8), in Sept., 1916; and was first attached to the submarine chasers at Newport, R.I. On March 21, 1917, he enlisted in the U.S.N.R.F., and served on Submarine Patrol No. 56, until Sept. 9. He was relieved and transferred to Naval Aviation Service, Sept. 15, 1917. In Oct. and Nov., he trained at the U.S.N.A. Station, M.I.T., and during the last four weeks was appointed Squadron Commander. In Dec. and Jan., he was attached to the Naval Air Station in Hampton Roads, Va. For the next three months he was at the Naval Air Station at Pensacola, Fla.; and was commissioned Ensign on March 15, 1918. At about this time he was appointed aide to Com. Ballinger. He returned to Hampton Roads for April and May, and was commissioned Lieut. (j.g.) on May 30, 1918. He sailed overseas and was stationed at U.S.N. Air Station, Killingholme, Eng., from June to Dec., 1918. Commissioned, Lieut. Nov., 1918.

In a flight over the North Sea on July 19, 1918, in Ensign Jay Scheffelin's plane, Lieut. Cutler dropped a bomb which destroyed the German U-boat 110, with 69 of its crew. He was appointed Senior Squadron Commander at Killingholme Station, in Oct., 1918. Returning to America, Lieut. Cutler was assigned to inactive duty on Jan. 15, 1919, at Boston.

Married, on Dec. 15, 1912, Leslie Bradley, of Boston.

Brothers in Service —

John W. Cutler, Major, U.S.A., Ordnance.
Eliot C. Cutler, Major, U.S.A., Medical.
George C. Cutler, Jr., Lieut. (j.g.), U.S.N.R.F., Destroyer Flotilla.
Robert B. Cutler, Capt., U.S.A., Infantry.

DONALD WILSON

ENSIGN, U.S.N.R.F.C., SQUADRON VI, N.A.S., PENSACOLA, FLORIDA

SON of Rev. John M. and Helen B. Wilson, of Lexington, Mass.; was born at Hudson, Mass., July 7, 1893. He was educated in the public schools of Fall River and Lexington, Mass.; at Phillips Exeter Academy, and at the Browne and Nichols School, Cambridge. He graduated from the Buildings Course, Lowell Institute School for Industrial Foremen.

He attended the 1st Plattsburg Camp in 1916. On May 28, 1917, he enlisted in the 14th Regulars, Railway Engineers, at Boston. He was assigned to Camp Rockingham, N.H., for training the latter part of June. On July 9, 1917, he was appointed Corporal, and was honorably discharged on July 24, to be enrolled in U.S.N.R.F. for Aviation Service. On Oct. 28 he was called for instruction at M.I.T. School of Naval Aeronautics. On Jan. 20, 1918, he was sent to Pensacola, Fla., for air training, and was assigned to Squadron II, night-bombers. After qualifying as a naval aviator, he acted as Instructor in Elementary Flying. He was commissioned Ensign on June 4, 1918, and appointed Instructor in H-boats and Navigation Pilot. He later became Chief Instructor in Squadron VI, Naval Air Station, Pensacola.

Ensign Wilson made successful experimental flights in the Gulf of Mexico, besides his routine work as Aviation Instructor. He was chosen as one of the pilots to fly from Pensacola to Cuba to join the Atlantic Fleet at Guantanamo. This flight began Feb. 6, 1919, with a journey to Tampa, Fla., and the second part was done on Feb. 8, from Tampa to Miami. From Miami on Feb. 13 the planes flew across to Sagua la Grande, on the north central shore of Cuba; and the next day to Nuevitas, also on the north shore of the island. On Saturday, Feb. 15, they made the last part of the journey around the east point of Cuba to Guantanamo Bay. The planes were heavily loaded with extra propellers, spare parts, and baggage, and each carried two pilots and two men.

NOEL CHADWICK

LIEUTENANT (*j.g.*), U.S. NAVAL RESERVE FLYING CORPS

SON of George W. and Ida May (Brooks) Chadwick; was born in Boston, Dec. 22, 1894. He was educated at the Noble and Greenough School, and at Harvard College, class of 1917. At school he was a member of the crew in 1910–11–12, and of the Noble track team, 1912–13. At college he was on the freshman crew and swimming team.

He left business to enlist at Boston, in the N.R.F.C., on June 11, 1917. He was sent at once with the first class to Akron, O., for training in dirigible work. He remained there from June 11, 1917, to Jan. 11, 1918. He was commissioned Ensign on Nov. 1, 1917, and dirigible pilot, in charge of the second class of cadets. From Jan. 11 to June 11, 1918, he was stationed at Key West, Fla., as Chief Dirigible Officer, to oversee the building and starting of the dirigible department of that station. He performed this duty practically alone, as he was the only Dirigible Officer. Within two months regular patrols were in operation up and down the Florida Keys, and to Cuba.

On June 11, 1918, he was transferred to Montauk, N.Y., Naval Air Station; where he remained for five months as Dirigible Officer and Navigating Officer, on patrol work until Dec. 11, 1918. He was commissioned Lieut. (j.g.), on Oct. 1, 1918. Lieut. Chadwick was later ordered to Cape May Naval Air Station, where he was released from active service on Jan. 8, 1919.

Married, July 12, 1919, Elizabeth Young, of Boston.

Brother in Service —

Theodore Chadwick, Capt., 102d F.A., 26th Division, A.E.F.

FRANCIS HARTLEY, Jr.

Ensign, U.S. Naval Reserve Flying Corps

Son of Frank and Anna C. (Duckworth) Hartley, of Belmont, Mass.; was born in Webster, Mass., July 9, 1895. He was educated at Phillips Andover Academy, and at the Yale Scientific School, graduating in 1917. He enlisted with the Naval Reserve Force, at Newport, R.I., and was transferred to Aviation in Aug., 1917. He was trained at M.I.T. Ground School in Jan., 1918, and sent from there to Pensacola, Fla., on April 1. He was commissioned Ensign on June 12, 1918, and was stationed at Rockaway, N.Y. He sailed overseas on July 31, 1918. In France he was stationed at Moutchic-Lacanau, and later at L'Aber Vrach, where he was trained as a pilot and in night-bombing, for two months. Later he engaged in night-bombing expeditions.

The day before the Armistice was signed, he had a narrow escape from death when the strut of his plane broke in crossing the English Channel, and he and his companion were thrown into the water. Their wireless was put out of commission and messages telling of their position were sent out by carrier pigeons. After battling for seven hours with the waves, they were rescued by a submarine sent out in search of them.

It is of interest to note that Ensign Hartley reports the great appreciation of what the Americans have done for them, which has been shown by the inhabitants of L'Aber Vrach. Although they have but the scantiest means, they have erected a monument to the Americans who lost their lives, and have issued a little history of their exploits for the native children to remember.

MORTON GOODSPEED

LIEUTENANT (*j.g.*), U.S. NAVAL RESERVE FLYING CORPS
EIGHTH NAVAL DISTRICT

SON of Joseph H. and Mabel (Morton) Goodspeed, of Boston, Mass.; was born in Boston on Feb. 3, 1895. He fitted for college at the Fay School, Southboro, Mass., and at St. George's School, Newport, R.I. At St. George's School he was captain of the base-ball and basket-ball teams, and received the athletic prize. He entered Princeton University with the class of 1918, and was half-back on the football team during his freshman year.

He left college to enlist in the U.S.N.R.F. at Newport, R.I., on March 24, 1917. He served on the Coast Patrol, U.S.S. *Celeritas*, off Newport, R.I., until Sept., 1917. On Sept. 13 he was transferred to the Aviation Corps, and on Oct. 15 ordered to the Ground School, M.I.T., for instruction. On graduating, March 18, 1918, he was sent to the U.S. Naval Air Station at Pensacola, Fla., where he reported for duty March 22, 1918. He was commissioned Ensign on July 3, 1918, and designated as Naval Aviator and Instructor. On Aug. 17, 1918, he was appointed Unit Commander in charge of Camp Sauftley, Santa Rosa Island, and of the Gunnery School of Instruction there. He was commissioned Lieut. (j.g.) on Jan. 1, 1919. He was relieved of active duty on Jan. 22.

Brother in Service —
Joseph H. Goodspeed, Jr., Seaman, U.S.N.R.F.

GEORGE CROMPTON, Jr.

Lieutenant, U.S. Naval Reserve Flying Corps

Son of George and Alice (Hastings) Crompton; was born in Worcester, Mass., May 7, 1897. He attended the Ridgefield School, and Milton Academy, graduating, 1916; entered Harvard College, class of 1920, completing his freshman year. At Milton he played on the football and tennis teams. At Harvard he was a member of the soccer team. He trained with the Harvard R.O.T.C. in 1916–17, and enlisted on June 8, 1917. He was ordered at once to the Naval Aviation Detachment at Akron, O., where he was trained in flying. He ranked as Naval Aviator from Sept. 21, 1917 (N.A. No. 100). On Oct. 13 he was sent to N.A. Station at Montauk, N.Y., where he was on duty patrolling in dirigibles. He was commissioned Ensign, U.S.N.R.F.C., Nov. 1, 1917, and Lieut. (j.g.) March 23, 1918.

Lieut. Crompton was ordered to Rockaway, N.Y., on June 4, and put in charge of dirigibles there from June 28 until Dec. 23. He was promoted to Lieut. on Oct. 1, 1918. On Sept. 18, 1918, he flew 600 miles in a dirigible across the States of Ohio, Pennsylvania, and New York, making the record cross-country dirigible flight for this country. He was also the first to successfully launch an airplane in air from a dirigible.

He was placed on the inactive list of the U.S.N.R.F. on Dec. 23, 1918, at Rockaway Beach, N.Y.

CHARLES E. HODGES, Jr.

Ensign, U.S. Naval Reserve Flying Corps, Northern Bombing Group

Son of Charles E. and Mary Elizabeth (O'Neill) Hodges; was born in Brookline, Mass., Nov. 29, 1897. He was educated at the Country Day School, and at Harvard College, class of 1919.

He attended the Plattsburg Training Camp, in 1915 and Harvard R.O.T.C. He enlisted on July 2, 1917, at Boston, and attended the Ground School, M.I.T., from Oct. 1 to Dec. 1; Naval Air Station, Hampton Roads, Va.; and N.A.S. Pensacola, Fla. (seaplanes). He was commissioned Ensign on Feb. 27, 1918, and sailed overseas on March 29, 1918. He trained at N.A.S. Moutchic-Lacanau, U.S. Army Bombing School, Clermont-Ferrand, Pilot's Pool, R.A.F., south of Calais. On July 18 he was attached to the 218th Squadron, R.A.F., near Calais, for active service. In Sept. he was transferred to the 5th Squadron Marines, U.S. Naval Region Base, Eastleigh, Eng., Headquarters of the Northern Bombing Group, U.S.N.A.F., where he remained until the Armistice. He was placed on inactive service list on Dec. 29, 1918, at Hampton Roads, Va.

From an account of his first bombing-raid, published in the *Harvard Bulletin:*

I went on my first raid yesterday, and for a first experience it was a knock-out. I dropped my bombs on a big city, while Archie put shell bursts all around me. I could n't keep up with the formation, got about 200 yards behind, and then the shell bursts stopped; and I took a look behind right away, and there was my observer, looking ahead instead of behind as he should have done, and five nice little scouts with black crosses on 'em about 300 yards away, behind my tail. If that observer could have been consumed by the heat of swear words he'd have been dead by now. Then he guessed from my hitting him that there was something wrong, turned around and began to shoot. I devoted my energies to getting all the speed I could, swearing worse than a trooper, and listening to the whistle of German steel. Then I took another look at the battle just in time to see one Hun stick his nose up in the air and go spinning down, and the rest turn around and go home. (One of the other members of the formation claimed the Hun, but if any one got him, my observer did; at any rate, it was n't confirmed.) Then Archie started again, sending up shrapnel and high-explosives, and a piece of shrapnel hit my tail. We all got safely home. I had about five bullet holes and a piece of shrapnel in the machine. It was my maiden-trip and also the machine's, and both a bit worse for it.

SCHUYLER ADAMS

ENSIGN, U.S.A.S. (NAVAL AVIATION)

SON of Enoch Case and Emma (Haff) Adams, of West Newton, Mass.; was born at Newburyport, Mass., June 19, 1893. He was prepared for college at the Newton High School, of which his father is Head-Master. He graduated from Harvard College, class of 1914. During 1916–17 he taught English in the Gilman Country Day School, Roland Park, Md.

In June, 1917, he enlisted in Naval Aviation; and in Aug. was assigned to the M.I.T. Ground School, after which he was taught practical aviation at Pensacola, Fla., in charge of Flight B. He was commissioned Ensign at Pensacola in Jan., 1918. Ensign Adams then trained in aerial gunnery at Fort Worth, Tex.; after which he was sent to Hampton Roads, Va., for work in large hydroplanes.

On account of his proficiency as an aviator, but much to his own regret, he was then detailed to teach Aviation at Bay Shore, N.Y., where he remained until flying at that station was suspended on account of the cold weather. He was then sent to Brunswick, Ga., where he remained but a short time, being detailed for office work in the Naval Operations Department, at Washington, D.C. Early in the spring of 1919 he was again transferred to Hampton Roads, where he is now in the experiment squadron of aviation.

Shortly after his return to Hampton Roads, Ensign Adams was enrolled in the Regular Navy.

ROGER AMORY

Major A.S.A., Detached Service

Son of Charles B. and Lily C. Amory; was born in Boston, Mass., March 28, 1887. He was educated at Milton Academy, and at Harvard College, A.B. 1910. Prior to the war he served three years in Troop B, 1st Squad, M.V.M., 1908 to 1911.

He enlisted at Newport News, Va., on May 3, 1917, and had preliminary training at the M.I.T. Ground School; flying training at Newport News, Va., and Mineola, N.Y. He was on duty at the School of Military Aeronautics, Austin, Tex.; Kelly Field, San Antonio, Tex.; and at Office of Director of Military Aeronautics, Washington, D.C. He was commissioned Capt., Sept., 1917; Major, Oct. 1918. He was honorably discharged at Washington, D.C., on Jan. 6, 1919.

Brothers in Service —

Charles B. Amory, Lieut.-Col. 26th Div., A.E.F.

John Austin Amory, Capt. (Chemical Warfare Service), 3d Div., A.E.F.

Father in Service —

Charles B. Amory, Major in Mass. Volunteers in the Civil War.

JOHN BAYARD CHEVALIER

First Lieutenant, A.S.A., U.S.A., Commanding Officer, Aviation Instruction Centre, Cazaux

Son of Charles N. and Elizabeth A. (Waterhouse) Chevalier, of Medford, Mass.; was born Jan. 31, 1887, at Providence, R.I. He was educated at Ogdensburg Academy, N.Y., Medford High School, class of 1904; Harvard College, class of 1908, B.A., A.M. He lived for nine years in the Far East and travelled extensively. Was vice-captain of the Shanghai Rowing Club, Shanghai, China.

For three years he served in the American Company, Shanghai, Volunteer Corps, Shanghai, China. He served through the Chinese Rebellion of 1913, and was honorably discharged in 1916, with the rank of Corporal. From Shanghai he returned to enlist in the S.E.R.C. at Cambridge, Mass., on Aug. 31, 1917. He attended the Ground School, M.I.T., from Sept. 13 to Nov. 10, 1917. He sailed overseas Nov. 27, 1917, as an enlisted man, flying cadet. In April, 1918, he took a machine-gun course at First Corps School, Gondrecourt. He had flying training also with the French Army at École de Voves, and was breveted as military pilot, June 24, 1918. (Farman planes). He was commissioned 2d Lieut. A.S.A.,U.S.A., June 10, 1918. From July 1 to Oct. 1, 1918, he was Commanding Officer of American Aviation Detachment, École d'Avord, advanced flying training; transferred to Sopwith planes, followed by chasse training on Nieuport planes. From Oct. 1 to Oct. 7, 1918, he had American pursuit training at Issoudun. From Oct. 19 to Dec. 8, 1918, he was Commanding Officer at Aviation Instruction Centre, Cazaux, the U.S. Camp attached to the French School of Aerial Gunnery. On Nov. 1, 1918, he was commissioned 1st Lieut., A.S. On Feb. 3, 1919, he was honorably discharged at the Air Service Dépôt, Garden City, N.Y.

Brothers in Service —

Elmer Harold Frye Chevalier, Private 21st U.S. Infantry; died in Service during Spanish-American War.

Godfrey de Courcelles Chevalier, Lieut.-Com., U.S.N.A.S.

GODFREY DE COURCELLES CHEVALIER

LIEUTENANT COMMANDER, U.S. NAVAL AVIATION SERVICE

SON of Charles N. and Elizabeth A. (Waterhouse) Chevalier, of Medford, Mass.; was born March 7, 1889, at Providence, R.I. He was educated at U.S. Naval Academy, and entered U.S. Service at Annapolis on June 28, 1906.

He entered U.S. Naval Aviation Service in 1912, and flew at Annapolis, Pensacola, Cuba, Vera Cruz, and elsewhere; in France at Tours, Avord, Pau, and Cazaux. He was Commanding Officer of U.S. Naval Air Station at Dunkirk, Seaplane Base, in 1917 and 1918. He was attached to the U.S. Naval Northern Bombing Group, and had special Aviation duty. He was commissioned Lieut. Commander in July, 1918. He served as Commanding Officer, Grand Fleet; U.S. Naval Aviation Repair Base, Eastleigh, Eng.

On March 9, 1919, Lieut.-Commander Chevalier was awarded the Croix de Guerre, by the French Government:

> For establishing the first seaplane base in France, and maintaining a high degree of efficiency and military valor in spite of numerous losses and frequent bombardments.

The Cross of the Legion of Honor was also awarded him, on April 9, 1919.

Married, June 14, 1919, Marguerite Jackson.

Brothers in Service —

Elmer Harold Frye Chevalier, Private, 21st Infantry; died in 1899, aged 20, on board the U.S. Transport *Hancock, en route* for the Philippines, during the Spanish-American War.

John Bayard Chevalier, 1st Lieut., U.S. Air Service, A.E.F.

MOSELEY TAYLOR

LIEUTENANT (*j.g.*), U.S.N.R.F.C., FIRST NORTHERN BOMBING GROUP

SON of William O. and Mary (Moseley) Taylor; was born in Boston, Mass., Jan. 30, 1895. He was educated at the Noble and Greenough School, Boston, at Phillips Andover Academy, and at Harvard College, class of 1918. He was an all-round athlete. At Noble and Greenough he played on the football team two years; track two years; crew two years, and was captain the last year. At Andover he was on the football, wrestling, hockey, and track teams. He was a member of the Harvard freshman crew; and played on the 'Varsity football team, and was on the crew in 1916.

On April 19, 1917, he enlisted in U.S.N.R.F.C., at Washington, D.C. He trained at Newport News, Va., and at the Naval Base, Jamestown, Va. He was commissioned Ensign Oct. 26, 1917. Exactly a month later he sailed for France. He trained near Bordeaux until Feb., 1918. He was stationed at Naval Base, Dunkirk, France, from Feb. 24 to May 10, and was commissioned Lieut. (j.g.) on March 28, 1918. Lieut. Taylor spent 12 weeks of the summer at Stonehenge, Eng., taking a course in night-bombing. In Aug. he was stationed at St.-Inglevert, France, with the Northern Bombing Group, U.S.N. During the last weeks of the war he served with the British 214th Squadron, R.A.F., running a Handley-Page bombing-machine, and seeing active service on sea and land. Lieut. Taylor was put on the reserve list in Jan., 1919, at Naval Base, Norfolk, Va.

ROBERT A. TALBOT

LIEUTENANT (*j.g.*), U.S.N.R.F., NAVAL AIR STATION, PENSACOLA
SQUADRON V

SON of Charles R. and Nellie E. (Cumner) Talbot, of Brookline, Mass.; was born in Lowell, Mass., June 11, 1896. He was educated at the Brookline High School, Stone School, class of 1915, and at Harvard College, class of 1919.

He enlisted in U.S.N.R.F. on April 20, 1917, at Charlestown, Mass. On Sept. 7, 1917, he reported at Naval Air Station, Pensacola, Fla., where he qualified as Fireman, 3d Class (A). On Nov. 23, 1917, he was ordered to M.I.T. Ground School, rating, Machine Mate, 2d Class (A). On Jan. 1, 1918, he received the rating of Chief Quartermaster (A). On Feb. 16 he reported to Naval Air Station, Pensacola, Fla., for flight instruction. On June 1, 1918, he qualified as Naval Aviator, and was commissioned Ensign on June 12, 1918.

Ensign Talbot was made Instructor in Advanced Boat Seaplane Flying, with Squadron V, June 14, 1918. He was appointed Chief Flight Instructor of Squadron V on Sept. 1, 1918, and commissioned Lieut. (j.g.) on Oct. 1, 1918. On Oct. 4, 1918, he was made Division Commander, Squadron V, Division A.

Lieut. Talbot received his inactive duty papers (ordered home) on March 7, 1919. His cruise expires April 20, 1921.

Brother in Service —
Cumner Talbot, U.S. Army.

HAROLD LYMAN RYAN

LIEUTENANT (*j.g.*), U.S. NAVAL RESERVE FORCE

SON of T. Harvey and Mary F. (Berry) Ryan, of Rio de Janeiro, Brazil; was born in Charlestown, Mass., April, 28, 1895. He was educated in Brazil, at the Somerville High School, class of 1914, and for three years at Tufts College, to which he returned after his discharge from the Service. He was class marshal, president of the Sword and Shield and Ivy (class honorary societies), and a member of Sigma Tau Alpha Fraternity at Tufts College.

He trained with the Tufts R.O.T.C. on May 24, 1917, he enlisted at Boston with the First Naval Aviation Detachment at the M.I.T. Ground School. On Aug. 25, 1917, he reported to the U.S.N.A.S., Hampton Roads, Va., for flying instruction. Here he had much experience in motor and seaplane construction. He was detached on Jan. 6, 1918, and sent to the Naval Aviation School, Pensacola, Fla., for final instruction in flying. He was commissioned Ensign on Feb. 19, 1918, and was detailed as Instructor at Pensacola, until receipt of orders for overseas service on March 12, 1918.

In France he was stationed at Moutchic-Lacanau from April 29 to Aug. 4, 1918, completing his course in ordnance training and bombing. He was ordered to active duty at Le Croisic, Loire Inférieure, where he was Chief Pilot, Chief Censor, and served on Court Martial and Survey Boards. He had a number of narrow escapes while training and in service. He fell once into the Bay, but escaped injury. He has had approximately 240 hours flying time, five hours in the air being his longest period for any continuous flight. His active service included convoy and patrol duty, flying 250 to 300 miles off the French coast. He was commissioned Lieut. (j.g.) on Oct. 1, 1918. After the Armistice he returned to America. He was placed on inactive duty on March 16, 1919, at Hampton Roads, Va.

Brother in Service —
Ernest T. Ryan, U.S.N.R.F.

MERRILL POTTER DELANO

LIEUTENANT, U.S. NAVAL RESERVE FLYING CORPS

SON of John M. and Grace Meade (Potter) Delano, of Newton, Mass.; was born at Boston, June 23, 1896. He attended Milton Academy, and graduated from Harvard College, in 1918. He was for two years on the 'Varsity baseball squad. He enlisted, April 24, 1917, and was assigned to active duty June 1, at the U.S. Naval Air Station at Akron, Ohio. He was commissioned Ensign, Oct. 4, 1917, sailed overseas on Nov. 13, and was stationed at the U.S. N.A.S., Paimbœuf, France, for eleven months, and at the U.S. N.A.S., Guipavas, for four months. On March 23, 1918, he was commissioned Lieut. (j.g.), and on Oct. 1, 1918, Lieut. He received inactive duty orders, March 2, 1919. Lieut. Delano was cited by the French Minister of the Marine, and received a letter of commendation from the U.S. Navy Department, for making a flight of twenty-four hours and forty minutes.

Married, Oct. 2, 1919, Hazel Holmes.

Left — Merrill Potter Delano.

CHARLES GRAY LITTLE

LIEUTENANT, U.S. NAVAL RESERVE FLYING CORPS

SON of Henry B. and Fanny (Gray) Little; was born in Newburyport, Mass., July 9, 1895. He was educated at the Noble and Greenough School, and at Harvard College.

He enlisted for Aviation Service in the Navy on May 9, 1917, at the Boston Navy Yard, and was assigned to the Naval Air Station at Akron, Ohio. He was commissioned Ensign, Oct. 31, 1917, sailed overseas on Nov. 12, and served at Rochefort and at Paimbœuf. On March 23, 1918, he was commissioned Lieut. (j.g.), and later appointed Senior Flight Commander. On April 21, 1918, he was awarded Brevet de Pilote de Dirigible. He was sent to Guipavas in Sept., 1918. Lieut. Little was Chief Pilot in charge of the dirigibles which went out to meet President Wilson when he arrived in France. On Oct. 1, 1918, he was commissioned Lieut.

He returned to the U.S. and was stationed at Cape May, N.J.

Brother in Service: Leon M. Little, Lieut., U.S.N.R.F.

Right — Charles Gray Little.

GEORGE M. ABBOTT

SECOND LIEUTENANT, U.S. MARINE CORPS, R.F.C., SEVENTH SQUADRON NORTHERN BOMBING GROUP, DAY WING

SON of George Chase and Emma (Afford) Abbott, of Waban, Mass.; was born in Melrose, Mass., March 8, 1897. He was educated at the Roxbury Latin School, Oak Grove Seminary, and Cornell University. At college he was a member of the Cornell cross-country team. He trained with the Cornell Cadet Corps.

He enlisted at Newport, R.I., on April 4, 1917; and was transferred to Naval Aviation, for U.S.N.R.F., on Sept. 18, 1917. He trained 10 weeks at M.I.T. Ground School, two months at Pensacola, Fla., and one month at Marine Field, Miami, Fla. He was commissioned 2d Lieut., dating from June 5, 1918.

On July 4, 1918, Lieut. Abbott was transferred to U.S. Marine Corps, R.F.C., and was ordered overseas. He landed in France Aug. 1, 1918, going directly to Calais, then to the site of the airdrome, at Dye, Pas de Calais, France. He was stationed there with the 7th Squadron, Northern Bombing Group, Day Wing, from Aug. 6 to Nov. 30, 1918. Much time was spent in getting the drome into suitable condition, during which period they were frequently subject to nocturnal visits by the Germans. Gradually the planes, De Haviland 4's and 9's, equipped with Liberty motors, began to arrive, and operations began, though upon a small scale. Then came the great British effort, when Ostend and Zeebrugge, the principal objective of the 7th Squadron, were captured by their allies, and their occupation was gone. The Squadron was moving to Knesseloere, Belgium, when rumors of the Armistice came, and it was ordered to cease moving material and personnel. Lieut. Abbott received home orders, which took effect Nov. 30, 1918. He was put upon the inactive service list, Feb. 1, 1919, in the Boston Reserve district.

EDWARD A. WENZ

LIEUTENANT (*j.g.*), U.S. NAVAL RESERVE FLYING CORPS

SON of Edward G. A. and Grace Eugenie (Vautrinot) Wenz, of Dedham, Mass.; was born at Roxbury, Mass., Aug. 1, 1893. He attended Boston College High School, and graduated from Boston College, class of 1914.

He enlisted in U.S.N.A. at the Boston Navy Yard on May 23, 1917. He trained at M.I.T. Ground School, graduating in the first class, and was sent to Pensacola, Fla., for flying instruction. He was commissioned Ensign on Dec. 29, 1917, and ordered abroad. He sailed overseas on Feb. 8, 1918, and was stationed at many places on the coast of England and Ireland, on patrol duty. While on duty at Budleigh Sallerton, Eng., he met with a severe accident on May 31, 1918. He and his observer had a narrow escape when his controls jammed. After a month in hospital he returned to duty.

For a time he was loaned to the Royal Flying Forces. He was commissioned Lieut. (j.g.) on Oct. 1, 1918, and has been a Chief Pilot for many months, still in service at Whiddy Island, Bantry Bay, Ireland, and expects to reënlist in the Service.

While on duty at Pensacola, before he had received his commission, Lieut. Wenz was cited for bravery in rescue work during a hurricane. From a copy of the citation:

> Chief Petty Officer MacLaughlin and his men of Group 8, who without suggestion swam out into the rough waters of the bay this morning at great bodily risk to themselves, bringing in safety many heavy wooden pilings which broke loose during the storm.

From the citation sent by the War Bureau, recommending official recognition of the bravery and generous action as indicated herein:

> The Bureau is pleased to note that your action in this case has demonstrated that you are willing to take advantage not only of the responsibilities of the naval service, but also of its opportunities for service outside the routine of duty. Your action in this case is heartily recommended.

Brother in Service —

Philip H. Wenz, Corp. Army Radio Section, Signal Corps; A.E.F.

WILLIAM WHEELWRIGHT TORREY

SECOND LIEUTENANT, U.S.M.C.R., NORTHERN BOMBING SQUADRON, FIELD E

SON of David C. and Jane C. (Wheelwright) Torrey, of Cambridge, Mass.; was born at Newbury, Mass., May 4, 1898. He was educated at Concord, Mass., High School, 1914; Phillips Andover Academy, 1915; and Harvard College, 1919. Previous to enlistment he trained with the Harvard R.O.T.C. in the spring of 1917.

He enlisted in U.S. Navy, July 2, 1917, and was a member of Naval Aviation Detachment, M.I.T., from Oct. 1, 1917, to Nov. 24, 1917. He trained at Naval Air Station, Hampton Roads, Va., Nov. 27, 1917, to Jan. 9, 1918, and at Pensacola, Fla., from Jan. 11 to April 11, 1918. He was commissioned Ensign, U.S.N.R.F., March 22, 1918. He was transferred to Marine Flying Field, Miami, Fla., from April 15 to July 15, 1918. On May 25 he was discharged from U.S.N.R.F., and enrolled as 2d Lieut. U.S.M.C.R., on the following day. In July he sailed overseas, and saw foreign service, attached to the Northern Bombing Squadron, Field E, from July 18, 1918, to Dec. 20, 1918. The Armistice being signed, he returned to America and was attached to the Marine Flying Field, Miami, Fla., Squadron C.

Brothers in Service —

Kenneth W. Torrey, Private, 106th Machine-Gun Co. Killed in action, Oct. 2, 1918.

Norman Z. Torrey, Corporal, Battery C, 101st F.A. Cited for bravery, D.S.C.

HURD HUTCHINS

LIEUTENANT, AVIATION CORPS, U.S. NAVAL RESERVE FORCE

SON of J. Hurd and Olivia (Endicott) Hutchins; was born in Boston, Mass., Feb. 25, 1894. He was educated at the Noble and Greenough School, and at Harvard College.

He started flying in April, 1917, under private instructions of the Curtiss Flying School, Newport News, Va. In May he joined the Navy and flew continuously as a Seaman (2d class), until Nov. of the same year, when he received his Naval Aviator's Certificate, and was commissioned Ensign, U.S.N.R.F.C.

For several months he occupied different positions, serving as Instructor and Flight Commander. In March, 1915, he was commissioned Lieut. (j.g.), and was given charge of the Quartermasters' School, which contained about 500 Quartermasters of the Navy, to serve when graduated as Mechanics in various degrees of the Aviation Service. This School ended in May, when Lieut. Hutchins resumed flying in the patrol service around the Virginia Capes. In this capacity he served as Patrol Pilot and as Division Commander for a short time, then as Flight Commander until Oct., 1918. While the German submarines were actively engaged off the Capes, he made one continuous patrol with full ordnance equipment out to sea and back, of eight hours and a half. This flight at the time was credited to him as the longest any naval plane had made. On Oct. 18, he was sent to Philadelphia in charge of flying three H-16's, twin motor machines, from Philadelphia to Pensacola *via* the Coast Line. The start was made from the Naval Aircraft factory at Philadelphia. Hampton Roads, Va.; Moorehead City, N.C.; Paris Island, S.C.; St. Augustine, Fla.; Miami, Fla.; and Tampa, Fla.; were the stations at which the boats made brief stops. At Pensacola, Lieut. Hutchins went through the Gunnery and the Bombing Schools, and had just completed the course when the Armistice was signed. On reaching Washington he was promoted to Lieut. in the Flying Corps. In Jan., 1919, he was placed on inactive duty, at Boston.

Brother in Service —

John Hutchins, 1st Lieut. 42d Division, A.E.F.

GARDINER COIT MEANS

Second Lieutenant, Infantry, Transferred to Air Service

Son of Rev. Frederick and Helen (Coit) Means; was born in Windham, Conn., June 7, 1896. He prepared for college at Exeter Academy, and attended Harvard College for three years. He was a member of the Harvard R.O.T.C., and in Aug., 1917, joined the R.O.T.C. at Plattsburg.

He was trained at Plattsburg from Aug. 23, 1917, to Dec. 17, when he was commissioned 2d Lieut. of Infantry. After further work at Camp Dix, N.J., he was transferred to the Aviation Section, Signal Corps, and sent to the Ground School at Ithaca, N.Y., Jan. 29, 1918. While training at Hazelhurst Field, Mineola, N.Y., Lieut. Means had a narrow escape in a tail-spin fall from 1800 feet. After further work at Camp Dick, Dallas, Tex., and Ellington Field, Houston, Tex., he was assigned to 4th Student Officers' Squadron, Sept., 1918.

Lieut. Means was honorably discharged from the Service Jan. 2, 1919, and is at present serving as a member of the Armenian Relief Expedition to the Near East.

Brothers in Service —

Paul Howard Means, Private, Medical Enlisted Reserve Corps.
Winthrop J. Means, Corporal, Harvard S.A.T.C.

THOMAS ROBESON MORSE

LIEUTENANT (*j.g.*), U.S. NAVAL AVIATION SERVICE

SON of Charles F. and Ellen H. Morse, of Boston; was born in Kansas City, Mo., May 29, 1895. He was educated at Groton School, and at Harvard College, class of 1918. He was on the freshman track team in 1915 at college.

On March 12, 1917, he enlisted in the Aviation Service at Charlestown, Mass., and was ordered to the Naval Station at Newport, R.I., on April 3. He responded to the call for naval aviators, and was sent to M.I.T. Ground School for instruction on Sept. 15, 1917. Having finished the course there on Nov. 10, he was ordered to the U.S. Naval Air Station, Pensacola, Fla. On Feb. 14, 1918, he was commissioned Ensign, and sailed for France on March 23. Until Aug. 1, 1918, he was stationed for bombing-training at Moutchic-Lacanau, Gironde. He was then ordered to U.S. Naval Air Station at Fromentine, Vendée, and served on patrol duty there until the end of the war. He was commissioned Lieut. (j.g.) on Oct. 1, 1918. He returned to the U.S. on Dec. 16, 1918, and was stationed at Hampton Roads, Va., until released from active service.

Brothers in Service —

Arthur H. Morse, Capt., 810th Pioneer Infantry, U.S.A.
Charles F. Morse, 102d Régiment, d'Artillerie, French Army.

HORACE SARGENT HINDS

ENSIGN, BOMBING SQUADRON, PENSACOLA, FLA.

SON of Fred C. and Emma R. Hinds, of Newtonville, Mass.; was born at Chelsea, Mass., Jan. 4, 1886. He was educated at the Newton High School, and Mass. Institute of Technology. He played on the football team at high school, and also at M.I.T.

On May 3, 1917, he enlisted in the Naval Reserve, at Newport, R.I., where he trained in the Seaman's branch. He then transferred to Aviation, and trained at the Ground School, M.I.T., from Feb., 1918. He had elementary flying at Miami, Fla., and advanced flying at Pensacola, Fla., where he was commissioned Ensign, on Sept. 6, 1918. At Miami he acted as submarine coast-patrol, and at Pensacola, served as bombing-pilot, and as instructor in bombing. In the spring of 1919 Ensign Hinds was promoted to Division Commander of the Bombing Squadron, at Pensacola, and is still in Service in that capacity.

DAVID B. ARNOLD

LIEUTENANT (*j.g.*), U.S.N.R.F.

SON of H. D. and I. Persis Arnold; was born in Boston, Mass., March 23, 1898. He was educated at Volkmann's School, and at Harvard College, class of 1918. In college he was manager of the Harvard crew. He attended the Junior Plattsburg Camp in 1915, and trained with the Harvard R.O.T.C. in 1916 and 1917. He enlisted in Boston in the U.S.N.R.F., on April 1, 1917, and trained at the M.I.T. Ground School, and at Key West, Fla. He was commissioned Ensign, March 25, 1918, and retained as Flight Instructor. In July, 1918, appointed Squadron Commander. Oct. 1, commissioned Lieut. (j.g.), and placed in charge of all flying at the station. On Jan. 24, 1919, he was placed on inactive duty from Key West, Fla.

Brother in Service —
Warren D. Arnold, Lieut. (j.g.), U.S.N.R.F.

Father in Service —
H. D. Arnold, Lieut.-Col. M.C.N.A.

A. MORRIS SONNABEND

Ensign, U.S. Naval Air Service

Son of Joseph and Esther Sonnabend; was born in Boston, Mass., Dec. 8, 1896. He was educated at Boston Latin School, class of 1914, and at Harvard College, class of 1918, A.B. 1917. At college he played on his class football team in 1915 and 1916. He trained with the Harvard Regiment and with the Harvard R.O.T.C.

On March 4, 1918, he enlisted in Naval Aviation, at the 3d Naval Reserve District, N.Y. April–June, 1918, he was trained with Flight 20, Naval Aviation Detachment, M.I.T. July–August, 1918, he had preliminary training at U.S.N.A. Station, Miami, Fla., with the 8th, 9th, and 10th Squadrons. He took advanced training Aug.–Nov. 1918, at U.S.N.A. Station, Pensacola, Fla., with the 3d, 4th, 2d, and 6th Squadrons. In Nov., 1918, he was commissioned Ensign, and ordered overseas. Because of the Armistice the orders were cancelled, and he was reordered to the Air Station at Miami, Fla., as Instructor. In Feb., 1919, he was still in Service.

JOHN W. ASHLEY

Lieutenant (*j.g.*), U.S. Naval Reserve Flying Corps

Son of Joseph and Edith C. (Johnson) Ashley, of Amesbury, Mass.; was born in New York City, Aug. 29, 1895. He graduated from the Amesbury High School in 1913, and during the previous summer attended a school of wireless telegraphy in Boston, receiving his diploma as state electrician, July 17, 1912. He entered the Wentworth Institute, where he won a year's scholarship, graduating, 1916.

In April, 1917, he enlisted in the N.R.F.C. at Boston Navy Yard. He attended M.I.T. Ground School, then the flying school at Pensacola, Fla., on Oct. 2, 1917. He was commissioned Ensign on Jan. 17, 1918, and sailed overseas on March 7, 1918; trained at Naval Air Station, Moutchic-Lacanau, until July 15, 1918; was then transferred to Brest as patrol pilot, convoying ships.

On Dec. 16, 1918, he sailed for the U.S.; and was ordered to U.S.N. Air Station at Chatham, Mass., on Jan. 15, 1919, where he is still in Service. He was promoted to Lieut. (j.g.) in March, 1919, dating from Oct., 1918.

WILLIAM SINCLAIR CORMACK, Jr.

Ensign, U.S. Naval Reserve Force, Northern Bombing Group

Son of William Sinclair and Myrtle A. (Leavitt) Cormack; was born at Newton, Mass., Sept. 12, 1896. He graduated from the Boston Latin School, class of 1913, and from Bowdoin College, A.B. 1917. He enlisted at Brunswick, Me., in April, 1917; trained in the Bowdoin College R.O.T.C. from April to June, 1917; was detached and enlisted in the Naval Air Service in June, 1917; attended the M.I.T. Ground School in Sept. and Oct., and continued training at Pensacola, Fla. He qualified as a pilot in March, 1918; was instructor in the Gunnery School at Pensacola from March till June, 1918; was commissioned Ensign on June 12, and ordered to Rockaway, N.Y., for convoy and patrol work, remaining until July, when he was sent overseas to France with the Northern Bombing Group, and stationed at Moutchic-Lacanau, in Aug., and at Paris in Sept. In Oct. he was at Brest, and in Nov. again at Moutchic-Lacanau. After the Armistice he returned to America, and was stationed at Bay Shore, N.Y., from Dec., 1918, till Jan. 15, 1919. Then ordered to inactive duty, at Bay Shore, N.Y.

JAMES COGGESHALL, Jr.

Ensign, U.S. Naval Reserve Flying Corps

Son of James and Hannah E. Coggeshall, of Allston, Mass.; was born in New York City, June 4, 1896. Educated at the Boston School of Commerce, and at Harvard College, A.B. 1917 (*honoris causa*). On Sept. 15, 1917, he enlisted in U.S.N.R.F.C., at Washington, D.C., and was sent to M.I.T. Ground School, completing his course on Nov. 25. He was ordered to the Naval Air Station at Hampton Roads, Va., Nov. 25 to Jan. 11, 1918. He was attached to N.A.S., Pensacola, Fla., Jan. 11 to Oct. 6, 1918. He was designated Naval Aviator, and commissioned Ensign, on March 4, 1918. Illness with typhoid fever prevented his flying from May 15 until Oct. 6, 1918. From the latter date until Dec. 13, 1918, he was attached to the Office of Naval Operations (Aviation) at Washington, D.C.; where he was relieved from active service. He was recommended for promotion to Lieut. (j.g.) as of Oct. 1, 1918.

Married, Aug. 15, 1917, to Esther Clarke.

JOHN ALEXANDER CASSIDY

SECOND LIEUTENANT, A.S.A., U.S.A.

SON of John and Helen (Robertson) Cassidy, of Saxonville, Mass.; was born in Berlin, Mass., Aug. 4, 1897. He was a graduate of Framingham High School, and had passed his examinations for Harvard College. He enlisted in U.S. Air Service on Nov. 13, 1917, at Boston; and on Feb. 2, 1918, entered Cornell Ground School. He graduated March 30, with Squadron 36. He then spent a month at Camp Dick, Dallas, Tex., from which place he was transferred to Call Field, Wichita Falls, Tex., for flying training. On Sept. 14, 1918, he was commissioned 2d Lieut., A.S.A. On Oct. 1 he was transferred to Love Field, Dallas, Tex., where he was honorably discharged on Jan. 21, 1919. On one occasion Lieut. Cassidy well-nigh established an altitude record, mounting nearly 30,000 feet.

Brother in Service —

Thomas A. Cassidy, 78th Division, 303d Supply Train.

LLOYD ROBERTS CLOWES

SECOND LIEUTENANT, A.S.A., U.S.A.

SON of George and Emily (Roberts) Clowes, of Bristol, R.I.; was born in Boston, April 3, 1896. He was educated at the Colt Memorial High School, Bristol, R.I., and at the R.I. State College (1918), leaving to enlist in his junior year. He trained at Plattsburg R.O.T.C. for three months, enlisting on May 12, 1917. He was recommended for a commission in the Artillery, Regular U.S. Army, but was transferred to Aviation on his request. He was sent to the M.I.T. Ground School; then to Mineola, N.Y., and to Lake Charles, La., for flying instruction. He was commissioned 2d Lieut. Feb. 5, 1918, at Gerstner Field, Lake Charles, La. After receiving his commission, he was transferred to Carlstrom Field, Arcadia, Fla., as Instructor in Scout Work and Acrobatics. On Oct. 31, 1918, he was given expert Aviator's Certificate No. 204, by the Aero Club of America. He was honorably discharged at Carlstrom Field, about March 1, 1919, and placed on the reserve list.

NELSON C. HINCKLEY

Second Lieutenant, A.S.A., U.S.A., Instructor at Ellington Field

Son of Herbert N. and May L. Hinckley; was born at Vineyard Haven, Mass., Jan. 19, 1893. Educated at Tisbury High School, Thayer Academy, and M.I.T., class of 1918. He enlisted at Boston on May 12, 1917, and attended the 3d Officers' Training Camp at Plattsburg, May 12 to Aug. 14, 1917. He was at M.I.T. Ground School, from Oct. 27 to Dec. 22, and trained at Kelly Field, San Antonio, Tex., from Jan. 8 to April 6, 1918, when he was commissioned 2d Lieut., Reserve Military Aviator, A.S.S.C. He was stationed at Camp Dick, Dallas, Tex., from April 25 to May 25, and at Ellington Field, Houston, Tex., from May 25 until the end of the war. Upon completion of the regular and post-graduate courses as a bombing-pilot at Ellington Field, he was assigned to the formation and advanced cross-country stage as an instructor. After the Armistice he was transferred to the R.M.A. stage to teach non-flying officers to become pilots.

Married, Dec. 26, 1918, Laura Howland Vincent.

HARRY C. HITCHCOCK

Second Lieutenant, A.S.A., U.S.A.

Son of Mr. and Mrs. George E. Hitchcock; was born at Malden, Mass., Feb. 26, 1887. He was educated at the Malden High School, where he played on the football, baseball, and basket-ball teams, and was a member of the track relay team. He enlisted in A.S.A. at Boston, on Dec. 6, 1917, and had training successively at S.M.A., Cornell University, Feb. 2, 1918, to April 6; Camp Dick, Dallas, Tex., April 12 to May 30; Scott Field, Belleville, Ill., June 1 to Nov. 4, 1918, where he had preliminary flying. He was commissioned 2d Lieut. A.S.A., Army Corps Pilot, on Sept. 4, 1918. From Nov. 1 to Dec. 10, 1918, he was stationed at Langley Field, Hampton, Va., for advanced flying as an Army Corps Pilot. He was honorably discharged at Langley Field on Dec. 10, 1918.

Married, Jan. 1, 1914, Margarita Bartlett.

WILLIAM TROTT KING, Jr.

SECOND LIEUTENANT, A.S.A., U.S.A.

SON of William Trott and Adell (Howe) King, of Bethel, Vt.; was born in St. Johnsbury, Vt., July 30, 1895. He was educated at the Whitcomb High School, Bethel, Vt.; at St. Johnsbury Academy; and Dartmouth College, class of 1917. He won the Powers Gold Medal in his freshman year at college, and was the champion ski-jumper in the following years. He enlisted in Aviation at Boston, in Nov., 1917. He began training at Cornell on Jan. 6, 1918. On March 8 he was ordered to Dallas, Tex. He was commissioned 2d Lieut. in the Air Service on June 28, 1918, and ordered overseas on Oct. 16. When the Armistice was signed, he was stationed at Issoudun. He was at Angers, awaiting orders home, when he was selected an interpreter on the staff of Brigadier-General McKinstry, of the Board of Indemnity Appraisers, on Jan. 20, 1919.

Brother in Service —
Benjamin H. King, Cadet Aviator.

LESLIE B. DUKE

SECOND LIEUTENANT, A.S.A., U.S.A.

SON of Mr. and Mrs. Charles S. Duke, of Wellesley Hills, Mass.; was born in Peoria, Ill., June 6, 1890. Educated at Mechanic Arts High School, Boston, and at M.I.T. He enlisted at Cambridge on Nov. 3, 1917, and trained at M.I.T. and Princeton Ground Schools, graduating on Jan. 12, 1918. He had preliminary flying at Kelly Field, San Antonio, Tex. On March 27 he was commissioned 2d Lieut. and took the Bombing Pilot's course at Ellington Field, graduating on Sept. 15. He had training in aerial gunnery at Taliaferro Field, from Oct. 5, 1918, to Jan. 25, 1919, then took a course in Aeronautical Engineering at M.I.T. At last accounts he was still in Service in the Technical Division, at Dayton, O.

MICHAEL FRANCIS McGRATH

SECOND LIEUTENANT, A.S.A., U.S.A.

SON of Thomas and Sarah (Henneberry) McGrath; was born in Bennington, Vt., March 24, 1887. He was educated at the public schools of Charlestown, Mass. He enlisted in the Air Service in Cambridge, Sept. 14, 1917. Attended the Ground Schools at M.I.T. and Princeton, and was transferred to Gerstner Field, where he was commissioned 2d Lieut. May 21, 1918. He was subsequently assigned to the Gunnery School at Wilbur Wright Field in Dayton, O.; and later to the Advanced Bombing School at Ellington Field, Houston, Tex. He had qualified as a day bombing pilot when the Armistice was signed, but had not been attached to any squadron.

Brothers in Service —

Matthew L. McGrath, Ch. Yeoman, U.S.N.R.F.
Joseph W. McGrath, Ch. Yeoman, U.S.N.R.F.

FORREST C. OSGOOD

ENSIGN, SQUADRON 1, PENSACOLA, FLORIDA

SON of Alvin F. and Caroline Robertson (Symmes) Osgood; was born in Ashmont, Mass., June 22, 1891. He graduated from the Arlington High School, where he made a record in athletics as a member of the track team and captain of the hockey team in 1912. For 5 years he was a member of the Boston Athletic Association hockey team. He enlisted in the Naval Reserves, 2d Naval District, at Newport, R.I., April, 1917, and was assigned duty on S.P. 428 *Mystery* (submarine-chaser), during the summer of 1917. He was transferred to Naval Aviation, and entered the Ground School, M.I.T., Oct. 30, 1917. On completing the course there, he was ordered to Pensacola, Fla., Jan. 19, 1918. He qualified as Gunnery Pilot in the U.S. Naval Flying Corps, and made an altitude record flight of 13,200 feet in the heavy-type bombing-plane H-12. Was commissioned Ensign, March 28, 1918. He was held at Pensacola as Instructor, and then as Division and Squadron Commander. From July, 1918, to Jan., 1919, four times recommended for promotion.

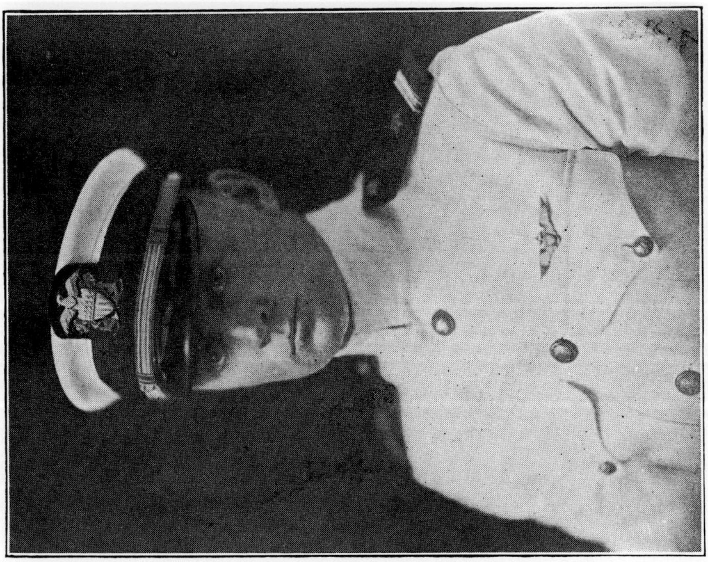

JOHN MORSE ELLIOT

Second Lieutenant, A.S.A., U.S.A.

Son of Dr. John Wheelock and Mary Lee (Morse) Elliot; was born in Boston, Nov. 5, 1891. He was educated at the Noble and Greenough School, Boston, Middlesex School, and at Harvard College. Previous to enlistment he trained with Battery A, M.V.M., for a year and a half. He attended the 1st Plattsburg Business Men's Training Camp in 1915, and the 2d Officers' Training Camp at Plattsburg in 1917. He enlisted in Boston in Jan., 1918, in the Aviation Service; was sent for training to Camp Dick, Dallas, Tex.; to Austin, Tex., S.M.A.; to Fortress Monroe, Va., Aerial Observation School; and later to Langley Field, Hampton, Va. He was commissioned 2d Lieut. Jan. 24, 1919, A.S.A., U.S.A. He was honorably discharged at Langley Field, Hampton, Va., on Jan. 27, 1919.

GARDNER DUNTON

Second Lieutenant, A.S.A., U.S.A.

Son of Charles and Mabel (Hooper) Dunton, of Allston, Mass.; was born in Boston, March 13, 1895. He was educated at the Boston Latin School and at Harvard College, class of 1918. He trained with the Harvard R.O.T.C. in 1916–17; attended the 1st Plattsburg Training Camp, from April 23, 1917; and enlisted there on May 12, 1917. Following this he trained at M.I.T. Ground School, from Oct. 20 to Dec. 15; and at Ellington Field, Houston, Tex., from Dec. 22, 1917, to May 10, 1918. He was commissioned 2d Lieut. March 25, 1918, and was stationed at Camp Dick Concentration Camp, Dallas, Tex., from April 12 to May 3, 1918; then at Fort Sill, Okla., for Corps d'Armée Pilot Training, from May 5, to June 8, 1918. He was detailed as Pilot Instructor in Aerial Gunnery at Selfridge Field, Mt. Clemens, Mich., from June 15, 1918, to Jan. 30, 1919. He was honorably discharged at Selfridge Field on Jan. 30, 1919, to return to college.

PAUL W. SHEDD

SECOND LIEUTENANT, A.S.A., U.S.A., FIRST PROVISIONAL TRAINING SQUADRON

SON of Charles Gale and Rhoda J. (Colburn) Shedd; was born in Keene, N.H., July 14, 1892. He was educated at Exeter Academy and at the M.I.T. He enlisted at Boston, on Dec. 1, 1917; was assigned to the Ground School, M.I.T., where he remained throughout Dec., 1917, and to the Ground School at Cornell, where he remained from Jan. 1 to Feb. 1, 1918. He was then transferred to Camp Dick, Dallas, Tex., March 1–April 15, and to Eberts Flying Field, Ark. April 15–Sept. 25. He was commissioned 2d Lieut., R.M.A., Aug. 15, 1918. Stationed from Sept. 25, 1918, to Jan. 10, 1919, at Ellington Field, Houston, Tex., where he was honorably discharged Jan. 10, 1919.

Twin Brother in Service —

Charles Gale Shedd, Jr., Capt., Ordnance Officer Corps; stationed at St.-Nazaire, France.

Father in Service —

Charles Gale Shedd, 1st Lieut., American Red Cross; served in Paris, France, April to Oct., 1918.

GEORGE PARKER MERRILL, JR.

SECOND LIEUTENANT, A.S.A., U.S.A.

SON of George Parker and Mary Alice (Jones) Merrill; was born in Melrose, Mass., March 6, 1894. He was educated at the Melrose High School, and at the Syracuse Forestry School, from which he graduated in 1915. He enlisted in Boston, Oct. 14, 1917, and was trained at the Ground School, M.I.T., at Cornell, and at Camp Dick, Dallas, Tex. He was assigned to Eberts Field, Lonoke, Ark., April 12, 1918. He was commissioned 2d Lieut., July 20, 1918, and subsequently held at Eberts Field as Instructor in Acrobatics. He was honorably discharged from the Service Dec. 9, 1918.

3902

FREDERICK B. CANN

SECOND LIEUTENANT, A.S.A., U.S.A.

SON of Bonman F. and Grace S. (Crosby) Cann, of Jaffrey, N.H.; was born at Cambridge, Mass., Dec. 12, 1885. He was educated at the Jaffrey High School, and the N.H. State College, at Durham, N.H. He attended the Plattsburg Training Camp for three months in 1916; and again in 1917. He graduated from the L.M.A. at Austin, Tex., from the Flying School at Kelly Field, San Antonio, Tex., and has since been Instructor at Park Field, Millington, Tenn. He was commissioned 2d Lieut. at Kelly Field.

HALSEY R. BAZLEY

SECOND LIEUTENANT, A.S.A., U.S.A., STAFF PILOT, TOURS, FRANCE

SON of William H. and Berta B. Bazley, of Everett, Mass.; was born in Whitman, Mass., May 7, 1896. He was educated at the Everett High School, and Northeastern College. In the summer of 1916 he attended the Plattsburg Training Camp. He enlisted, Oct. 30, 1917, at Cambridge, and was trained in Aviation at M.I.T. Ground School; elementary flying and aerial gunnery at Taliaferro Field, Fort Worth, Tex.; machine-gunnery at Wilbur Wright Field, Dayton, O. He was commissioned 2d Lieut. June 17, 1918, and sailed overseas on Sept. 16, 1918, reporting at Issoudun, France, for further training as pursuit pilot. After completing his instruction he was ordered to the 2d A.I.C. at Tours, France, for duty as staff pilot. He remained there until ordered back to the U.S. on March 1, 1919. He reported at Garden City and was assigned to a casual company of Air Service men to be brought to Camp Devens for discharge. After completion of duties at Camp Devens he was honorably discharged from Service on April 22, 1919.

Father in Service —

William H. Bazley, in the Spanish-American War.

HARRY FOSTER MURCHIE

SECOND LIEUTENANT, A.S.A., U.S.A.

SON of Henry S. and Harriet H. C. (Caldwell) Murchie, and grandson of Brigadier-General John C. Caldwell; was born in Calais, Me., Nov. 14, 1893. He was educated at the Calais High School, Phillips Academy, Andover, Mass., and Dartmouth College. At both school and college he was a 'Varsity letter man. Prior to his enlistment, Aug. 15, 1917, he had been in training at camp at Gettysburg, Pa., in 1913. He attended the Ground School, M.I.T., Aug.-Dec., 1917, and the Ground School at Princeton, beginning Jan., 1918. He was later transferred to Camp Dick, Dallas, Tex., and to Park Field, Memphis, Tenn., where he was commissioned 2d Lieut. Sept. 21, 1918. He was then ordered to Post Field, Fort Sill, Okla., and was stationed at Taliaferro Field, Fort Worth, Tex., where he received his honorable discharge, Jan. 28, 1919.

WILLIAM INGERSOLL BOWDITCH

SECOND LIEUTENANT, A.S.A., U.S.A.

SON of Ernest W. and Susan (Swann) Bowditch, of Milton, Mass.; was born in Boston, Mass., Dec. 8, 1893. He was educated at Milton Academy, at Hotchkiss School, Conn., and at M.I.T. He enlisted at Camp Devens on Nov. 19, 1917, and was attached to the 151st Dépôt Brigade Infantry at Camp Devens. He was then sent to Cornell School of Military Aeronautics, Feb. 16 to April 20, 1918; to Camp Dick, Dallas, Tex., April 27 to May 21; to Carlstrom Field, Arcadia, Fla., May 27 to July 27; to Dorr Field, Arcadia, July 27 to Aug. 20; and to Barron Field, Fort Worth, Tex., Aug. 23 to Dec. 10, 1918. He was commissioned 2d Lieut. on Dec. 10, 1918, and on the same date discharged in the Reserve, at Barron Field, Fort Worth, Tex.

ROSWELL EMORY DAVIS

Second Lieutenant, M.C., Tenth Squadron, Northern Bombing Group

Son of F. Irvin and Eunice S. Davis, of Hartford, Conn.; was born in New Britain, Conn., April 1, 1898. He attended the Hartford High School, and Phillips Exeter Academy, where he won his "E" in football, 1916 and 1917, and "E" in hockey and in rowing, 1917. He enlisted May 19, 1917, at Newport, R.I. On Oct. 29 he entered the M.I.T. Ground School. He left for Pensacola, Fla., on Jan. 19, 1918, making his first flight there on Jan. 23. On April 23 he went to Miami, Fla., to take up land-flying with the Marines. On June 1 he was discharged from the Navy and the same day enrolled in the Marine Corps. Commissioned 2d Lieut. on June 7, with rank dating from May 28, 1918, and attached to the 4th Squadron, 1st Marine Aviation Force. On Sept. 17, 1918, he sailed overseas, and was stationed at La Frene, France, until the Armistice, attached to 10th Squadron, Northern Bombing Group. Returning to America, he was ordered home Feb. 1, 1919. Placed on the inactive list, U.S. Marine Corps, Reserve Flying Corps, from Miami, Fla.

RALPH STARKWEATHER

Second Lieutenant, A.S.A., U.S.A.

Son of Oscar W. and S. Josephine Starkweather, of West Medford, Mass.; was born in South Boston, Mass., Aug. 29, 1891. He was educated in the Needham public schools, and at Bryant and Stratton Commercial School. He enlisted Sept. 5, 1917, at Cambridge, and trained at M.I.T. Ground School. He completed his course and training at Princeton, and later was sent to Love Field, Dallas, Tex. He was commissioned 2d Lieut. on June 6, 1918, and sent to Payne Field, West Point, Miss., and from there to Garden City, N.Y. Having received overseas orders, he sailed for France on Nov. 16, and finished his training at Issoudun, France.

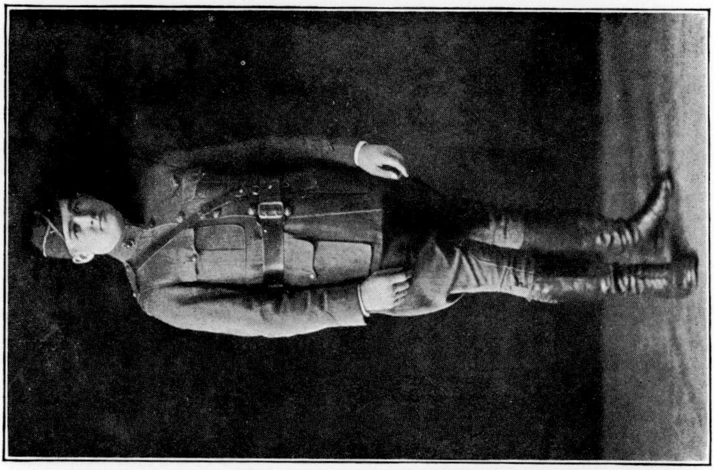

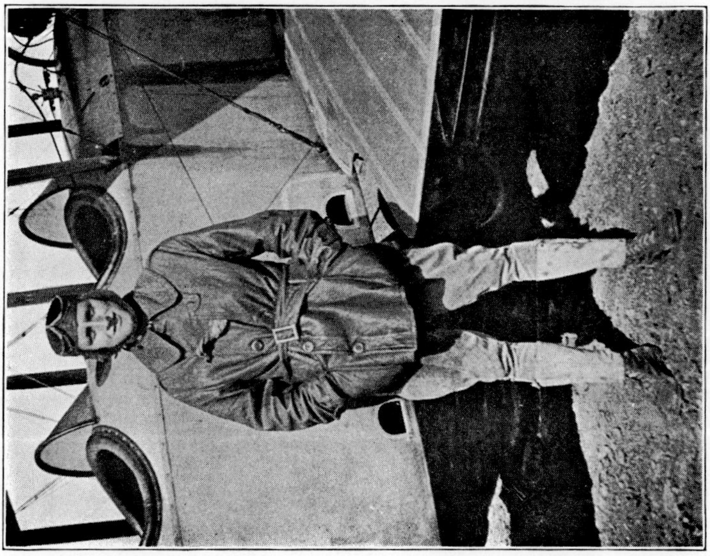

LEONARD L. STANLEY

First Lieutenant, A.S.A., U.S.A.

Son of William and Lila Wetmore (Courtney) Stanley; was born in Great Barrington, Mass., on June 19, 1891. He was educated at the Hotchkiss School, Lakeville. Conn., at Yale College, and at the M.I.T. He was on the Yale intercollegiate championship hockey team in 1908. Prior to the declaration of war he attended the 1st Officers' Training Camp at Plattsburg. On June 16, 1916, he enlisted in Squadron A, in New York City, for service at the Mexican Border. On his return he entered the Aviation Service. After training at the Princeton Ground School he proceeded overseas in the fall of 1917, was attached to the 2d A.I.C., at Tours, France, and to the Flying School of the 3d A.I.C. at Issoudun, France. Later he attended the school at Ford Junction, Eng. He was commissioned 1st Lieut., April 20, 1918. He was honorably discharged from the Service at Garden City, N.Y., Jan. 6, 1919.

CLARENCE STANLEY

Ensign, R.F., Naval Air Station, Pensacola, Florida

Son of William and Lila Wetmore (Courtney) Stanley; was born in Pittsfield, Mass., Jan. 14, 1897. He was educated at the Berkshire School, 1909–14, Sheffield, Mass., and at Yale College, 1915–17. He played on the hockey and baseball teams at Yale. He enlisted at the Boston Navy Yard on May 21, 1918, and was assigned to the Ground School at M.I.T. He took preliminary training at the Naval Air Station, Miami, Fla., and advanced training at Pensacola, Fla., where he was attached to Squadron 5 as Instructor. On Dec. 21, 1918, he was commissioned Ensign, R.F. On Feb. 10, 1919, was placed on inactive duty at Pensacola.

Brother in Service —

Gilbert Stanley, 1st Lieut., 96th Aero Squadron.

MICHAEL A. BUTLER

Second Lieutenant, A.S., U.S.A., Seventeenth Aero Squadron, Fourth Pursuit Group

Son of Michael J. and Sarah A. Butler; was born in Boston, Mass., in 1898. He attended the public schools of Boston, and later became an expert automobile mechanic and salesman. In March, 1917, he joined the American Ambulance Field Service, Section 12, at Paris, and remained in the service of the French Army until the United States declared war. He was transferred to the U.S. Air Service as a cadet in July, 1917, and served in France during the remainder of the war. He was commissioned 2d Lieut. in June, 1918. He was honorably discharged at Long Island, N.Y., on May 31, 1919.

Father in Service —

Michael J. Butler, Sergeant-Major, 11th Hussars, British Army; British Veteran of three wars; Egyptian Campaign, 1882–84; the Soudan, 1884–86; South African War, 1901–03.

HENRY W. VOGEL

Second Lieutenant, A.S.A., U.S.A.

Son of Henry W. and Mary J. Vogel; was born in Dedham, Mass., Feb. 6, 1897. He was educated at the Avery School, Dedham High School, the School of Business Administration and Finance, Boston, Y.M.C.A., and Boston University School of Business Administration. He enlisted at Boston on Dec. 18, 1917, and was trained first at S.M.A., Princeton, N.J., March 23 to June 22, 1918; at Air Service Flying School, Chanute Field, Rantoul, Ill., June 25 to Oct. 10, 1918, being commissioned 2d Lieut. on Oct. 2; at Payne Field, West Point, Miss., Oct. 12 to Nov. 7, 1918; and at Air Service Dépôt, Garden City, Field No. 2, N.Y., Nov. 10 to Dec. 19, 1918. He was honorably discharged at Air Service Dépôt, Garden City, on Dec. 19, 1918.

CARLETON WOODMAN BLANCHARD

SECOND LIEUTENANT, A.S.A., U.S.A.
FOURTEENTH SQUADRON R.A.F.

SON of George W. and Nellie H. (Forbes) Blanchard; was born at Somerville, Mass., July 30, 1895. He was educated at the Abington High School and M.I.T. At school he played football and baseball; and baseball at college. He trained with the Cadet Regiment, M.I.T. He enlisted Nov. 3, 1917, at Cambridge, and trained at M.I.T. and Princeton Ground Schools. He had flying training at Kelly Field, and Love Field, Tex., and took a gunnery-course at Dayton, O. He was commissioned 2d Lieut. March 28, 1918; sailed overseas and trained with the Royal Air Force at Montrose, Scotland, where he was attached to the 14th, or "Camel" Squadron, for service on the British front. He returned to America, and was honorably discharged at Camp Devens, Dec. 19, 1918.

Brother in Service—

George Kinson Blanchard, 2d Lieut. A.S.A., U.S.A.

Grandfather: Served in the Civil War; great-great grandfather served in the Revolutionary War.

GEORGE KINSON BLANCHARD

SECOND LIEUTENANT, A.S.A., U.S.A.

SON of George W. and Nellie H. (Forbes) Blanchard; was born at East Somerville, Mass., March 23, 1897. He was educated at Abington High School and Mass. Agricultural College, Amherst. He played football at high school and on the college team. He enlisted Nov. 16, 1917, at M.I.T., and had ground-school training at M.I.T. and Cornell. He trained for flying at Ellington Field, Houston, Tex., where he was commissioned 2d Lieut. on May 13, 1918. He was stationed for a short time at Love Field, Dallas, Tex., then went to West Point, Miss., for advanced flying. He was ordered overseas, and sailed from Hoboken in the latter part of Sept., 1918. He finished his training at Issoudun, France.

Brother in Service—

Carleton Woodman Blanchard, 2d Lieut. A.S.A., U.S.A.,

Grandfather: Served in the Civil War; great-great grandfather served in Revolutionary War.

ROBERT L. CLEVELAND

SECOND LIEUTENANT, A.S.A., U.S.A.

SON of E. C. and Camilla L. (Stedman) Cleveland; was born at North Adams, Mass., Feb. 23, 1891. He graduated from Drury High School, and from the Fitchburg Normal School. On July 9, 1917, he enlisted at M.I.T. Ground School, and was attached to Squadron 9. He received primary flying instructions at Mineola, N.Y., and was then stationed at Gerstner Field, Lake Charles, La., Dec. 20, 1917, to Feb. 27, 1918. On Feb. 14 he was commissioned 2d Lieut. March 1 to April 1 he was at Camp Dick, Dallas, Tex.; then transferred to Carruthers Field, Fort Worth, Tex., where he was stationed April 3 to Oct. 22. There he was Instructor of Acrobatic Flying and had charge of the acrobatic field. At Fort Worth he was recommended for a Lieutenantcy. On Oct. 28 he reported at Garden City for overseas service, but failed to get across. On Dec. 14 he was ordered to Carlstrom Field, Arcadia, Fla., where he was stationed until he resigned from Service on Jan. 13, 1919.

JOHN DE FOREST BARKER

SECOND LIEUTENANT, A.S.A., U.S.A., SEVENTY-FOURTH AERO SQUADRON

SON of Guy de Forest and Lillian (Lyon) Barker; was born at St. Albans, Vt., March 25, 1897. He graduated from the St. Albans High School, class of 1914, and entered Norwich University in Sept., 1915. At the end of his first year, June, 1916, he enlisted in the U.S. Army for service in Mexico. He was mustered out in Sept., 1916, and returned to the University to finish his course in Civil Engineering. In Sept., 1917, he enlisted in the Aviation Section, U.S.A., at Boston. On Dec. 8 he was ordered to M.I.T. Ground School. In Jan., 1918, he was transferred to Cornell, where he completed the ground course, and was sent to Camp Dick, Dallas, Tex. In April, 1918, he was sent to Call Field, Wichita Falls, Tex., and at the end of his course there was commissioned 2d Lieut. July, 1918, and was assigned to the Bombing Division. He was then sent to Love Field, Dallas, Tex., where he remained until ordered to Garden City, N.Y., Nov. 2, 1918. He was then attached to the 74th Aero Squadron, Roosevelt Field, Mineola, N.Y.

WALTER C. MOORE

CADET, A.S.A., U.S.A.

SON of Walter B. and Helen B. Moore; was born at Lynn, Mass., Jan. 13, 1897. He attended the Huntington Preparatory School, and entered Dartmouth College with the class of 1920. He was a member of the Dartmouth Regiment in 1916, and took a course in Advanced Military Training in 1917. He enlisted at Boston, Mass., Feb. 28, 1918. He entered the M.I.T. Ground School, June 20, 1918, and was later transferred to the School of Military Aeronautics at Cornell University, Ithaca, N.Y., on Sept. 7, 1918. He was ordered to Camp Dick, Dallas, Tex., on Sept. 24, 1918. On Oct. 16, 1918, he was detailed to Fort Monroe, Va., to the Aerial Observers' School. He was honorably discharged at Fort Monroe, on Nov. 26, 1918.

STANLEY B. POTTER

CADET, A.S.A., U.S.A.

SON of Hiram J. and M. Louise (Russell) Potter, of Brookline, Mass.; was born at Lawrence, Mass., Jan. 23, 1895. He was educated at the Manor School, Stamford, Conn.; at the Brookline High School, Brookline, Mass.; and at Harvard College. He enlisted in the Air Service at Boston, Dec. 13, 1917. He graduated from the U.S. School of Military Aeronautics, Princeton, N.J., on July 13, 1918, with honors, standing first in his class. He was then ordered to Camp Dick, Dallas, Tex., where he remained until Sept. 10, 1918. Subsequently he was sent to Rich Field, Waco, Tex., for flying training. He was honorably discharged at Rich Field, Waco, Tex., Dec. 7, 1918.

Married, July 15, 1918, M. Doris Hitchcock.